<u>God</u> on the Net

God on the Net

>> A guide to the best sites for study,
inspiration and resources

Year 2002 edition

Compiled by:// Vernon Blackmore

HarperCollins*Publishers*

HarperCollins*Publishers*
77–85 Fulham Palace Road, London W6 8JB

First published in Great Britain in 2001 by HarperCollins*Publishers*

10 9 8 7 6 5 4 3 2 1

© 1999, 2001 Vernon Blackmore

Vernon Blackmore asserts the moral right to be
identified as the compiler of this work

A catalogue record for this book is
available from the British Library

ISBN 0 00 712095 8

Printed and bound in Great Britain by
Martins the Printers Ltd, Berwick upon Tweed

Contents

INTRODUCTION

1 STARTING OUT 1
Starting Out – Counting the cost – An Internet service provider – Software to make it work

2 BROWSING THE WEB 14
Moving around – Understanding URLs – Links – Bookmarks or favorites – Menus and keyboard shortcuts – Saving pages – Searching for information

3 SEARCHING THE WEB 26
Search sites – Christian Directories – Using search engines – Meta search engines – Search agents – More search tips – Getting your church on the Web

4 SAFE SURFING 35
No sex, please – Shop till you (virtually) drop – Is it safe to shop on the web? – Viruses – Privacy

5 USING E-MAIL 48

Pros and cons – Sending and receiving mail – A little terminology – Using e-mail – Housekeeping – Informality rules OK – Easing the burden – Web-based e-mail – Mailing lists – Wider mailing lists – Other uses for your e-mail account

6 NEWSGROUPS, FORUMS, CHAT AND MESSAGING 64

Newsgroups – Web forums – Chat – instant Messaging – What about the future?

7 DIRECTORY OF SITES 74

8 ALPHABETICAL INDEX OF SITES 267

Introduction

A new person joins the Internet every half second. We are in the throes of an information revolution.

It's a very simple idea. And the simplest ideas have the greatest effect – the universe of all information, all of mankind's knowledge as one abstract information space. I thought of a lot of things to call it, but the thing I liked best was the World Wide Web.

Tim Berners-Lee, inventor of the World Wide Web

There are over 2 billion pages of information and entertainment on the World Wide Web, all accessible through a computer in your home or office. This is equivalent to fourteen million floppy disks which, if stacked one upon another, would be over five times higher than Mt. Everest. Every day another 50,000 more floppy disks of new material are added on. Some of this huge pile of resources is focused on the Christian faith and on helping church members not only grow in their own faith but be better equipped in their ministry to others. What's more, these resources are, by and large, completely free – though you will have to pay a few dollars or pounds a month for the Internet connection to gain access to them. True, there is much dross, as the Internet allows anyone to claim their 15MB of fame, but there is much, too, of real value.

This book is not a book on technology, however fascinating that is. Nor does it cover the history of the Internet or where we will be within a decade. It is a guide to finding resources in this vast, virtual world. In particular, it is a guide for Christians who want to discover resources on the web for their ministry and spiritual development.

The book is a traveller's guide, introducing you to a new world. It is split into two.

■ The first part looks at how to get on to the Internet, how to search for information, contribute a few e-mails to the 100 million sent every day, and maybe set up your own website. To continue with the travelling metaphor, this section describes how to reach the new world, its habits and customs. However, as a guide to this process it is hardly thorough: just enough to get you safely to your destination. Once on the Internet, there are more than enough guides to take you further.

■ The second, main, part is a directory of Christian websites, with references to general sites where appropriate. This may seem strange at first – a paper directory of electronic information – but the aim is not to provide an exhaustive list of every Christian site (which computers can do much better), but a tour guide to set a bewildered tourist on the road to some of the best views of this new world. Before long, as a seasoned traveller, you will be returning with tales of sights and sites you had not expected.

Not surprisingly, the first part draws on the second. Rather than endlessly repeat web addresses, the guide refers to the relevant section in the directory. This may require some skipping back and forth, but it does mean that once the earlier guide section has become redundant for you, you know that all the references remain in the directory.

In the fifteenth century some believed the first printed books were 'of the devil', for how otherwise could so many books look identical? On experiencing the Internet for the first time, the reaction is more likely to be amazement at its sheer variety. Yet, as Tim Berners-Lee, the man who coined the phrase 'World Wide Web', has said, 'If you think everything's over, you're completely wrong. This is just the start. So jump on board now because it's just speeding up.'

But where is God on the Net?

Vernon Blackmore
vernon@godonthenet.com

ACKNOWLEDGEMENTS

In creating a directory of websites I have inevitably drawn on existing lists, so I owe many thanks to unknown compilers across the web. I am also grateful to Jan Goddard-Jones and Jane Wigman for their work and to Becky Welch and Bob Carling for their additional research.

1

Starting Out

How do you 'get on the Internet'? What equipment is needed and how does it all work? In the pioneering days of this new medium (only a decade ago!) you needed to be a bit of a computer whiz to make sense of it all. But these days, any new computer comes with all the software you need. Your mobile phone, too, can be used to send e-mails. And your child's games console can link up with other players – over the Internet, of course. Not only is connecting using the Internet easier, but the range of devices you can use is expanding.

The desktop computer remains the most powerful way to use the Internet. An Internet-connected TV can be just as fast, but the TV screen is not designed for easy reading of text. Your mobile phone has an even more limited screen. However, British Telecom say that more Valentine's Day messages are now sent by mobile phone than by traditional cards, and some predict that with the next generation of mobile technology, phone use of the Internet will exceed that of desktop computers.

At heart, all these devices are doing the same job. They allow you to link your computer/TV/phone/ games console/pocket organizer/whatever into the big computer network we call the Internet. And once you're connected you can send and receive messages (e-mail) or view pages of information (web). The 'Internet' is the network of connected computers, 'e-mail' and the 'world wide web' are two of the most popular services which use this network.

The device you choose is up to you. But how do you make the connection? in general, you link up through your phone line. By means of your phone call to a special number, your ISP (Internet Service Provider) will make your phone line a temporary extension of the bigger, fatter permanent cables that connect many of the world's computers together. Think of if it like plugging an extension cable into an electrical wall socket. Your extension cable allows you temporarily to use the electricity with which the house is permanently wired. So, your ISP is permanently connected with the Internet and you temporarily share this connection through your phone line. Of course, if it is your TV you are using, the 'phone line' may be your cable and the Internet signals jostle down the cable along with the TV channels. If it is your mobile phone, the 'phone line' is the radio channel you use. You may never even see the letters ISP. As far as you are concerned, the cable company provides both TV and Internet. But, however it is dressed up, you will need these four things:

- A piece of technology on which you can read text and maybe type messages.
- A 'phone connection' to link you to others on the network.
- An ISP who agrees to link your phone connection into the Internet proper.

■ Some software or application installed on the device so you can send e-mails and browse pages on the World Wide Web.

If you use a computer, it may well be running 'Microsoft Windows'. Windows has excellent Internet software. In nine out of ten cases you should be able to plug a phone line into the back of any relatively new computer and follow a few on-screen prompts. When you get the hang of it, you may want to change your ISP, alter the settings in Windows or use different software. But that's for later.

Counting the cost

The phone connection is any standard telephone socket in your building. You can get an adaptor so that you can plug in both your modem and your normal phone. Just don't use both at the same time!

Telephone charges vary from country to country. Most Internet calls are to a local number (see the next section), so check out the costs of a local call. Your telephone company may also allow you to put your Internet service provider's number on your frequent calls list and so earn additional discount. Check the wording carefully: although charged at local call rates, calls to an ISP may in fact be classed as 'non-geographic' and be in a special band of their own.

When you browse the web you are connected all the time, so phone costs may mount. Budget for a few hours per week. On the other hand, exchanging e-mail takes very little on-line time, as reading your e-mail and composing your reply can be done without the phone being connected. Only transferring e-mail on and off the Internet requires a connection.

Some ISPs allow unlimited use for a fixed monthly fee. In reality, 'unlimited' means 'whenever you like but not all the time', but the fixed fee does allow you to budget accurately. This type of connection is called 'unmetered'. The next step up is a true 'always on' connection. For a larger monthly fee, the Internet is always connected to your computer. This is undoubtedly the thing of the future and houses will be wired for the Internet just as they are wired for 'always on' electricity today.

But somewhere, somehow, someone has to pay for your Internet access and use of Internet facilities such as e-mail and web space. There are five possibilities:

1. You pay your access provider a monthly connection fee.
2. You pay for your use of the telephone through call charges, and your ISP takes a cut from this.
4. You pay nothing, and advertisers foot all the bills.
5. You pay for additional technical help or an initial set-up fee.
6. You pay a subscription for additional services.

The second option (no monthly fee but you pay call charges) is common in the UK. It is often combined

---

with high charges for technical support (option 4).

In the US, where local calls can be free, the provider charges a monthly fee of $20+ for unlimited access. In Australia, the same fee may only get you 50 hours or so of access time per month; after that you are charged by the hour. The UK is going this way, too, where £10–£25 per month gives you 'unmetered' access to the Internet.

Advertisements are the method by which search sites and web directories make their money. You are free to use their facilities, as the advertisers hope to entice you away from the search page to their web sites. These days even some Internet software is driven by advertising: one of the panels on the software may be for advertisements and, as you browse the web, these are regularly updated.

Specialist services, such as financial information or professional journals, use subscriptions.

In order to calculate the monthly cost of, say, 25 hours on line, you need to:

- Check if there is a monthly fee – and for how many hours – and ask if there is any initial start-up charge.
- Calculate any call charges, using a mixture of cheap evening calls and normal day rates – and check that you can call a *local* number to connect to your ISP.
- Be realistic about needing technical support and budget for, say, three calls of 10 minutes each in the first month.

How fast is your connection?

Your computer uses some electrical wizardry called a modem to turn your phone line (which is usually used for talking) into a computer connection (which sends and receives digital data). New computers come with modems already in place, though you can upgrade an older machine by buying a separate modem. The current standard for modems is 'V90' although a new development called 'V92' improves the time it takes to connect and is optimised for web browsing. With a V90/92 connection, most web pages will load on to your screen within 5–20 seconds. Even with a fast modem, however, it may be that the Internet itself becomes clogged with users and slows everything down. In London after work on Fridays, getting home on a bicycle can be faster than in a sports car!

If you install ADSL (Asymmetric Digital Subscriber Line), you still have a modem but the connection at the telephone exchange has been modified to make it all work faster: much faster. The same is true with cable modems which can use the high speed cables that carry your TV signals. Your Internet connection may be up to ten times quicker. You may, however, be sharing your faster connection with others and the 'contention ratio' specifies the maximum number of people the ISP can load on to a single connection. This may be 20 or 50, depending on the depth of your wallet. Just as you pray for peaceful neighbours, so you now yearn for others in your street to be only occasional web surfers.

An Internet service provider

An Internet service provider (or ISP) is the company that receives the phone call from your computer and routes it on to the Internet itself. ISPs are permanently connected to the Internet and – for the duration of your phone call – allow you to share their connection.

Around the world there are huge, global ISPs such as AOL or Microsoft's MSN. Then within each country

In the UK many of the Internet Service Providers offer free access and their home pages offer extensive links to other sites.

there are large national companies, such as Virgin or Freeserve in the UK. Finally, alongside these are hundreds of smaller ISPs offering specialised services. The Internet magazines run tests to determine the best ISP. They balance connection speed with reliability and cost. Remember that a so-called 'free ISP' does bear a cost. You may need to pay for technical support, or you may have to pay phone charges to connect to the ISP.

A large national or international ISP will provide all you need on their CD. They will connect you to the internet, provide you with an e-mail address and set aside some space on their computers for any web pages you create. In short, you get 'dial-up', e-mail and web space as part of the package.

A package deal is certainly the best place to start. Over time, however, it may not be right for some users and certainly not for most organizations and churches. The snag with package deals is that the bundled e-mail and web space comes with addresses which show the ISP's name – for example, www.stmarys.demon.co.uk, for users of web pages on Demon or joe@bloggs142. freeserve.co.uk for e-mail with a FreeServe account. You would prefer the domain to be *your* name only, such as pastor@greenhillmethodist.co.uk. We can't go into registering a domain name (but see the articles on www.godonthenet.com). However, to use your own domain name you will need to move away from a free account and this is where a smaller, more specialised ISP can be valuable. Many organizations use one of the big names to connect them to the Internet and then use another ISP to register their domain name and provide web site storage ('hosting') and their e-mail accounts.

There are over 200 million people actively using the World Wide Web.

See **ISPs – General**
See **ISPs – Christian**

Double act

Traffic on the Internet is now doubling every 100 days.

Year	Host computers connected to the Internet
1969	4
1971	23
1974	62
1989	130,000
1990	300,000
1992	1,100,000
1995	6,600,000
1996	12,800,000
1997	19,500,000
1998	29,600,000
1999	44,400,000
2000	70,470,000
2001	106,000,000

Take a look at www.netsizer.com where you can see counters for new computers and users spinning around as you watch.

Most people can never be bothered to change their service provider. Certainly, changing your ISP can be difficult: you may have been bombarded with marketing brochures when the cable TV people dug up your area to lay their lines. Not only did they tell you that you would receive many more TV channels, but they promised to undercut your phone bills. The snag was you had to change your phone number. And your phone number is known to your family, your friends, your colleagues and even your enemies. Changing it was out the question.

The same can be true of e-mail. Once you have told people you may be reached at fredsmith@megacost-lyisp.com, then cancelling your subscription may save money but your e-mails will be returned to their senders. Your e-mail address will disappear with your subscription. The only lasting solution is to purchase your own domain name. This is all explained on www.godonthenet.com, along with details of sites where you can sign up for a more permanent e-mail address.

Software to make it work

You will need more than one software program to make the Internet work. On a standard Internet connection you can use separate software for each task *if you wish*. This enables you to select software that best suits your needs, but it can be confusing for those just starting out. Fortunately, the two main Internet software programs (Microsoft's *Internet Explorer* and Netscape's *Communicator* or *Navigator*) are really collections of programs that can turn their hand to most of the basic Internet services, and do it very well indeed. That's the good news. The even better news is that they are both free, so to begin with you need look no further than one of these two products. When you sign up with a service provider, the free CD will contain one or the other. It is in the service provider's interests to make your Internet experience as comfortable as possible, and most provide a good set of up-to-

If you are stuck on the meaning of computer terms, drop in on www.whatis.com

date software on their CDs. You can always update your software via the web itself or through the CDs on the covers of Internet magazines.

In Microsoft Windows, *Internet Explorer* is built seamlessly into Windows itself. Because of this, and because it is arguably better than Netscape's software, over 80% of people browsing the web use it. *Explorer*, both on Windows and on Apple Mac computers, contains a range of tools:

- A browser for viewing web pages.
- An e-mail program *(Outlook Express)* for sending and receiving e-mail.
- A newsreader for participating in discussion groups.
- A simple web page editor *(FrontPage Express)* for creating web pages.
- A FTP (File Transfer Protocol) function within the browser so that you can download files (such as MP3 music files) or send your church's web pages to the Internet so others can view them.
- *Messenger* for exchanging messages with friends or colleagues on-line at the same time as you.

So what don't you get that you need?

- You should buy some virus checking software from your local computer store. Viruses are malign programs which individuals around the world take perverse delight in embedding within normal software. If you run software which contains a virus, you may be lucky enough to get away with a simple warning message, or it may entirely wipe the contents of your hard disk. Viruses are a real danger, but a few precautions should ensure safe surfing. Always virus-check programs you obtain from the web before installing them on your computer, and only obtain software from reputable sources; an unknown website in Bulgaria is not a safe bet!

■ You will probably want to 'download' and try out software you find on the Internet. You can use your browser to retrieve the files. However, since software programs can take up a lot of disk space, they are usually 'compressed' by special techniques which reduce the sizes of the files. These compressed files take less time to transfer from the Internet to your computer, thus saving on time and telephone bills. You will need to decompress the file at your computer. The process is commonly called unzipping (nothing to do with Zip drives!) and you will need an unzipping program. Once on the web, you can retrieve one of these programs from a software library or from a computer store.

When you sign up with an ISP, they will usually send you a CD with the latest versions of *Internet Explorer* or *Netscape Communicator*. Your best option is to use this installation CD and phone the ISP's technical support line if you encounter difficulties. Once you've found your feet you can begin to experiment with different browsers or e-mail software.

See **Software – General**

2

Browsing the Web

Installing the software supplied by your Internet service provider will enable you to connect to the Internet. When you launch your browser by clicking on the icon on your computer's desktop, the browser will run the dial-up software and connect you to the Internet through your service provider. This will take about half a minute, or less. Once connected, the first page that displays is usually the start page of your service provider – once you become familiar with how the web works, you can change this to the website of your choice.

This is the beginning of your adventure. But how do you display the various websites listed in this book?

Moving around

When you want to go to another website, enter one of the many addresses given in this book into the long white box near the top of the screen and hit the return/enter key. If the address is a valid one, the screen will change in a few seconds to the new website. Because of the slow speed of modems and the heavy traffic on the Internet (which is not yet a superhighway!), some sites may take a minute or so to display the complete page. You can see that the browser is retrieving information as the logo at the top right of the screen becomes animated. If a page is taking a long time, you can always stop it by clicking once on the *Stop* button on the browser's toolbar and then click on *Home* to return to your initial starting point (or *Back* to return to the page you just left).

Much of the art of web browsing is effective navigation. As you move from page to page, you can use the *Back* and *Forward* buttons to retrace your steps. But you do not need to click repeatedly on the *Back* button to revisit sites, simply click the little black arrow next to the *Back* button (in *Internet Explorer*) or click and hold the back button (in Netscape *Communicator*), and a list of recently visited sites appears. Select the page you want. Right-clicking on the *Back* and *Forward* buttons also shows you where you have been, as does the drop down arrow at the end of the white address bar.

If you mistype an address, your browser may display a page that tells you that the site is 'unavailable'. Your browser can't tell the difference between a mistype and a site which is not responding because of computer failure. Check your typing and try again. Some browsers will be set up to jump automatically to a search engine if they can't display the page you want. In this case you will see a list of possible alternatives to what you typed. There is more on search engines in the next chapter.

You're living the web lifestyle when you just take it for granted that any purchase you make, any new thing you want to plan like a trip, you turn to the web as part of that process. People today live a phone lifestyle and a car lifestyle. They almost laugh when you say that to them because it's just so taken for granted.

Bill Gates, Microsoft

Understanding URLs

The address of a website – or Uniform Resource Locator – enables a web browser to find the precise page it needs among the millions of pages on the World Wide Web.

URLs are read from right to left. Take the URL http://www.harpercollins.co.uk

- *.uk* indicates this is an address in the UK.
- *.co* indicates it is a commercial company.
- *harpercollins* is the name of the company.
- *www* is the name of the computer holding the page within that company.
- *http://* tells the computer how to retrieve the information – web pages use the 'hypertext protocol' or http.

The *harpercollins.co.uk* section of the URL is the unique 'domain name' for that organization. A company or individual has to register a domain name before they can use it. Some domain names simply end in *.com* or *.net*. These are US or international domain names. Strictly speaking they should only be used by US-registered organizations or businesses with offices around the globe, but many other organizations use them as a matter of style.

UK domain name endings and rules

.co.uk – Commercial enterprises
.org.uk – Non-profit making organization
.net.uk – Host machines of ISPs
.ltd.uk – Registered companies
.plc.uk – Registered public companies
uk.com – Alternative to .co.uk
uk.net – Alternative to .co.uk

US domain name endings and rules

.com – Commercial enterprises
.biz – Commercial enterprises
.net – Internet related organization
.org – Non-profit organization
.edu – Education institutions
.coop – Cooperatives
.info – Information sites
.name – Individuals
.pro – Professionals

We register about 200,000 names a month. That's 4–5,000 a day. We register them in 90 seconds or less, and all of those customers are brought up on to the Net by the next day.

Gabe Battista, CEO of Network Solutions
who handle the .com domain.

The HarperCollins site contains hundreds of web pages, so how does your browser know which page to load? You can enter the folder or file name (if you know it!) after the domain name. For example, information on authors at HarperCollins is at http://www.fireandwater.com/authors/default.asp, where /authors/default.asp refers to the file default.asp within a folder called authors on the HarperCollins computer. If a file name is missed out, the computer at HarperCollins will assume you want the index.html file (or near variations), which is the standard name for the starting or index page. This is then sent to your computer for your browser to display.

URLs are usually written out in lowercase and the last part of the address (the page reference on the computer) is case sensitive, so www.ChristianBookshop.com will get you to the ChristianBookshop.com site just as well as www.christianbookshop.com .

Behind the scenes, each computer on the Internet is allocated a string of numbers to identify it. If you type in 62.232.85.229 you will also end up at Christianbookshop.com. You can either use the number or the address, as the latter is resolved into the former by a vast chain of directories scattered across the web called Domain Name Servers. When you go on to the Internet you, too, are given a unique number, but this varies every time you log on (the jargon calls it 'dynamic allocation'), so it is not much use telling your friends the number you used yesterday!

Typing in the numbers instead of the address does

not always work. It will only take you to the computer holding the site you want to access. Since most Internet servers hold hundreds, if not thousands, of websites, the computer will need the final part of the URL in order to direct you to the site you want.

You do not need to type web addresses in full. You can always miss off the *http://* as this is assumed. Also, browsers have an 'auto complete' feature that remembers the addresses of sites you have been to before and automatically completes them.

Some addresses may lead to dead ends. The individual or organization may have moved their website or even gone out of business. More likely, they may have reorganized the pages of their site and the address given in this book may no longer point to a valid page. Try shortening the address to the basic company name. For example, www.futurenet.com/internetworks/isps.asp refers to a list of ISPs held by *Internet Works Magazine*, which is part of the FutureNet group of magazines. If you shorten the address to www.futurenet.com/internetworks, you will find the home page of *Internet Works*, and if you shorten it yet further to www.futurenet.com you will visit the parent company's website. Once you have found a page that works, use the site's navigation buttons to take you to the page you were looking for – if it still exists!

L i n k s

The language of web browsers is called hypertext. The name implies that hypertext is more than just text on a computer screen, and its most important feature is the concept of a link. The coloured and/or underlined text you see on pages corresponds to links to other documents (or perhaps another section of the same document), either on the same website or on another website entirely. Clicking once on such a link will take you to the corresponding document. By clicking on links which interest you, you quickly find you are moving from site to site, country to country and topic to topic.

If you want to see where you are heading before you click, hold your mouse over a link without clicking: the cursor will change to a pointing hand and your browser will display the destination address somewhere on the screen (usually at the bottom, but exactly where depends on the browser you are using).

You are unlikely to get into trouble by clicking on whatever link interests you. You can always return to the previous page by using the *Back* button on your browser, and your browser has a 'History' or 'Go' list that allows you to return immediately to documents accessed earlier in the session. In the worst case, the *Home* button on the browser will rescue you from almost anything, taking you back to where you started. And do not worry about damaging any hardware or software on your computer by randomly clicking on hypertext links. You won't.

Your browser will usually distinguish visited from unvisited links: the colour of links you have already visited will be different from unvisited ones. Two common colours for visited and unvisited links are red and blue, but the exact colours depend on the browser and how the document that you are viewing has been written.

In addition to words, other objects on a page may also be links on which you can click. For example, images may be linked to something else. Many sites use buttons, much like the toolbars in software.

No one owns the Internet. No one controls the Internet. The Internet is the common heritage of all humankind.

Larry Ellison, founder of Oracle

Bookmarks or favorites

On the web, it is easy first to get distracted and then totally lost. One click leads to another, and pretty soon that promising virtual rest stop a few exits back is just a vague memory. And what about that site you visited last week? Unless you can remember addresses filled with slashes, dots, and unpronounceable clots of consonants, it is pretty much a lost cause.

To avoid web disorientation, make frequent use of your browser's favourites' 'bookmark' feature. Adding the page you are currently viewing as a bookmark stores a reference to that page's address on your computer, allowing you to return to it whenever you wish. To save the reference, right click on the page you want and select 'Add to favorites' or 'Add bookmark' from the pop-up menu. To return to the site, all you have to do is call up your list of favorites/bookmarks and select the one you want.

Using bookmarks

You do not need to bookmark every single page that grabs your interest. Concentrate on the prominent, content-rich sites that offer access to the information you need or list other, potentially-useful links. As long as the sites you want are within one or two clicks of a page you have bookmarked, you will have no problem finding what you want, when you want it. The easiest way to determine the best page to bookmark is to use your history list.

Go back with your history list. If you are browsing at high speed and forget to leave a bookmark somewhere important, don't panic. Your browser has a history list of the sites you most recently visited. You do not have to hit the back button until you get there: open the history list and select the site you want.

Sort bookmarks into categories. When (not if!) your bookmark list gets so big you can't find the bookmark you want, it is time to sift and sort. Browsers let you maintain lists or folders of bookmarks, and set up categories and subcategories. In this way you will be able to move quickly from general topics to specific areas of interest and then to the exact bookmarks you want. For example, in your bookmark list you may have a folder for Christian sites, and within that sub-folders for Christian directories, resource sites and local churches.

Have a Spring clean. Not every site stands the

test of time. That fascinating page that once caught your attention can look pretty dull after a while. If you are sure you want to forget it, just delete it. If you are not sure, move it into a category called 'Maybe', and every few months check whether you really do need it or not.

Menus and keyboard shortcuts

Browsers contain a wealth of functions beyond the scope of this book. Read the program's Help pages or buy one of the many introductory books. You will also find that your browser acts as an e-mail program and as a reader for newsgroups. It may also have an editor so that you can create your own web pages.

Most of these additional functions may be accessed through the toolbar and drop-down menus. Some of the more common actions also have keyboard short-cuts which allow you to press a set of keys rather than exercising your mouse – these are shown on the menus. Familiarizing yourself with some of these will make your browsing more efficient.

Saving pages

When you find something which interests you, you don't have to stop and read it all or take notes. Bookmark the page (so you can return to it easily) and then move on. The pages you view are temporarily stored on your hard disk, and until the memory (or 'cache') allocated for these pages is full, you can go back and view them at your leisure. You can do this browsing 'off line' without the phone meter ticking. Just collect the material you want, end your telephone connection, select 'Go offline' or 'Work off line' from the *File* menu and then return to the pages you wish to read.

If you want to make a permanent record of a page, select *File* from the toolbar and select one of the *Save As* options. All browsers will allow you to save the page as 'text only' – that is, without the images – and some will save both text and images. A more advanced form

A popular site, Christianity Today offers articles, information and search facilities.

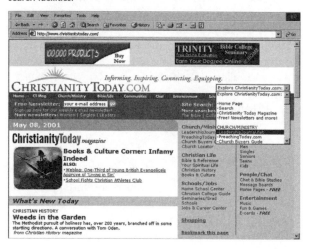

of saving is to save the page you are looking at and any pages on the same website that link to it. In this way, it is possible to capture a whole web site. (This may not work, however, on sites such as on-line shops. These sites may have thousands of products so you are asked to select a category or enter a search word in order to proceed.) Remember, too, that you can always copy and paste text and images from a web page straight into your word processor. Just mark the text or click on the image, right click, choose *Copy*, move to your word processor and paste it into the document.

See **Internet – Guides, Statistics and Security**

Searching for information

The addresses in this book will lead you to some excellent websites. These in turn will point you to others. Before long you will be surfing the web – although the busyness of some sites makes it seem more like 'Zimmer-framing the web'!

Soon you will need to find websites that are not mentioned here and which you don't have the address for. You will want to discover what the web has to offer a Christian musician, an innovative liturgist or a preacher with failing inspiration. The next section shows you how to search the web to find your own resources.

3

Searching the Web

There is an old proverb: 'Give someone a fish, and you feed them for three days. Teach someone to fish, and you feed them for life.' This book is full of references to excellent websites but soon it will become dated, and the site or information *you* want will not be listed. What then? To benefit from the web you should learn to be proficient in using the many search facilities it offers. A little time spent developing your own skills in web searching will be well worth it.

Search sites

As well as sites containing information, artwork, music, entertainment etc., there are sites dedicated to helping you find the content you want. These are well-frequented spots on the web and using them is completely free, as they make their money by selling advertising space or by charging sites for an entry in their lists.

The most well-known, and still the most visited, is Yahoo! It offers a vast directory of websites around the globe, categorized in a clear, tree-like structure. To find the sites Yahoo has listed under Christianity, first go to Yahoo by entering the address www.yahoo.com, then select *Society and Culture* from the opening screen, followed by *Religion and Spirituality*.

Yahoo also lets you enter a search word, and will scan the sites it has indexed for that word. The result is a list of links to websites it believes are relevant to your search. When you find a site in the list that you want to visit, simply click on the reference. Other search engines such as www.google.com place their first emphasis on searching for words; they offer a directory or category structure as a second option.

These search engines have indexed millions of pages. This means that a very general search request, such as 'Religion' will list thousands of possible pages to visit, rather like going into a large reference library and asking a librarian to fetch all the books that refer to 'religion'. The librarian's response will be to ask you to clarify in more detail what you are looking for: what religion? Are you interested in history? In doctrine? In styles of worship? etc.

In this chapter we will look at how to use these search engines and to narrow down the search request so that you only have a few dozen possible links to consider.

See **Search – General**

Christian directories

Smaller, specialized sites have grown up alongside the huge search engines. For example, CrossSearch in the

US searches Christian sites. You are likely to get more consistent results by using these search sites than the religious section of Yahoo.

There are also a whole host of specialist directories. None would claim to be exhaustive, but they have value because of their specialism. There are Christian music sites which offer links to Christian bands, university theology departments with lists of sites with material on New Testament theology, and liturgy sites with links to other similar ventures. Searching through these sites can be very rewarding, as one link leads to another fascinating link.

The larger Christian directories allow you to enter a search word or phrase, much as Yahoo does. The smaller ones ask you to navigate through their categories, defining and redefining your search subject. They are like a librarian's catalogue, with major sections splitting into sub-sections, and then into sub-sub-sections. The quality of the directory depends, of course, on the person (or persons) who compiled it.

See **Search – Christian**

Using search engines

Choose your search site. The starting point is to choose your search site carefully. If you do not want a mass of information from the US, however good, choose a search engine which concentrates on your country only. For example, use the UK Yahoo (www.yahoo.co.uk) or the Australian Yahoo (www.yahoo.com.au). If you are not searching for a particular word or phrase, use a directory site which allows you to browse through categories of topics. In the end, there is no best search engine though Google (www.google.com) is favoured by many for its simple interface and useful results. Each has its strengths, and each has its own style which may – or may not – suit your way of working.

Learn to use the site. No two search engines work in quite the same way. While some search engines are case sensitive by default (distinguishing between 'church' and 'Church'), others allow you to choose whether or not a search will be case sensitive. Many engines ignore words of three or fewer letters. And some search only indexes of keywords, while others search the complete text of pages. In most cases, you will get something you are interested in by entering a couple of relevant words in the search box – but usually the worthwhile stuff will be buried in a morass of irrelevancies. In short, before you go throwing words out into cyberspace, take a few moments to read the instructions!

Choose your words carefully. If you are interested in finding out about, say, bereavement counselling, do not simply use the single word 'death' or you will find irrelevant references to *Death in Venice*, or whatever. Think before you type: is the word too broad? Is there a synonym? Is there another, less common word that would also be on the site? Are there additional words which will narrow down the search (such as 'counselling')? If you can answer yes to any of these four questions, you will improve your search before you start.

Vary your spelling. Suppose you are looking for sites on bereavement counselling. You may not find too many in the US because they spell it 'counseling', with only one 'l'. A search for *liturgy* and *colour* needs to be *liturgy* and *color*.

Use the advanced search page. Most search sites have a page for more sophisticated searching. Make this page your friend. Sadly, only a tiny percentage of web surfers use these so-called advanced pages. But they can help you find what you want and reduce your frustration when the search engine says there are thousands of matches to your query.

The picture opposite shows the advanced search page for *Google*. You can see that you can choose to look for pages containing all the words you want to find (e.g. *Washington* and in the *UK*), an exact phrase, any of the words, or look for pages with one word in but not another (e.g. *Washington*, but not in the *UK*). You can also limit your searches to UK domains such as those ending in .co.uk, but remember that some UK companies may be using a .com domain. Finally, in *Google*, you can turn on a filter (*SafeSearch*) which will filter out known pornographic or offensive sites.

The search engine HotBot (www.hotbot.com) shows similar options right on its home page. Yahoo, like Google, refers you to an advanced page for these options. All search engines allow you to make selections in which you look for *all* words (e.g. flag AND red AND white AND blue for the US, UK and French flags)

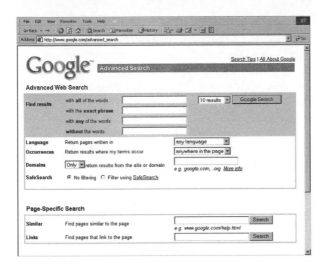

The 'advanced search' page on Google.

or for one or more possible words (e.g. liturgy OR worship OR praise). Some require you to type in the ANDs and ORs between your words, others use + before a word to include it and a – to exclude it (e.g. *Washington –UK* for any Washington outside the UK). Find your favourite search engine and learn its syntax. A half hour now will save hours later!

If at first you don't succeed ... Perhaps you find nothing or only half-useful results. There are plenty more search engines to choose from. Try another. You will be surprised how little overlap results from exactly the same search in two different web search tools. Conversely, two different engines may throw up *exactly* the same results. This is because they share the same technology or the same directory such as the widely used Open Directory Project (www.dmoz.org).

You may tire of chasing around the various search engines, visiting every one to find the site you need. If so, you can use one of the many 'meta search engines' which will submit your search request to a number of engines simultaneously. The best ones then collate the various responses and weed out the duplicates. The charmingly-named Dogpile will also search Usenet postings for relevant entries.

You can also install 'agent software' on your own computer such as the popular *Copernic*. Here you enter your search request into the software and then connect to the web. The software itself fires off your search request to a number of search engines then collates and, hopefully, weeds the results.

Save your search. Sometimes you get perfect results from a search and they are too good to throw away. You may be able to bookmark the URL and save it for later use. This is certainly true of the category pages in Yahoo or the Open Directory Project.

See **Search – General**

More search tips

■ To open a hypertext link you can simply click on it. But in *Internet Explorer* you can open a second, new window by holding down the shift key as you click. Returning to the original directory or search engine merely requires closing the second window rather than clicking on the *Back* button. You can also launch more than one window simultaneously if you wish to view a number of sites.

- Try browsing with 'view images' turned off. Viewing pages without images makes them much faster to load. If the page you find requires images, you can always turn them back on and reload.

- Once you have found an interesting page you can save the contents by using *File* then *Save As*. AskSam's *SurfSaver* allows you to capture a single page (with or without graphics) and then you can assign keywords and descriptive text before storing it away in a database for later reading and analysis. This is an excellent, yet inexpensive tool for serious researchers who need to capture a number of web pages.

- Keep an eye on www.searchenginewatch.com for new search engines and directories. This site is full of helpful hints on getting the best from your searches.

Getting your church on the web

With all this talk of finding sites you may be wondering how you can create your own church or organization site and list it in the various search engines and directories. This is an important area. Outside every church stands a church notice-board which advises passers-by of service times and welcomes people to attend. Every church should have a virtual notice-board on the

World Wide Web, linked to local community sites. Similarly, organizations and societies will want to have a page or two, however simple, so that people can find their contact details.

Rather than devote pages of explanation here, the *God on the Net* site has a whole section devoted to creating your own web site. You can read about setting objectives, about site creation software, domain names and submitting your site to search engines. And because it is on the web, you can more easily follow the links. There is also material from *Using your Church Web Site for Evangelism* to guide churches that see their web site as part of their mission strategy.

Alongside the general search engines, there are directories of Christian sites and resources such as 'Best of the Christian Web'.

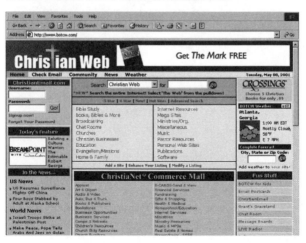

4

Safe Surfing

Is the Internet a 'Good Thing'? As with most technology, the issue lies more with how the technology is
used than with the underlying science. Radioactive
materials have been used to remove cancers or bomb
Hiroshima; printing has made the Bible a number one
bestseller yet enabled pornography to proliferate.

In this technological age, our life is at ever greater risk of
becoming an anonymous function of the productive process. Man
thus becomes unable to enjoy the beauties of creation and, even
more, to see the reflection of God's face in them.

Pope John Paul II

No sex, please

The ease of access to pornography for young, impres-
sionable minds is the moral mud usually slung at the
Internet. And there *is* a real danger. Not only are the
images and words explicit but they are more readily
viewable by an inquisitive teenager than the top-shelf
magazines in a shop. To overcome the problem,
governments can try to ban the sex sites (difficult in a
democracy which upholds values of personal freedom)
or individuals can use software which prevents access

to sites known to be offensive (far easier, but never one hundred per cent effective).

Making your Internet connection unusable with pornographic sites can occur at two places. Your internet service provider or favourite search engine may provide a 'filtered' service, which bars entrance to known sex sites and discussion groups. If you are looking for a service provider, this may be one of your 'must have' features along with low monthly cost and quality of software. Another approach is to install software on your computer which prevents access to known sex sites. The names of such packages indicate

There are plenty of Christian shopping sites on the Web. For example, Christianbookshop.com sells books direct from some of the UK's leading Christian publishers.

Tips for families

Set clear rules. Sit down with your children and work out an agreement governing Internet use – how many hours a week, what sort of use you hope to encourage, and a clear outline of the type of material or activity that you definitely will not tolerate.

Make the Internet a family activity. Keep the computer in a family room. As well as making parental control easier, this will help make the Internet something that the whole family can enjoy.

Choose a family-friendly ISP. There are various Internet Service Providers who offer access in a package tailored to the family. This will typically mean multiple e-mail addresses, filtering of material and a block on offensive newsgroups. Also, always use a search engine, such as *Google*, where you can filter out unsuitable sites.

Keep tabs. You can track what kind of sites your children have been visiting as browsers keep a summary list of sites visited (usually for a week or so, depending on the settings under *Options*). You can quickly scan through this history list to look for sites with suspicious names. As part of the agreement, emphasize that the browser's history is to be left intact: if anyone has cleared it, find out why!

Protect privacy. Make sure that the children realize the dangers of revealing personal details on the Internet, particularly in chat forums. They should never supply their name and address. On-line stalkers are rare, but you want to avoid offensive e-mails or receiving endless junk mail. Many parents ban chat systems (either chat forums or Internet Relay Chat), both for safety and to prevent excessive phone bills. If your child develops a friendship with someone in a chat room, go with them if they want to meet up. The 'new friend' from the web may not be who they claim to be.

Teach them manners. If your children join in discussions on the net, emphasize the need for them to use 'netiquette' – on-line manners. This is particularly important in newsgroups and mailing lists where debates can get heated. Impress on your children the need to understand what they are doing and to read the questions-and-answers page (FAQ) for the groups they use.

Watch for viruses. You should have a virus checker on your computer. If you download files, it is safest to restrict your use to one of the major commercial download sites as they are generally immune from viruses for fear of litigation-hungry Americans.

Use filters but be realistic. Install Internet filter software, but remember that there is no substitute for regular parental supervision. Today's techno-kids are adept at working out the weaknesses of filters, so don't become complacent. The best policy is to supervise your children as you do with any other media.

what they do: *Cyber Patrol, Net Nanny, Cybersitter, Surf Watch, Cyber Snoop.*

The browsers themselves offer some protection. *Internet Explorer*, for example, checks and filters out websites according to an external list in which sites are rated according to content. The ratings are provided by the Recreational Software Advisory Council, and you can check in at www.rsac.org to see how it works. The World Wide Web Consortium (W3C) has a set of technical standards called PICS (Platform for Internet Content Selection) which can control the sites accessed by browsers. The major search engines allow you to opt for 'safe' or 'family' searching. They do their best to filter out offensive sites from their search results. Since you can set your own preferences for using these search engines, you can turn on filtering as a permanent option.

One in three UK children have used the Internet, according to a study by NOP Research. Two-thirds of these say that it helps them learn. While boys prefer sports and games sites, girls tend to favour music and TV sites. Both sexes say they like to chat and make friends online. NOP estimates that while children typically spend one hour per week accessing the Internet, on average they spend 15 hours watching TV.

However, one in five say they have been 'upset' or 'embarrassed' by something they have accessed on the Internet. Two-fifths of these say they found something 'rude' on line, while a quarter believed they accessed information that would get them into trouble. One in seven were scared by something. Paedophiles are known to use chat rooms popular with children.

In the end, it's your call: you have to balance the benefits – education and entertainment – against the risk of your child being hurt. The physical world is a very dangerous place, so we teach our children road safety and not to take sweets from strangers. In the same way, develop a safety code for your child's virtual world.

Even with the combination of a safe Internet service provider – and *Cyber Snoop* watching your every move – there is still a need for responsible parenting. If a problem exists, talking it through may be better than simply banning use of the Internet. The creative teenager who is so helpful mastering the intricacies of your word processor in time for the church annual meeting is also developing the skills that could enable him to circumvent your software babysitter.

See **Family – General**

Shop till you (virtually) drop

Shopping, of course, is not simply about purchasing. It is also about browsing, comparing and finding all-important information to guide your final selection. Here the World Wide Web can excel for certain products.

Looking for a new car? Through the Internet you can scan through a number of lists from used car dealers. But you may still have to visit the showroom and take the car for a spin. Some things you have to see and touch before you buy. A virtual car showroom will not reveal if the exhaust is virtually missing. Yet other products you do not need to see first before you buy. If you want the latest Harry Potter novel, one bookshop is as good as another, and an Internet bookshop offers home delivery and possibly good discounts. The same can be said for CDs and fine wines, and these goods sell well over the web. Christian shopping sites are multiplying just as fast as others.

The respected Forrester Research has calculated that e-commerce could be worth as much as 5 per cent of all global sales by 2003 based on the assumption that online shopping will be simple and secure.

Is it safe to shop on the web?

A shop on the Internet will allow you to search for products and display information about them. If you want to buy a product, you click on a button to add it to your 'shopping cart', which is a list of the items you want to purchase. You can review this list and add or delete items at any point. When you have made your selection, simply enter your name, address and credit card details.

Is it safe to enter credit card details on the Internet? There may possibly be a highly sophisticated team of crooks with thousands of pounds', dollars' or yen's worth of computer equipment steaming open your electronic mail, but the chances are that such teams are more interested in the transactions in the national banks than your attempts to order a book. Technically, the risk is there; practically, the risk is far higher every time you hand your credit card to a sales person, use it to order over the phone or leave it unattended in your coat pocket.

There is a chance that a thief could intercept your credit card number as it travels from your computer to the website's server, but it is only a faint possibility. Most sites work with your browser to encrypt or encode your transaction information so that, if it is intercepted, it cannot be read. This encryption happens automatically and a padlock icon is shown on your browser's status line. As an example, Christianbookshop.com not only encrypts all transactions as you shop, but your card details are kept on their server in heavily coded form and the computer itself is in a secure building. Meanwhile, we worry about web security, while cheerfully discarding our credit card slips with our every-day rubbish!

If you have doubts about providing your credit card number or other personal information to a company's web site, check for the site's certificate by right clicking on the page that is asking for your card details. In *Explorer* look at *Properties*; in *Communicator* look at *View Info*. A website certificate, or digital signature, is an on line document that certifies the site's identity so you know your information is going where you intend it to go. It is also an indication that your transaction is being encrypted.

Shopping sites often use 'cookies' to hold details about your transaction. A cookie is a small amount of information stored on your computer by a website, such as the list of items currently in your shopping basket. Often a cookie is used to provide the site with information about you, such as your password for the site or the customized background colour you chose, in order to simplify your browsing. Cookies are common and harmless. They cannot be used to store information about you or your computer that you have not provided, but they can be used by certain services to create a profile of your interests based on the sites

If you are concerned about security and safety on the Net, read the introductory articles on Microsoft's site.

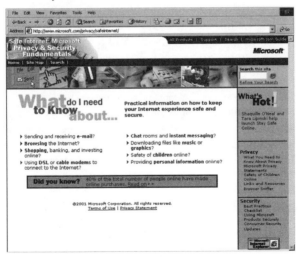

you visit. In this way advertisements on participating sites can be customized for you. Both *Communicator* and *Explorer* can alert you whenever a server tries to give you a cookie. If you don't wish to receive these cookies, or would like to control and limit the number you receive, the help file will give you details about how to disable or control cookies for your browser. If you turn cookies off, you may not be able to shop online.

In short, provided the shop you are dealing with is reputable and the Internet connection you are using is 'encrypted' (which means it scrambles the information before sending it across the net), you are secure.

E-commerce may be sweeping the world, but a while back they made a study of a town in California to see what the social effects would be. The Internet was in every home, and through the TV everyone could order anything from a paperback to a pizza. What was the item most requested? Postage stamps. There's hope yet.

There's no way to have a 2½ million-book physical bookstore. The largest physical bookstores in the world only have about 175,000 titles. If you were to print the Amazon.com catalogue it would be the size of more than 40 New York City phone-books.

Jeff Bezos, founder of Amazon.com

V i r u s e s

To protect yourself from viruses on the Internet, do not download files from sources that you do not know are safe. Viruses are usually hidden in programs and activated when the programs run. They also can be attached to certain other types of executable files, such as special-action web files, video files or apparently harmless e-mails.

If an unknown e-mail encourages you to look at, or run, a file attached to the message (which may promise you fame and fortune, and usually both), don't! Delete it immediately. This warning includes word processor files added as attachments as viruses can be transmitted using the macro language of the word processor. People can find security weaknesses in both your browser and your e-mail software, so keep these up to date as new versions are published as soon as security breaches are found.

Generally, when you are about to use a type of file that could contain a virus, your browser or e-mail software will display a warning and ask whether you want to open the file or save it to disk. If you are confident that the file comes from a trustworthy source, you can continue. If you are not sure, you may want to cancel your action. There are many anti-virus programs that can scan your computer for viruses, inoculate against known viruses, and even repair damage caused by a virus. Make sure you use one regularly and keep it up to date.

As our use of the Internet becomes more sophisticated, more and more homes and businesses have connections that are always on. Since these connections are accessing public sites, the reverse is also true: hackers can attempt to access your computer through the same connections. You will therefore need to watch the security on your own computer or network and install a *firewall* such as ZoneAlarm which locks out others from seeing information on your computer.

See **Internet – Guides, Statistics and Security**

Privacy

Any website you visit can tell who and where your Internet service provider is, what site you were last at, what web browser you are using, and which pages you visit on the site. By asking you to register, a site can collect additional information from you such as your name, e-mail address, postal address, income level and interests. It is entirely up to you whether you provide this.

If you are listed in the UK or US telephone book, your name, address, and telephone number are probably in databases on the web, available for others to search. Try looking yourself up in the Yahoo! People Search, available from the opening page of the Yahoo search engine. You may be able to find out if your name appears elsewhere by searching for your name using a search engine.

Messages you post to Usenet newsgroups are available to anyone on the Internet, and they are archived and can be searched, so do not think of them as private. Also, spam e-mailers (those who send mass e-mail messages, often for advertising) pick up addresses from newsgroups. This may be another reason for picking up a free web-based e-mail address.

Some sites will ask to register you as a user. They may require a password so that your details are only available to you. Remembering passwords is difficult and it is easy to get locked out of a site because you have forgotten the magic combination. The danger is that you use only one password for all the sites you visit and also make the password too simple. Even passwords such as your dog's name or your favourite football team are easy to crack. Ideally you need a combination of letters and numbers. Why not find an obscure verse of the Bible (not John 3:16!) and use the letters and numbers these present?

We have become used to security measures in our everyday lives. We never write down our bank account PIN code, we lock the door when we go out, we fasten our bag as we walk down the street. The Internet is no different. There are crooks about, but a few security precautions will keep browsing safe.

See **Internet – Guides, Statistics and Security**

5

Using E-mail

When people refer to 'the Internet', they often have in mind browsing through the innumerable pages of information on the World Wide Web – a library brought to your own desktop computer down your telephone line.

True, the web is useful. It is not just about helping young Elsie-May with her homework, but everything from reading the archbishop's press releases to checking the value of a secondhand car or getting it insured. But this mass of interconnected computers carries services other than a global *Yellow Pages* cum *Encyclopaedia Britannica*. It can be used to send and receive e-mail. And for many it is this service which makes it all worthwhile.

E-mail! Baby, that's number one.

Steve Ballmer, Executive Vice President, Microsoft

Pros and cons

What is e-mail? The letter you write on your computer can be sent to the intended recipient by sending it down the telephone line. No printing, no search for stamps, no dash to the post box. And it is not like the fax machine which requires an available fax machine at the other end to reply. Your e-mail wends its way from your computer to the computer of the company that provides you with an Internet connection, and from there to the computer of the Internet service provider of the intended recipient. There it stays, and when your colleague or friend next connects to the Internet, your message is transferred to his (or her) computer.

E-mail will not replace letters or faxes, nor personal visits. It is just another means of communication. It has its weak points: if your recipient only connects to the Internet once in a blue moon then it would be quicker to use the post; nor could you include a cutting from a newspaper as you would if you popped it into an envelope. But on the other hand, you do not have to wait until the person is at home – nor will you disturb him if he is. And, if your recipient regularly checks his electronic mail box, communication can be very quick. And although you can't tear out an article from a newspaper, you can cut and paste from documents on the World Wide Web (including on line newspapers) or attach a church report from your word processor.

If Jesus were walking the earth today, I'm convinced He would have an e-mail address.'

Bishop Paul Loverde,
Chairman of the US Bishop's Vocations Committee

Sending and receiving mail

To send and receive electronic-mail messages, or e-mail, over the Internet you need an account. You can get this through an Internet Service Provider, and when you sign up with an ISP you are usually offered an integrated service which includes both web browsing and e-mail. You also need e-mail software for your computer, and a good starting point is to use the e-mail software that comes with your web browser. If you install Microsoft's *Internet Explorer*, for example, you also install their free e-mail software called *Outlook Express*.

When you click on the *Retrieve mail* or *Get mail* button in e-mail software, the program links to your ISP, enters your account details and retrieves any new messages. The messages are saved as short files on your hard disk, and your e-mail software allows you to scan through them and select the ones you want to read or delete. After retrieving any new mail messages, the software sends to your ISP any messages you have created and then ends the telephone connection. The whole sequence may only take a minute.

With a web browser, you are using the telephone all the time that you browse the web. With e-mail you usually read and compose your messages 'off line'. Only when you want to fetch new mail and send out mail do you connect to the Internet. So you might connect twice a day: once in the morning to retrieve messages sent to you overnight, and later in the day to send your replies to the morning's mail and to retrieve any sent to you during the day. Equally, and especially if you have an 'always on' connection, you can leave your e-mail ticking away in the background; it will check for mail every five minutes or so and alert you if new mail arrives.

A little terminology

There are many acronyms associated with e-mail. The three main ones are:

SMTP Simple Mail Transport Protocol, the standard method that e-mail software uses to handle *outgoing* e-mail messages.
POP3 Post Office Protocol version 3, the standard method that e-mail software uses to handle *incoming* e-mail messages. This is gradually being replaced by a more powerful protocol called **IMAP.**
MIME Multipurpose Internet Mail Extensions, a format for turning files such as a spreadsheet or formatted document (from, say, *Word*) into simple text so it can be sent via e-mail.

To set up your e-mail software, you will need to know your SMTP server address and your POP3 server address. For an e-mail service such as Mailbox's, these server addresses are pop3.mailbox.co.uk and smtp.mailbox.co.uk. You can think of these as specialised web pages. Your e-mail software visits your SMTP site to deliver mail and your POP3 site to send it. Your service provider (ISP) will give you the information for its servers. These addresses, along with your account name and password, need to be entered into the configuration screen for your software. More recent software will prompt you to fill in these details when you first install the software using your ISP's CD.

Using e-mail

Describing how to use e-mail software is not as easy as a guide to browsers. Each e-mail program has differently named buttons on differently designed screens. However, the principles are the same for all.

To send a message to someone, you click on the *New mail* or *Compose message* button. This brings up a screen with, typically, three boxes. In the *To* section you enter the e-mail address of the intended recipient, in the *Subject* box you enter a brief description of the message you want to send, and in the *Message* box itself you type your message. When you have finished, click on the *Save* or *Send* button. If you are already on the Internet, your message may be sent at once; if you are being frugal on phone bills by writing your messages off line, your message will be saved in your 'out box' or 'out tray'. The next time you connect to the Internet, you can click on the *Send and Receive* button and all the messages in the out box will be sent.

When writing your message there may be other boxes on the screen. For example, you should be able to enter the addresses of people to whom you wish to send a copy of your message. You should also be able to enter the name of a file on your computer which you want to send as an 'attachment'. The attachment is sent along with your message and the recipient can then place the file on his or her computer. In this way you can pass complex Word documents, image files or even programs. However, the person who receives your e-mail with an attachment can open the attachment only if they have the program in which the attachment was originally created. If the recipient does not have the program you used to create your attachment, they may be able to get the appropriate viewer. A viewer contains the components of a program needed to display (but not edit) a file created with the full version of the program.

The *Send and Receive* button does what it says: it sends out to the Internet any messages in your out box. It also retrieves any messages waiting for you and stores them as files in your inbox. The subject for each message is displayed in a list, so you can see at a glance what the mail is about. With most programs you can sort this mail by subject title, by date or by sender. Clicking on a subject line will open the full message. To reply to a message, you simply have to click the *Reply* button and a new, blank message screen will appear, but with the sender's address already entered in the *To* box.

E-mail addresses

The e-mail address you use in the *To* box is made up of two parts. Consider an address fredsmith@postbox.co.uk: the section after the @ indicates the computer on which the recipient has his or her e-mail account; the section before indicates the account, which may be a name (here Fred Smith's account) or it may be a department (for example, sales@postbox.co.uk) within a company.

If you take out a standard account with a service provider, the computer server used for e-mails will belong to the provider. Your e-mail address will end with the provider's name, such as transaction@compuserve.com, where TransAction is a company which uses CompuServe's e-mail services. If you register your own domain name (see the *God on the Net* site for details), you have a choice. The ISP who registered your domain can automatically forward all mail received by that domain to any existing e-mail account. So TransAction could continue to use transaction@compuserve.com and forward to it any mail sent to *anyone*@transaction.co.uk. A neater approach would be for TransAction to forget the Compuserve account and arrange to pick up their mail directly from their new ISP's mail server.

I looked at my keyboard. The one that was most obvious was the @ sign, because this person was 'at' this other computer. So it seemed fairly obvious, and I just chose it.

Ray Tomlinson, inventor of e-mail on the Internet

Housekeeping

As with paper correspondence, e-mails need to be sorted, filed and possibly thrown away. Your e-mail software allows you to store messages you want to keep in folders with descriptive names, such as 'Work', 'Personal' or 'Hobby'. The program should also give you the means to find a message, with search facilities to look for words in the subject lines or in the body of the messages.

You will also build up a valuable list of e-mail addresses. Addresses can be saved, along with the real name of the person, in the software's *Address book*. Some e-mail programs will look at every incoming e-mail and check whether the sender's address is in your address book. If it is not, it will offer to save it for you.

A survey of UK and Irish businesses found that junk mail could be costing them over $8 billion per year and that it may become such a problem that specialized software will have to be employed to put a stop to it. Three out of four of those surveyed said they received up to five junk e-mails per day, while 16 percent said they received between 6 and 25 junk e-mails per day.

A collection of e-mails is a vital source of information for many users. The list of e-mails which require a response becomes a to-do list, the folders with past messages becomes a vital repository of birthdays to remember, telephone numbers and personal names. Some people sometimes send reminder notes to themselves via e-mail, rather than use another to-do system!

Informality rules OK

E-mail has generated a culture of informality. An e-mail from a colleague may simply say, 'John, When is the next church council meeting? Regards, Simon.' And your reply may be equally terse: 'Simon, It's on Friday. See you there! John.' There is seldom 'Dear John ...' and rarely 'Yours sincerely ...' Although every decent e-mail program has a spelling checker, many ignore it! The medium encourages brief, but frequent communication.

The medium also encourages wider communication. Because sending a copy of a message to another recipient is so simple, you may find that you receive many *copies* of e-mails primarily addressed to someone else, just because the sender 'thought you might like to be kept in the picture'. Thus the e-mails flowing back and forth between members of the mission committee may be routinely copied to both the minister and the youth worker so they know what is being planned. In the days of paper and post, these additional copies would seldom have been sent.

Research from KPMG Management Consulting finds that UK directors spend more than five working weeks a year trawling through their mail. This equates to 75 million days a year or 11 per cent of an individual's time.

Your e-mail software may allow you to format your text by adding bold, italics, colours and even different fonts. It works much like a word processor. By all means, add formatting if you need to in order to make your document clearer. But the essence of e-mail is simple communication and formatting makes e-mails more bulky (so slower to retrieve) and possibly unreadable by some e-mail software. If you want to permanently turn off formatting (as many do), check through your software's *Options.*

Easing the burden

You may not save on stamps by signing up with an Internet service provider and getting an e-mail account. With a monthly charge from your service provider plus the cost of calls to connect to the Internet, you would need to be sending 20–50 messages by e-mail which you would have previously sent by post to make it worth your while. And this assumes you already own the equipment.

But you may ease the burden on people trying to reach you. Take for example a busy central church office trying to re-arrange a meeting: the administrator simply copies the e-mail to all who need to attend (with a copy to the bishop for information, etc.), and 30 seconds of local telephone charges sends dozens of 'letters' on their way. It is so easy and cheap to send multiple copies that many organizations send out newsletters this way.

Your church council may be wary of giving an Internet connection to your youth worker to 'surf the net'. But if the same Internet connection puts him or her in better touch with area experts, other members of the team and resource organizations which can help in the work, e-mail has postage stamps licked.

Web-based e-mail

The account you obtain from your Internet service provider is usually a 'POP3' account – that is, whenever you are connected to the Internet, you use your e-mail software to send and retrieve messages. It does not matter how you get on to the Internet (you could be using a friend's computer), provided the e-mail software knows the addresses of your POP3 and SMTP servers, together with your account name and password, it will handle e-mail for you. If you regularly log on from a second computer, you may wish to set up the e-mail software so that it reads your e-mails but does not delete them from the server. Then, on returning to your usual computer, you can retrieve the messages a second time so you can file them. With this type of e-mail account you can use all the power of specialist e-mail software, and reduce your phone costs by composing your mail off line and simply logging on to exchange mail.

But there is another type of e-mail account which uses a web page as its e-mail 'software'. Using a web browser, you can fill in a form on a web site that mimics e-mail software, with a *To* address and *Message* box. When you've completed the form, it is converted to the e-mail format and the message is sent. The advantage is that you can use such sites wherever you are, provided you have web access. For example, you could send your own personal e-mail messages while browsing the web at work. The disadvantage is that you are connected to the Internet all the time you are reading and composing your messages, which could be expensive.

You could have a second, web-based e-mail account for personal or church purposes only. On most of the systems you can either retrieve mail by going to the website or ask for e-mail sent to that web account to be forwarded to your standard dial-up account. You

Some service providers can give you access to your e-mail via the web. Here (on the author's account) clicking on each subject line brings up a web page that displays the e-mail message with further links to reply to or delete the message.

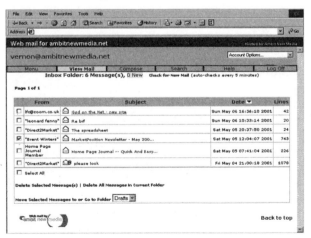

can often use web e-mail to retrieve mail waiting in your dial-up account, so even on holiday you could pop into the nearest cyber café, access the web page and read about the worries back home! Web-based e-mail can be a helpful supplement to your standard dial-up, especially as the e-mail address may be more attractive.

Web-based e-mail is often free. Most of the main web search engines offer accounts or there are specialist providers. Probably the best known is *HotMail*, now owned by Microsoft. Its very popularity means that the connections are often very busy and you may be subject to unwanted advertising e-mails. Finding a smaller provider may be a better option. Your ISP may also allow web access to your standard POP3 account and this is the best of both worlds: an e-mail account you can use with standard e-mail software yet also visit through a web browser from anywhere in the world.

See **Internet – Free Services**

M a i l i n g   l i s t s

Your e-mail account can be used for more than personal messages from colleagues and friends. You can place your name on a list of those who want to be regularly informed via e-mail about some subject which interests you all.

As you browse through websites, you will notice that some sites have a button inviting you to subscribe to their mailing list. The word 'subscribe' is misleading as there is seldom any payment or need to provide details of your credit card. Suppose, for example, you want to be kept up to date with new books from a particular publisher. The publisher's website may have a 'subscribe to mailing list' button, and by clicking this you will be invited to fill in your name and e-mail address. Thereafter, the publisher will e-mail you with their news, every week or month depending on the regularity of their mailing list.

These mailing lists can be a very effective way of keeping in touch. The material arrives unobtrusively in your e-mail in-basket; you do not have to do anything more. However, if you find you no longer need the mailing – or you subscribed to too many and your mail basket is overflowing – simply follow the instructions on the bottom of the mailing to 'unsubscribe' or 'sign off'. This usually includes sending a simple e-mail back to the administrator asking for your name to be removed from the list. Make sure you get the words and format of this sign-off e-mail correct as the list maintenance is almost certainly done automatically and computers are very unforgiving: SIGNOF will not be read as SIGNOFF!

Wider mailing lists

You may be interested in a broad subject area, such as liturgy, rather than the products of one particular website. Fine. There are thousands of mailing lists to which you can subscribe. You can also start your own.

You may also be able to use your own e-mail software to create a mailing list. It will not have the facilities for people to subscribe and sign off automatically, but it will enable you to send a single e-mail to a large number of people with a single mouse click. Most mail programs have a way of doing this: look up 'mailing lists' in the help. If your e-mail software cannot create mailing lists, use a copy of Pegasus Mail (it is free) from www.pmail.com. You an also automate a welcome message to new subscribers using fillers and stationery.

See **Search – E-mail and Phone**

Other uses for your e-mail account

Beyond personal e-mail and mailing lists, there are a few other uses for your e-mail account.

- **Send someone a fax.** If the person you are trying to reach does not have e-mail but has a fax machine, you can convert your e-mail into fax. This is useful if you wish to include some members on a mailing list who do not yet have Internet access.
- **Ask for a reminder on a specified date.** If you are worried about forgetting someone's birthday,

ask a reminder service to e-mail you just before the day.

■ **Be informed on any changes to a website.** If you are waiting anxiously for a new website to go live or to be updated, you can set up a free account to monitor it and send you an e-mail whenever it detects a change.

■ **Be posted with today's news.** If you would rather the news came to you than you having to log on to *The Times*'s site, some news sites will add you to their mailing list.

See **Internet – Free Services**

6

Newsgroups, Forums, Chat and Messaging

The World Wide Web is largely all one way. You view what others have created and the most you get to do is fill in a form or click on a button to respond by e-mail. Newsgroups, forums, chat and messaging, however, are all about talking with someone using your keyboard, computer and the Internet as the medium.

Newsgroups

Newsgroups are a bit like e-mails, but you send your messages to a public notice-board where others can read your wisdom and you theirs. In this way a discussion can take place, especially as the software keeps track of who has replied to what message and the threads of the discussion are easy to follow. Over 250,000 articles are posted to Usenet (the official name for the newsgroup system) each day.

One gigantic notice-board would be impossible to manage, so there are 35,000 of them divided into (almost) every subject under the sun – and a fair few that seem further out of orbit! The number of groups you can browse depends on your Internet Service Provider. Some ISPs filter out some of the junk and the groups that might offend. If all members of your family have access to the Internet, you should use an ISP who uses this filtering. Even so, you will end up with 25,000+ groups to browse through, which is enough for most tastes and interests.

A good way to start is to use www.deja.com to access the newsgroups through a website using your browser. The opening page allows you to search for entries with key words, or to browse through the list of newsgroups available.

As with website addresses, newsgroup names are peppered with full stops. But whereas the dots in a web address indicate its location and type, the dots in a newsgroup name reveal subject or interest divisions, and these form a hierarchy. For example, rec.sport.cricket.info offers information about cricket under the sports section of the recreational category.

Use Deja to select a few groups and read the message 'postings' as they are called. If you want to reply, simply click on the *Post* button on the screen. You will have to register with that newsgroup as part of the process, but Deja will take you through all this. However, before you go adding your opinions to the world's knowledge bank, take time to read a number of the current postings to learn the approach commonly used and the interests of its members. Most groups have a file relating to frequently asked questions (the FAQ file); read it before you join in. On some groups a 'newbie' entering in without an awareness of how the group operates will receive some very curt replies. So before you seek to evangelize the alt.satan-worshippers group, spend time reading what's been written before.

Some groups are 'moderated', which means that one person acts as an editor with the right to exclude your posting. Moderators can also help new people to keep the discussion going. A good moderator can be a real asset to a group.

The new Internet user is Mary Bloggs, an ordinary person living an ordinary life. The typical internet user is no longer an atavistic nerd but a fully integrated member of society who wants to do their shopping and conduct personal business on the Internet.

Frank Gens, Senior Analyst at International Data Corporation

Deja is a web front end to the Usenet system. With Deja you can use your web browser to read and respond to postings. Reading and posting to news-groups through a browser may be easy, but it will run up your phone bill.

If newsgroups are for you, use a newsgroup 'reader' – a software program which can download the groups of interest to you. You can then browse through the threads without the phone meter ticking away, compose your carefully crafted riposte, and go back on line to post it. The browsers *Explorer* and *Communicator* both have good newsgroup readers built-in. Click on *Help* to get some instructions for setting the software up to work with your ISP and the groups you want. There are also specialist readers such as Forté's *Agent*. Pop over to Tucows to find the news readers available.

Usenet messages may look like e-mail but are in fact transferred using a protocol called NNTP (Network News Transport Protocol). Your ISP maintains their own database of Usenet messages, which it updates periodically with neighbouring databases. This means that a posting to a newsgroup does not appear instantaneously the world over, even though it may appear immediately you post it on your screen. It will take a little while as one database updates another. These days, however, this process can be almost as fast as e-mail.

No ISP can hold all the messages for all groups for

You can read newsgroups using your browser. Deja is one of the most popular web interfaces to thousands of newsgroups.

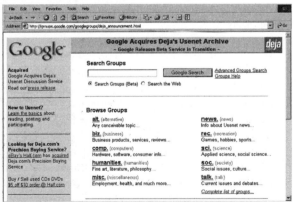

Newsgroup categories

The newsgroups are organized in a tree structure which has seven major categories:

Comp Topics of interest to both computer professionals and hobbyists, including topics in computer science, software sources, and information on hardware and software systems.

Rec Groups oriented towards hobbies and recreational activities.

Sci Discussions marked by special knowledge relating to research in or application of the established sciences.

Soc Groups primarily addressing social issues and socializing. Included are discussions relating to many different world cultures and religions.

Talk Groups largely debate-oriented and tending to feature long discussions without resolution and without appreciable amounts of general information.

News Groups concerned with the news network, group maintenance, and software.

Misc Groups addressing themes not easily classified into any of the other headings, or which incorporate themes from multiple categories. Subjects include fitness, job-hunting, law and investments.

> There are also dozens of other areas that are not part of these 'big seven'. The most famous is the **alt** hierarchy, created by people who wanted to bypass those who control the big seven groups. Other areas are controlled by individual organizations.

all time. So it is usual to delete messages after 3–4 days. If you want to dig back further, use Deja News on the web, which keeps everything as far back as 1995!

See **Software – General**
See **Newsgroups**

What groups should you subscribe to? The directory in the second half of the book gives some indications of where to find Christian and religious newsgroups.

See **Newsgroups**

Web forums

Web forums are another way to collaborate on the Internet. They are in essence a bulletin board system, navigated with a web browser. Users must visit the web site that hosts the forum in order to read messages from others and 'post' their own. Typically the web page will allow you to select a discussion subject and then display all the posts made for that subject since a particular time. You can click on any item to read it and then, if you wish, enter a reply. Your reply will be added to the page, either immediately or after acceptance by the moderator or web site's owner.

You can add discussion forums to your own web site though, depending on the software you use, you may need to obtain the permission of your ISP. Sites such as Delphi (forums.delphi.com) will host a free public or private discussion forum for you. As a further alternative, if you believe your discussion subject is of wide appeal within the Christian community, ask a Christian ISP or magazine if they will host it for you.

See **Web Design – Hosting, Domains and Services**
See **Internet – Free Services**
See **ISPs – Christian**

The Internet boom hasn't even started. We're just beginning to scratch ... I think we're in the roaring 20s.

Scott McNealy, founder of Sun Microsystems

Chat

A chat room is a web site, or part of a web site, that provides a venue for communities of users with a common interest to converse in real time. Forums and newsgroups allow users to post messages but don't have the capacity for interactive talking. In chat rooms what you type is instantly seen by others.

Most chat rooms don't need any special software. Those that do, such as Internet Relay Chat, allow users to download it from the Internet. Chat room users register for the chat room of their choice, choose a user name and password, and log into a particular room as most sites have multiple chat rooms. Inside the chat room, there is usually a list of the people currently online and these people are alerted that another person has entered the chat room. To chat, users type a message into a text box. The message is almost immediately visible in the larger communal message area and other users respond. Users can enter chat rooms and read messages without sending any, a practice known as 'lurking'.

Within chat rooms you can build up relationships and discuss any subject of mutual interest. But because of the possibility of intimacy, you should take care not to reveal information about yourself and use a nick-name rather than your own name. Parents should be vigilant if their teenagers are using chat rooms. Although the interaction can be great fun, there is a danger of older people participating in the chat and masquerading as teenagers themselves. It is better always to use chat rooms that have a moderator who can monitor what is going on and to whom you can complain if someone is harassing you. It is foolish to meet someone from a chat room friendship unless you are accompanied by an adult.

See **Networks, Communities and Centres**

Instant Messaging

Instant messaging (sometimes called IM or IMing) is the ability to easily see whether a chosen friend or colleague is connected to the Internet and, if they are, to exchange messages with them. Instant messaging differs from ordinary e-mail in that you can have a real conversation, back and forth.

AOL first popularized instant messaging but Microsoft has also produced widely-used software called *Messenger* which is part of their *Internet Explorer* package. An alternative tool is called Jabber.

In order for Instant Messaging to work, both users must subscribe to the service and must be online at the same time. Also, the intended recipient must have set his or software to accept instant messages. (An attempt to send an IM to someone who is not online, or who is not willing to accept IMs, will result in a message that the transmission cannot be completed.) On receiving a message, the software alerts the recipient with a distinctive sound to indicate that an IM has arrived, allowing the recipient to accept or reject it. The recipient can then open a window to view the incoming message.

Under most conditions, IMing is truly 'instant'. Even during peak Internet usage periods, the delay is rarely more than a second or two. It is possible for two people to have a real-time online 'conversation' by IMing each other back and forth.

What about the future?

What does the future hold? Whereas books, magazines, radio and TV are largely one-way media, the

Internet has the potential to be truly interactive. This is where it is likely to be most popular. The crude chat and messaging systems of today, where entries are typed and conversation speeds can be sluggish, will give way to three dimensional, virtual worlds where we can speak to and see others. Perhaps the Church, with its focus on community and service for others, can play a significant part by being involved, just as her Lord entered into the networks and communities of his day.

7

Directory of Sites

In creating a directory of Christian websites, the difficulty is not only what to leave out but under what heading to classify some of the sites.

The larger Christian search engines in the US have over 10,000 entries. This book has space for only some of these! I have therefore omitted local church sites and concentrated on organizations and sites which offer further links to a particular subject. I am also very aware that I have omitted those sites I have never found! So if, on your web travels, you discover a site which ought to be listed in this book, please fill in the submission form at www.godonthenet.com. Inevitably, this guide is a starting point, not a definitive directory.

Classifying some of the sites in this book is difficult. A large site, such as *Christianity Today* (www.christianitytoday.com) has community sections for church leaders, youth and women, alongside many others. I have placed a few sites in two categories, but (for reasons of space) have resisted doing this generally. So please hunt around, and in particular look at the *Magazines and Journals – Christian* section where many of the more general sites are listed.

Classifying beliefs is also difficult. How broad is the Christian umbrella? As a working classification, I have taken my lead from the World Council of Churches. And what of other religions? Placing Islamic sites in the same category as some strange cult implies a derogatory view of Islam, which is certainly not intended. But numerous sections and sub-sections also do not help, so all beliefs, both respected worldwide religions and suspect cults, are grouped in the one category *Other beliefs*.

In order to increase the number of sites listed, I have added sites to the end of some sections without any descriptive comment. This is usually because the name of the site – such as the name of a well-known aid agency or Christian mission society – says it all.

Some links will not work. In revising the first edition of this book I discovered that one in seven sites had moved, gone out of business, changed their domain name or had amalgamated with another site. Although every site in this new edition has been checked, by the time this book is published there will already be a handful or so of false trails. Please let me know of them via the *God On the Net* web site. I have noticed that many more organizations and societies now have their own domain name, rather than using the web space provided by their ISP. So I'm hopeful that their domain name will follow them around the web as they move from one hosting service to another and for the next edition there will be fewer changes to make.

The Web is, of course, World Wide and this directory includes English-speaking sites from around the globe. There is a bias towards UK sites, partly because this book is first published in the UK and partly because UK sites are not well represented in the large, US-based Christian directories.

You may want to add your own site to the list. Many sent me e-mails of recommendations, and I have visited those sites. Some are now in the directory, others are not. If you are thinking of creating your own site, this edition has dropped the chapter on getting your church on the web. However, the content is still on the *God on the Net* site so you can go there to learn about creating web pages and obtaining your own domain name. There is also material from another of my books, *Using your Church Web Site for Evangelism*.

William Booth, founder of the Salvation Army, said, 'Why should the devil have all the good music?' The same can be said for websites. Christians have produced a few extremely good sites, although the highest rating awarded to any Christian site by *Encyclopaedia Britannica* is only two stars out of a maximum of five. In comparison with the large web search sites and the pages from *Time* magazine and Disney, this rating is understandable. Certainly, in preparing a sermon, investigating the church music of Bach, being a parent or having a good laugh, the general sites must be included alongside the specifi-cally Christian ones as they have so much to offer. In most categories, therefore, I have listed *general* sites wherever I think they will support Christian ministry and spirituality.

Browsing the general World Wide Web as a Christian is salutary. In most of the main search directories, 'religion' (let alone Christianity) is not one of the main subject areas listed on the first page. You have to hunt for it. It may be under 'society', 'personal', or even be listed under 'leisure'. In the World Wide Web, Christianity appears as a minor interest and God a mere hyperlink among millions of others. The sense of relativism, pick 'n' mix culture and a loss of absolutes is profound.

Finally, I need to emphasize that the sites listed do not pass some invisible test of orthodoxy nor, necessarily, score high marks for good style. I have sought to be inclusive, crossing denominations and spirituality for sites which may open a gateway into *your* interests. I wish you happy surfing.

Directory of
Sites - Contents

Aid 81
Bible 84
Bible Study and Groups 87
Biblical Studies and Theology 91
Books – On-line Texts 96
Books – Publishers 99
Cards 102
Children – Christian 103
Children – General 105
Churches – National/International Societies 109
Drama 118
Education – Bible and Theology 119
Education – General 122
Environment – General and Christian 124
Events 128
Family – Christian 129
Family – General 130
Graphics – Christian 133
Graphics – General 136
Health – General and Christian 137
History – General and Christian 139
Humour – Christian 141

Humour – General 142
Internet – Free Services 143
Internet – Guides, Statistics and Security 145
ISPs – Christian 147
ISPs – General 149
Leadership 150
Magazines and Journals – Christian 151
Magazines and Journals – General 154
Maps and Travel 155
Miscellaneous 157
Mission – Apologetics and Evangelism 159
Mission – Organizations 166
Music – Christian 172
Music – General 177
Networks, Communities and Centres 180
News – Christian 185
News – General 187
Newsgroups 191
Other Beliefs 192
Politics and Government 199
Reference – General 203
Search – Christian Directories and Gateways 207
Search – E-mail and Phone 214
Search – General 217
Sermons and Preaching 222
Shopping 224
Social Issues 227
Software – Christian 231
Software – General 232
Spirituality 235
Support and Counselling 237

TV/Radio/Film 243
Web Design – Creating Pages 246
Web Design – Hosting, Domains and Services 249
Women – Christian and General 253
Worship and Liturgy 256
Youth – Christian 258
Youth – General 264

A I D

Charity Net
http://charitynet.org/
Excellent for information on charities, especially those in the UK. To track down details of a charity, try their links section at http://www.charitynet.org/resources/charitylinks/.

Amnesty International USA
http://www.amnestyusa.org
Information about this Nobel Prize-winning grassroots activist organization.

Book Aid
http://www.bookaid.org
Provides books and other reading material to developing countries and arranges World Book Day.

Charity Christmas Cards
http://www.charitychristmascards.org
Non-profit group that designs Christmas cards for businesses, with proceeds going to charity.

Charity Net
http://www.charitynet.org
Excellent for information on charities, especially those in the UK. To track down details of a charity, try their links section at http://www.charitynet.org/resources/charitylinks/.

Christian Vocations
http://www.christianvocations.org
Advice and information for those who wish to become involved in Christian mission.

Comic Relief
http://www.comicrelief.co.uk
Using celebrities to tackle poverty, promote social justice in UK and Africa.

Compassion International
http://www.compassion.com
Christian child sponsorship.

Cool Planet
http://www.oxfam.org.uk/coolplanet/
Oxfam's site for children and teachers.

Fair Trade
http://www.fairtrade.net
Fair-trading labelling organisations world-wide.

Jubilee 2000
http://www.jubilee2000uk.org
Jubilee 2000 is an international movement in over 40 countries advocating a debt-free start to the Millennium for a billion people.

Jubilee Kids
http://www.jubilee-kids.org
Aims to help children 'live the story' as they find out facts, take action, and learn about justice in the debt crisis issue.

Native Web
http://www.nativeweb.org
An extensive listing of resources for indigenous people around the world.

One World
http://www.oneworld.org
A community of over 350 leading global justice organizations. Good for links to organizations such as Oxfam and Save the Children.

President for a Day
http://www.presidentforaday.org
Sponsored by Tearfund and World Vision, this is a site for the educational computer game that enables players to act as president of a fictional African country.

ReliefWeb
http://www.reliefweb.int/w/rwb.nsf
An electronic clearing house for those needing information on humanitarian emergenices and natural disasters.

Traidcraft
http://www.traidcraft.co.uk
Traidcraft is a leading fair trade organization which believes in giving poor workers in 'third world' countries the opportunity to use their skills with dignity.

World Relief
http://www.worldrelief.org
This organisation is all about helping the hurting by addressing the physical and spiritual needs of those it serves.

World Service Enquiry
http://www.wse.org.uk
Information and advice about working or volunteering over-seas in the developing world for peace, justice, development or mission.

CAFOD http://www.cafod.org.uk

Catholic Relief Services http://www.catholicrelief.org

Christian Aid http://www.christian-aid.org.uk

Christians Abroad http://www.cabroad.org.uk

Church Urban Fund http://www.cuf.org.uk

Compassion UK http://www.compassionuk.org

Food and Agriculture Organization http://www.fao.org

Food for the Hungry International http://www.fh.org

Foreign and Commonwealth Office http://www.fco.gov.uk

International Committee of the Red Cross (ICRC)
http://www.icrc.org

International Federation of Red Cross and Red Crescent Societies http://www.ifrc.org

International Orthodox Christian Charities (IOCC)
http://www.ioc.org

Leprosy Mission International
http://www.leprosymission.org

LESEA Global: Feed the Hungry
http://www.feedthehungry.org

Oxfam http://www.oxfam.org.uk

Red Cross, The http://www.redcross.org

Rotary Foundation http://www.rotary.org

Save the Children http://www.oneworld.org/scf/

Tear Fund http://www.tearfund.org

United Nations Childrens Fund (UNICEF)
http://www.unicef.org

United Nations Development Programme (UNDP)
http://www.undp.org

United Nations: Humanitarian Affairs
http://www.un.org/ha/

Voluntary Service Overseas http://www.vso.org.uk

World Trade Organisation (WTO) http://www.wto.org

World Vision International http://www.wvi.org

BIBLE

Amazing Facts
http://amazing-facts.org
Some of the most interesting facts found in the Bible. Family
fun Bible triva.

Audio-Bible
http://www.audiobible.com
Hear the King James Version narrated by Alexander Scourby
online.

Back to the Bible
http://www.backtothebible.org/minute/
Short devotions from the Back to the Bible radio ministry.

Bible Browser
http://mama.stg.brown.edu/webs/bible_browser/pbeasy.shtml
A concordance on the web. You can search for chapters, verses, words and even parts of words in three translations : KJV, RSV and Vulgate (Latin).

Bible Gateway
http://bible.gospelcom.net
Search the Bible in eleven languages and various Bible versions.

Bible Gateway, The
http://www.bible.gospelcom.net
Tool to search by word in a variety of Bible translations and languages.

Bible Reading Fellowship
http://www.brf.org.uk
Bible reading notes and books, with extracts.

Bible Site, The
http://www.thebiblesite.org
Donate Bibles to persecuted Christians worldwide.

Bibles: Public Domain Reference
http://www.bible.org/docs/public/readme.htm
Public domain Bibles and commentaries.

Blue Letter Bible
http://www.blueletterbible.org
Look up any Bible verse and link it to over 165,000 pages of concordances, lexicons, dictionaries and commentaries.

Daily Bible Reading Plan
http://users.aol.com/bible2007/dailypln.htm
A daily Bible reading plan for the whole year.

Daily Bible readings
http://www.americanbible.org/DailyReading/today.cfm
Daily Bible readings from the American Bible Society.

Gideons International
http://www.gideons.org
Did you know that Gideons annually distribute 45,000,000 Scriptures worldwide? That's 86 a minute!

God's Word for Each Day
http://www.godsworld.org
Daily Scripture passages to lead you through the Bible in a year.

Journey of Faith
http://www.crusade.org/cgi/journey.cgi
Daily passages to guide you through the Bible in 365 days.

Journey of Faith
http://www.crusade.org/journey/
Year-long Bible reading programme from Campus Crusade in Canada.

Keys For Kids
http://www.gospelcom.net/cbh/kfk/
Bible material for children from Children's Bible Hour Ministries.

New Media Bible
http://www.newmediabible.org
New Media Bible traces the Bible's evolution: from ancient orally-transmitted stories to hand-written manuscripts to Gutenberg's press.

On-line Bibles
http://www.geocities.com/Heartland/Acres/3964/bibles/
Over 120 on-line Bibles.

Our Daily Bread
http://www.gospelcom.net/rbc/odb/
Pick the month, the day of the week, and up pops a biblical thought for the day, chosen and turned into a mini-sermon by America's Gospel Communication Network.

Read the Bible in a Year
http://www.bibleinayear.org
Bible texts e-mailed to you daily.

Resurrected
http://www.resurrected.co.uk
The site for those who can't read the Bible at a regular time each day, or don't have a Bible to hand when they want one.

Study, The
http://www.lexalt.com/spirituallife/thestudy.shtml
Access devotional aids such as 'Daily Bread' and 'Read Through the Bible in One Year'. Also provides Bible seach facility.

Unbound Bible, The
http://www.unboundbible.org
A collection of searchable Bibles: 10 English versions, Greek and Hebrew texts, 4 ancient versions and over 4 versions in other languages.

Bible on the Web http://www.bibleontheweb.com

Jewish Bible Association http://www.jewishbible.org

Summer Institute of Linguistics http://www.sil.org

Wycliffe Bible Translators http://www.wycliffe.org

BIBLE STUDY AND GROUPS

Acts 17.11
http://www.acts17-11.com/studies.html
A small collection of Bible studies on various topics concerning Christian living, growth and faith.

Alpha
http://www.alpha.org.uk
Developed at Holy Trinity Church, London, Alpha is a 15-session practical introduction to the Christian faith. The church itself is at www.htb.org.uk.

BibArch
http://www.bibarch.com
Learn from biblical archaeology about the ancient cultures of Bible lands.

Bible Answer Machine
http://bibleanswermachine.ww7.com
Answers to your Bible questions.

Bible Information Online
http://www.bibleinfo.com
Over 340 Bible topics are available to 'help you find answers to life's questions and struggles'.

Bible Learning Centre
http://www.biblelearning.org
A site from the American Bible Society that focuses on the new methods of studying Scripture online. The site encourages Bible exploration with tutorials and interactive programmes for young people.

Bible Studies Foundation
http://www.bible.org
Over 3,000 studies organized by topic or book of the Bible.

Bible Visuals
http://www.nd.edu/~kcoblent/theo.html
Kelley Coblentz of Notre Dame University has gathered together a variety of Internet images relevant to the study of the Bible. Visit this site for busts of Roman emperors, maps of ancient Jerusalem and more.

Biblical Studies Foundation
http://www.bible.org
Home of the free-over-the-internet New English Translation and good set of links to other sites concerned with Bible study.

Cell-Church Website
http://www.cell-church.org
A cell church believes its small groups are the basic building blocks of church life more than the Sunday-by-Sunday congregation. This site has articles, reports and links to cell churches.

Children's Bible Study
http://www.childrensbiblestudy.com
Animated introduction to some Bible study material, much of it from a creationist viewpoint.

Christianity On-line – Bible and Reference
http://www.christianityonline.com/bible/
Comprehensive research and reference tool. Search for Bible verses from a variety of translations. Library of resources includes dictionaries, commentaries, concordances.

Connect Bible Studies
http://www.connectbiblestudies.com
Bible studies aimed to help think through topical issues in a current popular film, book, television programme or album.

Cover to Cover
http://www.cover2cover.org
Reading the Bible, cover to cover.

Darkness to Light
http://www.dtl.org
Resources from Reformed Baptist perspective arranged by topic.

Devotional Bible Study, A
http://mydevotion.com
On-line Bible study including topical verses on faith, anger, stress, etc. Have fun with a talking screen-saver.

Explore the Word
http://www.exploretheword.com
An excellent site for serious Bible study. Also has notes on history, spirituality and sermons.

GOSHEN
http://www.biblestudytools.net
Bible study tools on GOSHEN. At the core of the Bible Study Tools are several cross-indexed topical and dictionary resources: Nave's Topical Bible, Easton's Bible Dictionary, Torrey's New Topical Textbook and Hitchcock's Bible Names Dictionary.

Grace Notes
http://www.villageministries.org/grace-notes/
Grace Notes is a Christian publication ministry for distributing verse-by-verse Bible lessons, topical articles (word studies) and historical studies.

Grow with the Bible
http://www.grow-with-the-bible.org.uk
A resource designed for churches to encourage regular Bible reading.

Illustrated Lectionary Texts
http://divinity.library.vanderbilt.edu/lectionary/
Illustrated lectionary readings at Vanderbilt Divinity Library.

Prophecy Central
http://www.bible-prophecy.com
A world of information about biblical prophecy, all you could want to know.

Shepherd Recordings
http://members.netscapeonline.co.uk/jimwlp/
Exists to spread understanding of God's Word through the use of tape recorded ministry. Borrow tapes for free.

Study Bible Forum
http://www.studybibleforum.com
On this site you can post your questions on verses of the Bible and await the answer.

Truth on Fire
http://truth-on-fire.com
Devotionals, Bible studies and resources from Pastor Kevin Lynch.

Various studies
http://www.joshhunt.com/goodindex.html
Sunday school lessons, church growth articles, Bible studies.

Virtual Jerusalem
http://www.imaginevr.co.il/vrjerusa.htm
Tour of Jerusalem, the 3,000-year-old City of David and cross-roads for three of the world's major religions – Judaism, Islam and Christianity. You will need Viscape software, which can be downloaded from the site.

Whisper of Thunder, A
http://www.godsbook.com
Bible study guide which may be viewed on-line or down-loaded. Uses KJV or NIV.

Word of Life
http://www.word.org.uk
Bible correspondence course

Believer.com http://www.believer.com

Berean Bible Studies Page http://www.afn.org/~leo/

Bible Studies from Yes Lord Ministries
http://ourworld.compuserve.com/homepages/YesLord/

Bible Study http://www.biblestudy.org

K-House Interactive http://www.khouse.org

Sunday School Lessons
http://www.sundayschoollessons.com

BIBLICAL STUDIES AND THEOLOGY

Amazing Discoveries in Bible Archaeology
http://www.concentric.net/~extraord/archaeology.htm
Delve into the archaeological discoveries of Bible times.

APS Research Guide – Theology
http://www.utoronto.ca/stmikes/theobook.htm
Guide to resources for theological and religious studies. Covers major religions and includes texts.

Bible-Links Page
http://www1.uni-bremen.de/~wie/bibel.html
Lots of links of interest to New Testament scholars.

Biblical Archaeology Society
http://www.bib-arch.org
Information about the Society: publications, videos, seminars and digs.

Biblical Hebrew Made Easy
http://www.biblicalhebrew.com
Useful information for anyone interested in Biblical Hebrew. Site gives details of distance learning course.

Catechism of the Catholic Church
http://www.christusrex.org/www1/CDHN/ccc.html
Summary of Catholic teaching with a useful search facility that will enable you to find out about Church teaching for the topic you type in.

Catholic Doctrinal Concordance
http://www.infpage.com/concordance/
A doctrinal concordance that gives people interested in Catholicism a quick reference for the most common items of the faith.

Catholic Encyclopedia, The
http://newadvent.org/cathen
The Catholic Encyclopedia aims to give its readers full and authoritative information on the entire cycle of Catholic interests, action and doctrine.

Center for Reformed Theology and Apologetics
http://www.reformed.org
This comprehensive site is dedicated to the provision of what they hold to be biblically sound resources.

Christian Origins
http://www.christianorigins.org
A site specializing in resources for the study of New Testament and Christian origins: anthropology, archaeology, dictionaries, libraries, journals, religious studies sites etc.

Computer-Assisted Theology
http://info.ox.ac.uk/ctitext/theology/
Oxford University's index of Internet resources relating to theological studies.

Dig the Bible
http://www.digbible.org
Useful for layperson seeking a greater understanding of the Bible through archaeology. Take an on-line guided tour of the Holy Lands, learn about archaeological methods or maybe take part in a dig.

E-grace.net
http://www.e-grace.net
Search by theme from list of links to theology sites.

Ecole Initiative
http://cedar.evansville.edu/~ecoleweb/
A clearly written and growing encyclopaedia of early church history with a chronology, glossary and documents.

Evangelical Philosophical Society
http://www.epsociety.org
Site of Evangelical Philosophical Society which is committed to offering teaching on philosophy, apologetics and ethics.

Fides Quaerens Internetum – Christian Theology
http://www.bu.edu/people/bpstone/theology/theology.html
Comprehensive list of Internet resources for use by students and scholars of Christian theology.

Guide to Early Church Documents
http://www.iclnet.org/pub/resources/christian-history.html
Contains pointers to Internet-accessible files relating to the early church, including canonical documents, creeds, the writings of the Apostolic Fathers and other historical texts relevant to church history.

Internet Encylopaedia of Philosophy, The
http://www.utm.edu/research/iep/
A vast resource containing articles on philosophers, philosophical and ethical theories, terms and movements. Easy to navigate with its own search engine and time line of thinking, this site has authoritative content and is useful for students and teacher.

Jonathan Edwards
http://www.jonathanedwards.com
Largest body of Edwards' writings on the Internet.

Mark Goodacre's Web Resources
http://www.ntgateway.com
An excellent set of links to scholarly resources on the New Testament. Among the usual references to Greek culture, Patristics and the Synoptic problem lies a fascinating section on the films made about Jesus.

New Testament Gateway, The
http://www.ntgateway.com
Gateway to commentaries, Greek New Testament Texts, and much more.

Okeanos
http://faculty.washington.edu/snoegel/okeanos.html
Website for Biblical, Classical and Ancient Near Eastern Studies.

Philosophy in Cyberspace
http://www-personal.monash.edu.au/~dey/phil/
A substantial philosophy links site divided into sections and sub sections.

RE Directory
http://www.theredirectory.org.uk
Directory of RE sites and organizations.

RE Site, The
http://www.resite.org.uk
A good starting point for RE on the web.

Religious Education Sources
http://members.aol.com/wardfreman/alevelre/
Links to sources for UK secondary school religious education topics.

Religious Studies Resources on the Internet
http://fn2.freenet.edmonton.ab.ca/~cstier/religion/toc.htm
Links to general religious studies sites and to specific faith sites.

Reluctant Journey
http://www.gseh65.freeserve.co.uk/contents.htm
On-line book about a homophobic man who changed his mind about what the Bible says about homosexuality.

Resource Pages for Biblical Studies
http://www.hivolda.no/asf/kkf/rel-stud.html
Resource for serious, scholarly studies of early Christian writings and their social world.

Resources for Greek Grammar and Exegesis
http://faculty.bbc.edu/RDecker/rd_rsrc.htm
Resource materials related to the study of the New Testament in the original Greek.

Stanford Encyclopedia of Philosophy
http://plato.stanford.edu
Claims to be the first dynamic encyclopaedia in which each entry is maintained and kept up to date by an expert or group of experts in the field.

Synoptic Problem
http://www.mindspring.com/~scarlson/synopt/
A site devoted to the Synoptic problem.

Theological Research Exchange Network
http://www.tren.com
TREN is a library of over 8,000 theological thesis/dissertation titles representing research from many different institutions.

Tyndale House
http://www.tyndale.cam.ac.uk
A major centre for biblical research with links to other centres.

Virtual Religion Index
http://religion.rutgers.edu/links/vrindex.html
A comprehensive listing (with commentary) of Internet resources for religious studies and theology.

Wabash Centre
http://www.wabashcenter.wabash.edu/Internet/front.htm
A selective, annotated guide to a wide variety of electronic resources of interest to those who are involved in the study and practice of religion.

Early Church Documents
http://web.mit.edu/afs/athena.mit.edu/activity/c/csa/www/documents/README

Glossary of Religious Terms
http://www.religioustolerance.org/glossary.htm

Interpretation: A Journal of Bible and Theology
http://www.interpretation.org

BOOKS - ON-LINE TEXTS

Alex Catalogue of Electronic Texts
http://sunsite.berkeley.edu/alex/
Collection of digital documents in English literature, American literature and Western philosophy.

Anglican Online Hymnal
http://www.oremus.org/hymnal/
Public domain texts from nine Anglican hymnals from the second half of the twentieth century.

Books and Literature
http://digital.library.upenn.edu/books/
Index of on-line books plus pointers to text and special exhibits archives.

Books On Line
http://www.books-on-line.com
Over 16,000 free books plus information on new titles.

Christian Classics Ethereal Library

http://ccel.org

Classic Christian books in electronic format. There is enough good reading material here to last you a lifetime! All of the books are in the public domain in the US.

Creeds of Christendom

http://www.creeds.net

Good collection of credal and confessional documents from a wide range of groups.

Electric Library

http://www.elibrary.com

Search databases of newspapers, magazines, classic books, maps, photographs and major artworks.

English Server

http://eserver.org

The reference section of the 'English Server' at Carnegie Mellon University, Pittsburgh. It offers more than 20,000 texts in many disciplines.

Guide to Christian Literature on the Internet

http://www.iclnet.org/pub/resources/christian-books3.html

ICLnet offers pointers to Internet-accessible literature related to Christianity.

Internet History Sourcebooks

http://www.fordham.edu/halsall/

The Paul Halsall/Fordham University has (avidly) collected public domain and copy-permitted historical texts.

Internet Public Library

http://ipl.sils.umich.edu

Links to thousands of online books, magazines, and newspapers.

Into the Wardrobe

http://cslewis.drzeus.net

For those fascinated by the 'Narnian Chronicles', or other C. S. Lewis works, wander through this site's various links. More a site for adults and researchers than for children.

IPL Online Texts on Religion
http://readroom.ipl.org/bin/ipl/ipl.books-
idx.pl?type=deweystem&q1=200
On-line texts from the Internet Public Library's section on
Religion. The home page for the library is http://www.ipl.org.

Methodist Archives and Research Centre
http://rylibweb.man.ac.uk/data1/dg/text/method.html
Guide to collection of manuscripts and printed materials on
the British Methodist Church from the John Rylands University
Library.

New Advent
http://www.newadvent.org
This site has an index of over 4,000 articles on Catholicism
and is a superb resource for study and links. There are also
ancient Christian writings and a Catholic Encyclopedia.

On-line Books Page, The
http://digital.library.upenn.edu/books/
If you are looking for something to read on Christianity, try a
few of the 700 or so on-line texts linked by this site.

Order of St Benedict
http://www.osb.org/osb/gen/topics/lectio
From the Order of St Benedict, a directory to the Bible and
Christian authors.

Project Gutenburg
http://promo.net/pg/
The Project places out of copyright texts as electronic books
on the Internet.

Project Wittenberg
http://www.iclnet.org/pub/resources/text/wittenberg/witten-
berg-home.html
Home to works by and about Martin Luther and other
Lutherans. All manner of texts from quotations to commentaries, hymns to statements of faith, theological treatises to
biographies.

Religion-online.org
http://www.religion-online.org
Full texts on numerous subjects by recognized scholars. Topics include sociology, ethics, communication and pastoral care to name a few.

St Pachomius Library
http://www.ocf.org/orthodoxpage/reading/St.Pachomius/
A vast library of Christian writings, from Greek sources to Syriac writers and African orthodoxy.

Texas Christain University
http://library.tcu.edu
Library catalogue plus on-line books for use.

Wheaton College
http://www.wheaton.edu/learnres/
Library catalogue of learning resources, archives and special collections.

WWW Virtual Library
http://vlib.org/Overview.html
Online texts a-plenty. Categorized into subject areas.

BOOKS - PUBLISHERS

Areopagus Publications
http://www.churchnet.org.uk/areopagus
Resources, including a magazine, for Christian writers.

Bible Reading Fellowship
http://www.brf.org.uk
Bible reading notes and books, with extracts.

BookFinder.com
http://www.bookfinder.com
Searches from 15 million new, rare and out-of-print titles.

Christian Book Promotions Trust
http://www.christianbookpromotions.org.uk
A charity devoted to promoting Christian books, videos and CD-ROMs.

Christian Cartoons Showcase, The
http://www.ChristianCartoons.com
Resource and showcase for Christian cartoonists.

Christian Comics
http://members.aol.com/ChriCom
News and reviews of Christian comic products and projects.

Christian Comics International
http://members.aol.com/ChriCom/
A long-established site which claims to be the definitive source for information on Christian comics.

Church House Publishing
http://www.chpublishing.co.uk
The publishing arm of the Church of England with a full catalogue at http://www.chbookshop.co.uk/.

Finding Publishers
http://www.lights.com/publisher/
Links to publishers' home pages.

HarperCollins*Publishers* – religious books
http://www.christian-publishing.com
Religious section of HarperCollins and publisher of this guide. The main site is at http://www.fireandwater.com.

Lion Publishing
http://www.lion-publishing.co.uk
On-line magazine and book purchasing from one of the UK's foremost Christian publishers.

Perivale Christian Distributors
http://www.christnetbooks.co.uk/Peribooks/
Supplies American Christian books to Christians and Christian bookshops throughout the UK and Europe.

Scripture Union
http://www.scriptureunion.org.uk
Christian publications with special ministry to children and young people.

SharpWriter.Com
http://www.sharpwriter.com
Ready reference links and advice for writers.

SPCK
http://www.spck.org.uk
A mission society known throughout the world for its grants, support of theological education and distribution of Christian literature.

United Media
http://www.unitedmedia.com/comics/
A simple way to find a comic strip on the web. If you want to colour a Peanuts picture for someone special, this is for you.

Ayer Company Publishers http://www.scry.com/ayer/

Baker Book House http://www.bakerbooks.com

Banner of Truth http://www.banneroftruth.co.uk

Barbour Publishing http://www.barbourbooks.com

Cambridge University Press http://www.cup.cam.ac.uk

Christian Focus Publications http://www.christianfocus.com

Christian Publishing Organisation http://www.cpo-online.org

Concordia Publishing House (LCMS) http://www.cph.org

Forward Movement Publications http://www.forwardmovement.org

Good Book Company, The http://www.thegoodbook.co.uk

Gospel Light http://www.gospellight.com

HarperCollins US http://www.harpercollins.com

Ignatius Press http://www.ignatius.com

InterVarsity Press http://www.gospelcom.net/ivpress/

IVP Publishers http://www.ivpbooks.com

Kingsway Communications http://www.kingsway.co.uk

Lutterworth Press http://www.lutterworth.com

Mennonite Publishing House http://www.mph.org

Navigators http://www.gospelcom.net/navs/NP

Pastoral Press Trinity Music http://www.pastoralpress.com

STL http://www.stl.org

Thomas Nelson Publishers http://www.thomasnelson.com

WesleyOwen Online Bookshop
http://www.wesleyowen.com

Zondervan Publishing House http://www.zondervan.com

CARDS

Bible Cards
http://www.bibleverseart.com
A good source of Bible verses and photographic images to
make your own e-cards.

Blue Mountain
http://www.bluemountain.com
Send an electronic greeting card. This site offers a large
choice including Christian images and Bible verses.

Christian Postcards
http://www.christianpostcards.com
E-mail a friend with an electronic postcard.

Disney Cards
http://www.postcards.org
Lots of postcards to choose from on this site including Disney
animations.

Faith Cards
http://faithcards.digitracts.com/faithcard/
Good quality cards from DigiTracts which help you share your
faith.

Heart Gallery
http://www.heartlight.org/gallery/
Electronic greeting cards you can send to friends and family. Select from a variety of Bible verses.

Nature Cards
http://www.e-cards.com
An e-card site where advertising on the cards supports the World Wildlife Fund.

CHILDREN - CHRISTIAN

Abundant Life Kids
http://members.truepath.com/KIDS/
Christian fun site for children with on-line games and Bible stories.

Apple Sauce Kids
http://home.dmv.com/~aplsauce/
Resources for anyone who works with children and young people. Everything is copyright free.

Assemblies Website
http://www.assemblies.org.uk
Instant assemblies materials for primary schools.

Bible Quizzes from TwoPaths
http://www.twopaths.com/biblequizzes.html
Automatically scored quizzes, some with illustrations and music.

Boys Brigade
http://www.boys-brigade.org.uk
This Christian organization for 6–18 year-olds is the oldest voluntary uniformed youth organization in the world. Now embracing the most up-to-date technology.

Children's Bible Study
http://www.childrensbiblestudy.com
Animated introduction to some Bible study material, much of it from a creationist viewpoint.

ChildrensMinistry.net
http://www.childrensministry.net
Claims to be the biggest and best children's ministry resource site on the web. Take a look and see.

Christian Links for Kids
http://www.kids-teens.org
Christian site for kids that includes testimonies, games, homework help, birthday book and a video club.

Christianity On-line Games
http://www.christianityonline.com/fun/
Lots of games here ranging from checkers, Etch-a-Sketch to sports games.

Christianity Online – Kids
http://www.christianityonline.com/community/kids/
On-line games both old and new linked to Bible stories.

Church Lads and Church Girls Brigade
http://www.church-brigade.syol.com
A uniformed Anglican youth organization offering fun and fellowship for boys and girls between the ages of 5 and 21.

Church Pastoral Aid Society (CPAS)
http://www.cpas.org.uk
UK mission society mainly working with Anglican churches. Best known for its youth and children's work (Explorers, Climbers, Scramblers, Pathfinders and CYFA).

Guideposts for Kids
http://www.gp4k.com
Home page of colourful Christian magazine for children crammed with features such as art studio and phone booth to call up stories, songs and Scripture verses.

Keys For Kids
http://www.gospelcom.net/cbh/kfk/
Bible material for children from Children's Bible Hour Ministries.

Kid's Sunday School Place
http://www.kidssundayschool.com
Ideas and resources for Sunday school teachers.

Kidzweb
http://www.kidzweb.org
On-line comics and stories for children.

Scripture Union
http://www.scriptureunion.org.uk
Christian publications with special ministry to children and young people.

Talks to Children
http://www.talks2children.itsforministry.org
Over 150 talk oultines from the Church of Scotland Board of Parish Education.

Two Edged Sword, The
http://hooray2u.com
This comic book for children (and parents!) of seven to fourteen years makes Bible lessons fun.

Ultimate Veggie Tales Web Site
http://www.veggietales.net
The Internet's largest and most exhaustive resource for fans of Bob the Tomato and Larry the Cucumber.

Children's Ministry from Kingsway
http://www.childrensministry.co.uk

Children's Society http://www.the-childrens-society.org.uk

Ethics for children http://gonow.to/ethics/

Kids and Stuff http://www.angelfire.com/ca/kidsandstuff/

National Christian Education Council
http://www.ncec.org.uk

Teknon Trust http://www.teknon.org

CHILDREN - GENERAL

Ask Jeeves for Kids
http://www.ajkids.com
Excellent search engine for children which allows them to type in sentences such as, 'Why is the sky blue?'

Awesome Library
http://www.awesomelibrary.org
Awesome Library has over 16,000 carefully reviewed educational resources.

Baby World
http://www.babyworld.co.uk
One of the UK's leading mother and child information sites. Stock up on Calpol from here.

Barnados
http://www.barnados.org.uk
Informative site of the largest child-care charity in UK.

Berit's Best Sites for Children
http://www.beritsbest.com
Directory of safe, recommended general websites for children up to age 12.

Child Alert
http://www.childalert.co.uk
Information, education and advice regarding child safety and relevant products.

Child Fun
http://www.childfun.com
Useful source of crafts and activities for pre-school children.

DaKidz
http://www.dakidz.com
Site to help children get the most out of computers.

Destination: Earth
http://www.earth.nasa.gov/
Official site of NASA's Earth Science enterprise. With educational materials and images, it has a great section for children.

EduWeb
http://www.eduweb.co.uk
The leading Internet education service in the UK providing education resources for teachers and pupils.

Fun Brain
http://www.funbrain.com
Excellent US site features quizzes and games to enhance learning.

Kid Info
http://www.kidinfo.com
This American site has childrens' stories, games and reference sources to help with homework plus teachers' manuals and lesson plans.

Kids Channel
http://www.kids-channel.co.uk
Games, puzzles, stories and printable colouring sheets. Promotes itself as the safe place for children of all ages to play and explore the internet.

Kids Domain
http://www.kidsdomain.co.uk
Online activities, tips for safe surfing, stories for children of all ages, games, colouring pages.

Kids Earth
http://kids.earth.nasa.gov
A marvellous childrens' resource from NASA about earth science.

Kids Jokes
http://www.kidsjokes.co.uk
What every parent dreads: the A-Z collection of knock, knock jokes. But an essential site for children's workers.

Kids Web
http://www.kidsvista.com
US site which offers selective but helpful guide to topics, including the arts, sciences, social studies and miscellaneous reference material.

Kids' Almanac
http://kids.infoplease.com
Children's on-line dictionary, encyclopedia and homework help.

KidsLink
http://www.kidslink.co.uk
Offers a 'safe haven' with over 11,000 links to the best education and fun.

OneKey
http://www.onekey.com
Large, categorised database of sites suitable for children.

Peter Rabbit
http://www.peterrabbit.co.uk
Not much to do with Christianity, but how could we leave out this favourite?

Sassy's Place for Kids
http://www.geocities.com/Heartland/Plains/7316/
Activities and stories for children aged three to eleven years.

UK Children's Directory
http://www.ukchildrensdirectory.com
Umbrella site hosting a comprehensive list of links to children's and parenting sites.

UK Kids
http://www.ukkids.co.uk
Cool site for older children with entertainment, careers, hobbies, health and advice channels.

Under Fives
http://www.underfives.co.uk
Ideas, activities and that all-important recipe for play dough.

Yahooligans
http://www.yahooligans.com
Child-friendly web guide organized into subject groups like dinosaurs, hobbies and homework answers. Excellent.

Children's Society, The http://www.the-childrens-society.org.uk

Ecology http://www.eco-pros.com

United Nations Childrens Fund (UNICEF)
http://www.unicef.org

CHURCHES - NATIONAL/
INTERNATIONAL SOCIETIES

Alliance of Lesbian and Gay Anglicans
http://www.alga.org
Membership details, statements and other resources.

Anglican Communion Virtual Tour
http://www.anglicancommunion.org/virtualtour
The Anglican family of churches spans 164 countries in all
parts of the globe. This site offers a glimpse into the ministry
of some of these churches.

Anglicans Online
http://www.anglican.org/online/
Anglican news and resources, with material for youth minis-
ters and young Anglicans, a section on music and religious
orders.

Archbishop of Canterbury
http://www.archbishopofcanterbury.org
Official site, including speeches, CV, personal history and
press releases.

Assemblies of God
http://www.aog.org.uk
Assemblies of God, information about Pentecostal churches
doing evangelical work worldwide.

Baptist Org
http://www.baptist.org
The website with the most extensive collection of Baptist
resources and information. This is a community web site for
all Baptists.

Baptist Union of Great Britain
http://www.baptist.org.uk
Information about Baptist churches – mainly in the UK but
encompasses the 'family' of 40 million followers worldwide.
Links to resources, Baptist sites and e-mail directory.

Catholic Info Net (CIN)
http://www.cin.org
Roman Catholic information site.

Catholic Information Center
http://www.catholic.net
Information, Papal encyclicals, teachings, documents, Catholic directories and news.

Catholic Online
http://www.catholic.org
A centre for the exchange of information for Catholics.

Catholic Pages
http://www.catholic-pages.com
Portal site for Roman Catholics with links, discussion, cards, humour etc.

Catholic Resources on the Net
http://www.cs.cmu.edu/People/spok/catholic.html
An unofficial index of Catholic-related resources.

Cell Church
http://www.cellchurch.co.uk
News on cell churches in the UK, plus some articles.

Cell Life Resources
http://nlc.hypermart.net/cell/
Keep up to date with the cell church movement.

Church of England
http://www.church-of-england.org
Information and news site. The site may also be reached through http://www.cofe.anglican.org/.

Church of England Yellow Pages
http://www.blackburn.anglican.org/yellow_pages
An A–Z directory of Anglican churches and church organizations throughout the UK. Lists addresses, telephone numbers and clergy.

Church of Scotland
http://www.cofs.org.uk
Official pages from the Church of Scotland featuring information on the Church's history and constitution plus a directory of congregations.

Church of the Brethren
http://www.brethren.org
Unofficial web site of the Church of the Brethren, an ecumenical and evangelical Protestant denomination with churches in most of the US states and a few other countries.

Church of the Province of Southern Africa
http://www.cpsa.org.za

Congregational Federation
http://www.congregational.org.uk
There are probably at least 500 Congregational Churches in Britain, though the three main groups are the Congregational Federation, Evangelical Fellowship of Congregational Churches and Unaffiliated Congregational Churches.

Ecumenical Links
http://www.geocities.com/Heartland/Ranch/9925/ecumenical.html
If you need to find the website of a national or denominational church, consult this comprehensive list. The World Council of Churches (http://www.wcc-coe.org/) is also a good place to look.

Episcopalian.org
http://www.episcopalian.org
Designed to inform and encourage those who support worldwide evangelism and discipleship, particularly in the Anglican Communion. Offers news stories with a special eye towards missions. Also helps with website development and hosting.

Evangelical Alliance
http://www.eauk.org
An umbrella body covering one million Christians in the UK, through 65,000 individual members, 3,500 member churches and 800 societies.

EWTN
http://www.ewtn.com
Portal site for Roman Catholics.

First Church of Cyberspace
http://www.godweb.org/index1.html
The site makes use of RealAudio, animation techniques and heavy graphics to showcase music, sermons and a multimedia Bible.

Ichthus Christian Fellowship
http://www.ichthus.org.uk
Began in 1974 under the leadership of Roger Forster and now includes 26 congregations in London, Hertfordshire and Kent, and a further 130 other linked churches in the UK and Europe.

Jesuit Resources
http://www.jesuit.org
Site for The Society of Jesus. Links to history, documents, retreat centres and other web resources.

Jesus Army (Jesus Fellowship Church)
http://www.jesus.org.uk
Home of the Jesus Army. Site has comprehensive links and a search page that sends searches to the main Christian engines. New Creation Christian Community may be found at http://www.jesus.org.uk/nccc/.

Lutherans.Net
http://www.lutherans.net
A website for Lutherans with Bible study tools, discussion, prayer and free web space at http://www.luther95.org.

Methodist Church of Great Britain
http://www.methodist.org.uk
A guide to Methodist beliefs, history and work. Includes the Church's e-zine and links to churches' sites.

New Frontiers International
http://www.n-f-i.org
NFI is a family of over 250 churches.

Orthodox Christian Foundation
http://www.ocf.org
Resources for Christian Orthodox worship. Includes a library of articles on Orthodox history, belief, and practice, news from Orthodox churches and organizations, and links to associated sites.

Pentecostal and Charismatic Churches in the UK
http://www.upcc.com
Directory of UK Pentecostal churches.

Quakers
http://www.quaker.org
Extensive links to Quaker information and other websites.

Reformed Ecumenical Council
http://www.gospelcom.net/rec/
A council of churches that seeks to promote and express the unity of the growing family of Reformed Churches worldwide. Has news and lists of members.

Roman Catholic Church, Holy See, Vatican City
http://www.vatican.va
Central site for the Roman Catholic Church. Guide in six languages, with details on the Church, Catholic news, the Vatican museums and an archive of texts. Visit the Catacombs at http://www.catacombe.roma.it/.

Salvation Army (UK)
http://www.salvationarmy.org.uk
A Church with an evangelistic emphasis, doing extensive social work.

United Methodist Church (Unofficial)
http://www.netins.net/showcase/umsource
This site is not officially endorsed by the UMC, but contains information on the Methodist Church, United Methodist churches, colleges, seminaries on the Internet, ministry resources, and other information.

United Methodist Church
http://www.umc.org
News and information on the UMC. Church locator to find churches.

University of St. Mary of the Lake
http://www.vocations.org/library
Excellent links to other Catholic sites and documents.

Word is Alive, The
http://www.geocities.com/Athens/Forum/1853
Aims to convey information on Roman Catholicism as it relates to society today.

World Council of Churches
http://www.wcc-coe.org
Excellent links to national churches and organizations around the world.

American Baptist Churches in the USA http://www.abc-usa.org

Anglican Africa http://www.anglicanafrica.org/saia/

Anglican Catholic Church http://www.anglicancatholic.org

Anglican Church of Canada http://www.anglican.ca

Anglican Communion http://www.anglicancommunion.org

Antiochian Catholic Church in America
http://www.geocities.com/athens/forum/7951/

Antiochian Orthodox Christian Archdiocese of North America http://antiochian.org

Assemblies of God http://www.ag.org

Associate Reformed Presbyterian Church
http://www.arpsynod.org

Association of Vineyard Churches
http://www.vineyard.org.uk

Baptist Men's Movement
http://easyweb.easynet.co.uk/~aeptypog/bmmhp.html

Baptist World Alliance http://www.bwanet.org

Canadian Conference of Mennonite Brethren Churches
http://www.mbconf.ca/

Canadian Conference of Catholic Bishops
http://www.cccb.ca

Canadian Council of Churches
http://www.web.net/~ccchurch/

Chinese Church in London http://www.ccil.org.uk

Christadelphians http://www.christadelphian.org.uk

Christian Church (Disciples of Christ) in the US
http://www.disciples.org

Christian Reformed Church in North America
http://www.crcna.org

Church Army http://www.churcharmy.org.uk

Church in Wales http://www.churchinwales.org.uk

Church of God, International http://www.cgi.org/cgi/

Church of the Brethren Network http://www.cob-net.org

Church of the Nazarene http://www.nazarene.org

Church Union http://www.netcomuk.co.uk/~lnagel/
churchunion.htm

Church Union, The http://www.churchunion.care4free.net

Church Urban Fund http://www.cuf.org.uk

Confraternity of the Blessed Sacrament
http://www.netcomuk.co.uk/~lnagel/cbs.html

Council of European Bishops Conferences (CCEE)
http://communio.hcbc.hu

Diaconal Association of the Church of England
http://www.societies.anglican.org/dace/

Ecumenical Patriarchate of Constantinople
http://www.goarch.org/patriarchate

Elim Pentecostal Church http://www.elim.org.uk

Episcopal Church http://www.dfms.org

Episcopal Church in the United States of America
http://www.ecusa.org

Evangelical Covenant Church http://www.covchurch.org

Evangelical Free Church of America http://www.efca.org

Free Church of Scotland http://www.freechurch.org

Greek Orthodox Archdiocese of America
http://www.goarch.org

Hong Kong Christian Council
http://www.hk.super.net/~hkcc

International Church of the Foursquare Gospel
http://www.foursquare.org

**International Community of the Charismatic Episcopal
Church** http://www.iccec.org

International Council of Community Churches
http://www.akcache.com/community/iccc-nat.html

International Union of Gospel Missions
http://www.iugm.org

London Mennonite Centre
http://www.btinternet.com/~lmc/

Lutheran Church of Australia http://www.lca.org.au

Lutheran World Federation http://lutheranworld.org

Moravian Church http://www.moravian.org

National Conference of Catholic Bishops
http://www.nccbuscc.org

National Council of Churches in the USA
http://ncccusa.org

New Frontier
http://ourworld.compuserve.com/homepages/nfi/

Orthodox Christian Page in America
http://www.ocf.org/OrthodoxPage/

Orthodox Church in America http://www.oca.org

Orthodox Presbyterian Church http://opc.org

Peniel Pentecostal Church http://www.peniel.org

Pentecostal World Conference
http://www.pentecostalworldconf.org

Pioneer http://www.pioneer.org.uk

Presbyterian Church: USA http://www.pcusa.org

Reformed Church in America http://www.rca.org

Reformed Churches of Australia http://www.rca.org.au/

Reformed Episcopal Church http://www.recus.org

Religious Society of Friends (Quakers)
http://www.quaker.org

Reorganized Church of Jesus Christ of Latter-Day Saints
http://cofchrist.org

Seventh-Day Adventists http://www.adventist.org

South African Council of Churches http://www.sacc.org.za

Southern Baptist Convention http://www.sbc.net

United Church of Christ http://www.ucc.org

United Free Church of Scotland http://www.ufcos.org.uk

United Reformed Church: UK http://www.urc.org.uk

World Alliance of Reformed Churches http://warc.ch

World Evangelical Fellowship
http://www.worldevangelical.org

DRAMA

Creative Church
http://www.creativechurch.org.uk
Extensive and regularly updated listing of Christian contemporary music, drama scripts and video clips. Registration fee required.

Drama for the Church
http://www.drama4church.com
Database of sketches for Christian theatre and worship services. Contains descriptions of over 1300 scripts.

DramaShare
http://www.dramashare.org
Aims to assist Christian drama worldwide by providing royalty-free Christian drama scripts and 'How-to' manuals on organization and training.

Dramatix
http://www.carey.ac.nz/drama/
Dramatix is a community effort sharing theatrical works written by Christians around the world. The majority of scripts may be used free of charge.

Free Christian drama scripts
http://www.nlc.net.au/~jw/
Christian drama scripts suitable for Church, youth group, Sunday school, camps, variety nights, or just clowning around.

IScriptdb
http://www.iscriptdb.com
A vast resource for tracking down free film scripts on the internet.

Kingdom Dance Resources
http://www.bensley.clara.co.uk
Flags, streamers, ribbons, books, workshops.

Lifelines Drama Group
http://www.lifelines.org.uk
UK drama group. Many of LifeLines' scripts are available for downloading plus links to other drama resources.

EDUCATION - BIBLE AND THEOLOGY

All Nations Christian College
http://www.allnations.ac.uk
Offers courses in Christian missionary and cross-cultural training, designed to equip its students to reach unreached peoples and administer practical hope to a broken world.

BBC Education Webguide: Religion
http://www.bbc.co.uk/religion/
BBC's guide to religion split into material suitable at primary, secondary and adult levels.

Belief, Culture and Learning Information Gateway
http://www.becal.net
Peer-reviewed educational and research resources concerning belief, culture and values.

Birdies RE Resource Centre
http://www.ajbird.demon.co.uk
Religious education resources including lesson plans.

CALM Online
http://www.calmonline.org.uk
CALMonline is a comprehensive database of adult Christian courses, sources and resources in England and Wales.

Cambridge Theological Federation
http://www.theofed.cam.ac.uk
Home for seven theological institutions in the Cambridge (UK) area.

Christian College Guide
http://www.whatsthebest-college.com
Guide to Christian colleges in USA.

Christian Education Movement
http://www.cem.org.uk
An ecumenical educational charity which works throughout the UK to support religious education in schools.

Christian Education Links and Resources
http://www.tcmnet.com/~cc/edu/edulinks.html
Christian and general educational resources, home schooling
and miscellaneous resources.

Christian History Institute
http://www.gospelcom.net/chi/
The American History Institute is keen to make Christian
history accessible and interesting. It features 'What Happened
on this Date in Christian History'.

Christian Homeschool Forum
http://www.gocin.com/homeschool/
Members from the Forum share support and encouragement
for those interested in home schooling.

Christian student groups
http://www.churchnet.org.uk/ukgroups/campus/
List of UK student and campus groups on ChurchNet.

Christians in Science Education
http://www.cis.org.uk/cise
Provides a service to Christians who are involved in science
education. It is sponsored by Christians in Science and
Association of Christian Teachers.

European Institute of Protestant Studies
http://www.ianpaisley.org
The domain name tells its own story. The Institute's purpose is
to 'expound the Bible, expose the Papacy, and to promote,
defend and maintain Bible Protestantism'.

Farmington Institute
http://www.farmington.ac.uk
The Farmington Institute was founded to improve Christian
education in schools, colleges and universities. It is
ecumenical in its commitment to the Christian faith and takes
a particular interest in other world religions.

Gsus On
http://www.gsuson.com
Christian resources for school RE lessons.

ICLNet
http://www.iclnet.org/pub/resources/xn-dir.html
Directory of Christian and theological colleges in the US.

Omnilist Education
http://members.aol.com/clinksgold/omnschol.htm
List of US colleges and other education links.

RE-XS for Schools
http://re-xs.ucsm.ac.uk
Offers information and links on over 20 religions and belief
systems, major contemporary moral issues and RE teaching.

Regents Theological College
http://www.regents-tc.ac.uk
Bible College for Elim Pentecostal Church

Association of Christian Teachers http://www.christian-
teachers.org

Bible College of Wales
http://members.netscapeonline.co.uk/philaedwards

Birmingham Bible Institute http://www.charis.co.uk/bbi/

Calvin College http://www.calvin.edu/

Christ for the Nations http://www.christforthenationsuk.org

Christian Home and School
http://www.gospelcom.net/csi/chs/

Gordon College http://www.gordon.edu/

London Bible College http://www.londonbiblecollege.ac.uk

Moody College http://www.moody.edu/

Moorlands Bible College http://www.moorlands.ac.uk

New College, University of Edinburgh
http://www.div.ed.ac.uk

Oak Hill Theological College http://www.oakhill.ac.uk

Pusey House, Oxford
http://parishes.oxford.anglican.org/puseyhouse/

Religious Education Council of England and Wales
http://re-xs.ucsm.ac.uk/re-council/

Spurgeon's College http://www.spurgeons.ac.uk

Westcott House http://www.ely.anglican.org/westcott/

Wycliffe Hall, Oxford http://www.wycliffe.ox.ac.uk

EDUCATION - GENERAL

Argosphere.net
http://www.argosphere.net
Child-friendly site packed with support and learning material.

BBC Education Webguide
http://www.bbc.co.uk/education/webguide/
Guide to sites classified according to school key stages.

BBC Schools
http://www.bbc.co.uk/education/schools
Wide range of resources packed with information for all ages.

Campus Tours
http://www.campustours.com
Virtual tours of USA colleges with maps and web cams.

College is Possible
http://www.collegeispossible.org
Comprehensive information on American colleges and universities.

College Quest
http://www.collegequest.com
Decribes colleges in USA, gives financial advice and includes on-line application.

CollegeNET
http://www.collegenet.com
Search engine for USA colleges and universities provides information and advice on graduate programs and financial aid.

Educate the Children
http://www.educate.org.uk
Exclusively for primary school education featuring the whole curriculum.

Education Index
http://www.educationindex.com
American guide to education-related sites which can be selected by subject or age. Incudes games and chat groups.

EduNet
http://www.edunet.com
Wide range of information on courses, programmes and online materials for students.

EduWeb
http://www.eduweb.co.uk
The leading Internet education service in the UK providing education resources for teachers and pupils.

Govern Your School
http://www.governyourschool.co.uk
Brilliant site for school governors and would-be school governors.

Guardian NetClass
http://education.guardian.co.uk/netclass/
Articles and links on education for parents and educators.

National Grid for Learning
http://www.ngfl.gov.uk
UK Government portal site for learning.

Parents Online
http://www.parents.org.uk
Helps parents guide children through primary school.

Religious Eduication and Environment Programme
http://www.reep.org
Multifaith educational programmes, a schools programme (RE), speakers, trainers and materials in the fields of spirituality, ecology and religion.

Sixthform UK
http://www.sixthform.co.uk
Guidance on careers and help on studying.

Student World
http://www.student-world.co.uk
Plenty here for all students!

StudyWeb
http://www.studyweb.com
Over 150,000 links for learning. Homework begins here!

Department of Education and Employment
http://www.dfee.gov.uk

IDS – Institute of Development Studies
http://www.ids.ac.uk/ids/

Times Educational Supplement http://www.tes.co.uk

United Nations Educational, Scientific and Cultural Organization (UNESCO) http://www.unesco.org

ENVIRONMENT – GENERAL AND CHRISTIAN

ARM Education Centre
http://www.arm.gov/docs/education/warming.html
An excellent educational site for children to learn about global warming.

Best Environmental Resources Directories
http://www.ulb.ac.be/ceese/meta/cds.html
This site contains several environmental directories.

Christian Ecology Link
http://www.christian-ecology.org.uk
A multi-denominational UK Christian movement for people concerned about the environment.

Earth Observatory
http://earthobservatory.nasa.gov
Excellent resource featuring real satellite data from NASA.

Eco-Congregation
http://www.tidybritain.org.uk/gfg/
A programme for churches to help them take spiritual and practical steps to care for God's creation.

Ecotheology
http://www.ecotheology.org
An ecumenical theological journal focusing on key ecological concerns.

EnviroWeb
http://envirolink.org
Claims to be the largest on-line environmental information service on the planet.

European Christian Environmental Network
http://www.ecen.org
A network of churches and Christian organizations involved in environmental issues.

Evangelical Environmental Network (USA)
http://www.creationcare.org
An evangelical ministry initiated by World Vision and Evangelicals for Social Action to be faithful as stewards of God's creation.

Evangelical Environmental Network
http://homepages.tcp.co.uk/~carling/een/
An informal group of individuals – including environmentalists, scientists, and theologians – who are concerned about caring for God's creation.

Friends of the Earth
http://www.foe.org.uk
In-depth analysis of current environment issues.

Friends of the Earth and GM
http://www.foe.co.uk/campaigns/food_and_biotechnology
Friends of the Earth debate on GM foods.

Genetic Modification Issues
http://www.gm-info.gov.uk
Key facts on GM issues from the UK government.

Global Change Master Directory
http://gcmd.gsfc.nasa.gov
Huge, if rather technical directory of global change data.

Good Steward, The
http://www.thegoodsteward.com
Biblical principles of stewardship: time, money and the environment.

GreenSpirit
http://www.greenspirit.org.uk
GreenSpirit celebrates all existence as sacred and deeply connected. It is the trading name for the Association for Creation Spirituality.

John Ray Initiative
http://www.jri.org.uk
Aims to bring together scientific and Christian understandings of the environment.

Medina Valley Centre
http://www.medinavalleycentre.org.uk
An outdoor education centre offering environmental education and field studies for schools, colleges and universities. It offers RYA sailing courses and sailing and activity holidays.

Miss Maggie
http://www.missmaggie.org
Children's site to learn about the environment.

Nature Cards
http://www.e-cards.com
An e-card site where advertising on the cards supports the World Wildlife Fund.

New Economics Foundation
http://www.neweconomics.org
Independent think tank working to construct a new economy centred on people and the environment.

Quaker Network of Green Concern
http://www.quakergreenconcern.org.uk/about.html
A quaker based environmental network set up to to explore and promote awareness of the need for a green lifestyle.

Religious Eduication and Environment Programme
http://www.reep.org
Multifaith educational programmes, a schools programme
(RE), speakers, trainers and materials in the fields of spirituality, ecology and religion.

Rocha, A
http://www.arocha.org
An international Christian conservation organisation with
projects in Portugal, France, Lebanon, Kenya, Czech Republic
and Canada.

Society, Religion and Technology Project
http://www.srtp.org.uk/srtpage3.shtml
Examines the ethics of technology, with resources on genetic
engineering, cloning, risk and climate change.

World Wildlife Fund
http://www.worldwildlife.org
This site, with well-known panda logo, is devoted to conservation of nature. Lots of information about endangered
species and their environment.

Earth Island Institute http://www.earthisland.org

EarthAction http://www.oneworld.org/earthaction/

Ecology http://www.eco-pros.com

Environment and Nature http://www.nrpe.org

European Environment Agency, The http://www.eea.eu.int

Greenpeace International http://greenpeace.org

Natural History Museum http://www.nhm.ac.uk

Project Earth http://www.projectearth.com

Sustainable Development (United Nations)
http://www.un.org/esa/sustdev/

World Conservation Union (IUCN) http://www.iucn.org

World Wide Fund for Nature http://www.panda.org

EVENTS

Christian Bed and Breakfast
http://www.icbbn.com/icbbn.html
This is a private hospitality network for Christians to enjoy fellowship with one another and to provide lodging at affordable prices.

Christian Resources Exhibition
http://www.crexhib.co.uk
News on forthcoming exhibitions.

Greenbelt Festival
http://www.greenbelt.org.uk
Annual music and arts festival in the UK. See also http://www.beltup.freeserve.co.uk.

New Wine
http://www.new-wine.org
Organizes conferences and regional events in the UK. Also has a ministry through a magazine, tapes, albums and videos.

Soul Survivor Watford
http://www.soulsurvivor.com
Through festivals and events, Soul Survivor provide a place for young people to get connected with God in lifestyles of worship that make sense to them.

Spring Harvest
http://www.springh.org
Everything you need to know about the Spring Harvest weeks is here. So, as the site says, 'Explore and enjoy'.

Easter People http://www.robfrost.org/ep.html

Global March for Jesus http://www.gmfj.org

Stoneleigh Bible Week http://www.n-f-i.org/sbw.htm

FAMILY – CHRISTIAN

Amazing Facts
http://amazing-facts.org
Some of the most interesting facts found in the Bible. Family fun Bible triva.

American Family Association
http://www.afa.net
AFA stands for traditional family values, focusing primarily on the influence of television and other media – including pornography – on our society.

BiblicalParenting.com
http://www.biblicalparenting.com
Not much more than a set of links to other sites, but these could be helpful.

Christian Movies Theater On-Line
http://www.angelfire.com/mt/BibleTruths/MovieCenter.html
Fun, family site with downloadable real audio and video player.

Christmas Eternal
http://members.carol.net/~asmsmsks/xristmas.htm
The meaning and history behind Christmas customs and symbols from a traditional Christian perspective.

Christmas in Cyber space
http://www.njwebworks.net/christmas/
A directory of Christmas and Advent sites as an antidote to the usual commercialization of this festival.

Concerned Women for America
http://www.cwfa.org
Aims to restore the family to its traditional purpose.

Family Research Council
http://www.frc.org
Promotes the traditional family unit and the Judeo-Christian value system upon which it is built.

FamilyLife
http://www.familylife.com
A division of Campus Crusade for Christ, this provides practical, biblical tools to strengthen marriage and family relationships.

Focus on the Family
http://www.fotf.org
The official site of Focus on the Family offers practical advice on marriage and raising children.

James Dobson
http://www.family.org
Support and advice on parenting from Dr James Dobson.

Parentalk
http://www.parentalk.co.uk
Inspiring articles for parents.

Promise Keepers
http://www.promisekeepers.org
Dedicated to social reform through revitalization of the father's role within the family.

Search for the Meaning of Christmas
http://techdirect.com/christmas
This site invites you to join in sharing the Christmas tradition.

Family Values Network http://www.fvn.com

Marriage Resources http://www.marriageresource.org.uk

FAMILY - GENERAL

2-in-2-1
http://www.2-in-2-1.co.uk
Resources to shape, enrich or repair your marriage. The site offers a Christian bias and promotes religious marriage.

ABC's of Parenting
http://www.abcparenting.com
Comprehensive site covering all aspects of parenting with loads of links.

Ask Jeeves for Kids
http://www.ajkids.com
Excellent search engine for children which allows them to type in sentences such as, 'Why is the sky blue?'

Child Poverty Action Group
http://www.cpag.org.uk
Researches family poverty in UK and provides welfare benefits advice and training courses.

Families.co.uk
http://www.families.co.uk
Aims to provide a great source of useful and interesting information for the whole family.

Family at Go.com
http://family.go.com
There are all sorts of things on this site including advice on parenting, health, holidays plus ideas for activities, birthdays, recipes.

Family Click
http://www.familyclick.com
Family site which filters its content.

Family Education Network
http://www.familyeducation.com
US site which aims to help parents and their children learn and succeed. Has sections on homework help and college admissions.

Family Play
http://www.familyplay.com/activities/
A good place to find activities for the family. You can select by age, occasion, location etc.

Family Point
http://www.familypoint.com
Provides web tools to help far-flung families stay in closer contact: address book, group calendar, photo album, chat room … Easy to use.

Family.com
http://www.family.com
In typical Disney style, Family.com celebrates the best of parenting and parenting ideas, with topics ranging from projects to recipes, travel and education.

Moms Online
http://www.momsonline.com
Plenty of easy-to-prepare menus, child-rearing advice, stories and chat groups.

Parent Soup
http://www.parentsoup.com
Parent Soup's active chat groups and message boards are a good place to find advice and help.

ParentsPlace.com
http://www.parentsplace.com
A supportive site where new parents can get all sorts of information. The easy-to-navigate site features lots of information presented in a simple Q&A format.

Practical Parent
http://www.practicalparent.org.uk
Free advice for parents on children's behaviour problems.

Search Engine Watch
http://searchenginewatch.com/facts/kids.html
Links here to child-safe search options and articles that explain how filtering of Internet sites works.

Smart Marriages
http://www.smartmarriages.com
The coalition for marriage, family and couples education.

UK Mums
http://www.ukmums.co.uk
See UK Parents.

WholeFamily Centre
http://www.wholefamily.com
An interactive site geared to everyone in every family.

National Council for One Parent Families
http://www.oneparentfamilies.org.uk

Parents News Online http://www.parents-news.co.uk

UK Parents http://www.ukparents.co.uk

GRAPHICS - CHRISTIAN

Atlantic Fish
http://members.tripod.com/~chr4/
Free Christian clipart.

Bible Verse Art
http://bibleverseart.com
Gallery of Christian art, e-cards and wallpapers.

Bible Visuals
http://www.nd.edu/~kcoblent/theo.html
Kelley Coblentz of Notre Dame University has gathered together a variety of Internet images relevant to the study of the Bible. Visit this site for busts of Roman emperors, maps of ancient Jerusalem and more.

BiblePower
http://www.biblepower.com
Selection of Christian clipart, screensavers, wallpaper and sounds.

BibleVerse Art.com
http://bibleverseart.com
Christian images: wallpaper, e-cards and screen savers.

Byzantine Images
http://www.bway.net/~halsall/images.html
There is a growing amount of Byzantine art on the Internet. This site contains some images, with links to other sites.

Cartoon Works
http://www.gospelcom.net/cartoonworks/
Home of cartoonist Ron Wheeler.

Christian Computer Art
http://www.cc-art.com
A collection of over 6,000 professionally presented images from simple clipart to full colour pictures.

Christian Wallpapers
http://www.christianwallpapers.freeservers.com
Like the name says: Christian-themed computer wallpaper.

Cross Daily images
http://graphics.crossdaily.com
Graphics from Cross Daily plus links to other image sites.

Cross Search
http://www.crosssearch.com/Art/Clip_Art/
Clipart directory on Cross Search.

Desktop Themes
http://www.infonet.ee/arthemes/
Themes spiritual and artistic.

Free Christian Images
http://www.fci.crossnet.se/
FCI make contemporary Christian images which are free for non-profit use.

Inspired Christian Technologies
http://www.inspired-tech.com/gallery.html
Christian radio and television broadcasts and feature-length motion pictures by RealVideo. Free Christian animated graphics.

Jesus Christ – Images, Art and Photographs
http://www.clark.net/pub/webbge/jesus.htm
This site holds 400 images of Jesus created down the centuries by artists both known and unknown.

John Bell's Christian Art Gallery
http://jrbell.crossdaily.com
Lots of free pictures for not-for-profit or evangelistic sites and literature

On-line Icons
http://www.mit.edu:8001/activities/ocf/icons.html
A collection of religious icons, including Jesus, Theotokos and
various saints. Images are freely available for personal use.

Religious Borders
http://windyweb.com/design/gallery.htm
A collection of religious backgrounds and buttons from
Windy's Web Designs. Original artwork suitable for your
church website.

Religious Christmas in Art
http://www.execpc.com/~tmuth/st_john/xmas/art.htm
A collection of links to many paintings on websites across the
world which portray the events of the Christmas story.

Religious Icon and Image Archive
http://www.aphids.com/susan/relimage/
Collection of religious and Christian images and graphics for
use on non-commercial web pages.

Reverend Fun
http://www.gospelcom.net/rev-fun/
Daily full-colour cartoons which may be freely used in any
non-profit bulletin or newsletter.

WhyteHouse, The
http://www.whytehouse.com
A place to go for free Christian web graphics and Javascripts.

Byzantine Orthodox Christian Icon Studio
http://www.sacredicons.com

Christ Art http://www.christart.com

Christian Computing
http://www.gospelcom.net/ccmag/clipart

Free Christian Images http://www.fci.crossnet.se

Timo's Christian Clipart Site
http://members.theglobe.com/timoclipart/

GRAPHICS - GENERAL

AltaVista
http://www.altavista.com
Impressive service with millions of pictures listed, most obtained by crawling the web. Search on any topic and matching images are displayed as thumbnail images.

Art Today
http://www.arttoday.com
Over 1 million images from this subscription site.

Artcyclopedia
http://www.artcyclopedia.com
Directory of artists and museums. Useful links to view art on-line. Best to search by artist name.

Earth Observatory
http://earthobservatory.nasa.gov
Excellent resource featuring real satellite data from NASA.

Free Site: graphics, The
http://www.thefreesite.com/freegraphics.htm
List of sources for free clipart, images, borders, backgrounds etc.

Graphic Designers Paradise
http://desktoppublishing.com/design.html
A good selection of graphic design links and articles.

Lycos Picture Search
http://multimedia.lycos.com
Now you can search for photos, art designs, videos, music, noises … Pick from 80,000 free images, including some with religious themes.

Microsoft Design Gallery
http://dgl.microsoft.com
Huge resource of images for web design, etc.

Pictures of Earth
http://seds.lpl.arizona.edu/billa/tnp/pxearth.html
Satellite pictures.

World Wide Art Resources
http://www.world-arts-resources.com
Huge index on the art world – a kind of Yahoo for art with
plenty of art history links.

HEALTH - GENERAL AND
CHRISTIAN

About on Ancient History
http://www.ancienthistory.about.com
Vast subject by subject resource with articles, maps and
source material.

American Medical Association
http://www.ama-assn.org/consumer/gnrl.htm
On-line health information from the American Medical
Association.

Christians in Health Care
http://www.christian-healthcare.org.uk
Helps Christians working in healthcare to be more effective in
their day-to-day witness at work.

Department of Health
http://www.doh.gov.uk
Social and public health issues.

Elder Web and AgeInfo
http://www.elderweb.com
4,000 reviewed links related to care of the frail and elderly. In
the UK look at AgeInfo (http://www.cpa.org.uk/ageinfo/
ageinfo.html) which has information for everyone concerned
with older people, including a database of over 32,000 books
and articles.

Health and Safety
http://www.healthandsafety.co.uk
Everything you need to know about safety in the workplace.

Health Web
http://healthweb.org
This US site provides links to evaluated information on the www. Useful for both the health care professional and the layman. Parental guidance may be required for some topics.

Healthfinder
http://www.healthfinder.gov
US Government-funded directory with links to a selection of health resources.

Healthy Kids
http://www.healthykids.org.uk
Online health centre for children over three years.

KidsDoctor
http://www.kidsdoctor.com
Access to database of childrens' health topics. Question-and-answer section with a reading room of books and articles.

KidsHealth
http://www.kidshealth.org
A site created by US medical experts that focuses on children's health and tries to use language that parents can understand.

Pharm Web
http://www.pharmweb.net
Pharmaceutical Yellow Pages.

Virtual Children's Hospital Home Page
http://vch.vh.org
Medical reference and health promotion tool for patients, families and health care professionals.

Women's Health
http://womenshealth.about.com
Frequently updated comprehensive resource provides articles and thousands of annotated links.

British Red Cross, The http://www.redcross.org.uk

Christian Medical and Dental Associations
http://www.cmds.org

Christian Medical Fellowship http://www.cmf.org.uk

Episcopal Medical Missions Foundation
http://www.emmf.com

World Health Organization (WHO) http://www.who.int/

HISTORY - GENERAL AND CHRISTIAN

Anglican Timeline
http://justus.anglican.org/resources/timeline/
A time line of Anglican history created by Ed Friedlander.

Biographical Sketches of Christians
http://justus.anglican.org/resources/bio/
Stories of the people who, through the centuries, have made the Christian Church what it is today.

Christian History
http://www.christianitytoday.com/history/
Seeks to 'make the heritage of Christianity come to life'. Contains sample articles on such issues as Christian involvement in the abolition of slavery and modern urban decay.

Christian History Institute
http://www.gospelcom.net/chi/
The American History Institute is keen to make Christian history accessible and interesting. It features 'What Happened on this Date in Christian History'.

Ecole Initiative
http://cedar.evansville.edu/~ecoleweb/
A clearly written and growing encyclopedia of early church history with a chronology, glossary and documents.

Hall of Church History
http://www.gty.org/~phil/hall.htm
Subtitled with the wonderful name 'Theology from a Bunch of Dead Guys', this site explores Christian history and theology.

History Channel
http://www.historychannel.com
If you are into history, drop in on the History Channel. Very useful search engine if you ever need a short biography on a famous preacher or leader.

History Index
http://www.ukans.edu/history/VL/
Indexed list of history sites: 3,500 connections arranged alphabetically by subject and name.

HistoryNet, The
http://www.thehistorynet.com
This is a great place to find out about events in history. Includes eye-witness reports and picture gallery.

Internet History Sourcebooks
http://www.fordham.edu/halsall/
The Paul Halsall/Fordham University has (avidly) collected public domain and copy-permitted historical texts.

Learning Curve Gallery
http://learningcurve.pro.gov.uk/virtualmuseum
One of the best general historical resource sites for older children, teenagers and adults.

Roman Empire
http://www.roman-empire.net
Incredibly comprehensive site featuring interactive maps and a separate children's section.

Today in History
http://www.9online.com/today/today.htm
If you want to illustrate what happened in history on a certain day, call in here.

Twentieth Century, The
http://www.thecentury.com
All you've ever wanted to know about the twentieth century shown in a variety of formats including audio and video.

Early Church Documents
http://web.mit.edu/afs/athena.mit.edu/activity/c/csa/www/documents/README

European History http://history.hanover.edu/europe.htm

London Jewish Cultural Centre http://www.ljcc.org.uk

Tudor History http://www.tudorhistory.org

HUMOUR - CHRISTIAN

Cartoons and Illustrations
http://www.borg.com/~rjgtoons/cpub.html
Cartoons for Christian publishers, religious education, church bulletins and newsletters from Randy Glasbergen

Christian Jokes
http://www.christianjokes.co.uk
Contains only clean, family jokes and is run solely by Christians.

Comic Break
http://www.webcom.com/~ctt/comic.html
Do you want to know how many Episcopalians it takes to change a light bulb? Answer: six. One to change the bulb and five to form a society to preserve the memory of the old light bulb.

EcuLaugh
http://www.ecunet.org
For over a decade, members have contributed good, clean, religious humour to EcuLaugh.

Heaven
http://www.catholicdigest.org
Magazine intended to 'offer fresh, insightful, humorous play on inspirational issues for people of all faiths', with most of the material drawn from Catholic Digest.

Humour from About
http://christianity.about.com/religion/christianity/cs/christian humor/
About's guide to humour sites.

Pastor Tim's Clean Laughs
http://www.cybersalt.org/cleanlaugh/
Jokes, images, videos and even 'funny files to run on your computer'.

Reverend Fun
http://www.gospelcom.net/rev-fun/
Daily full-colour cartoons which may be freely used in any non-profit bulletin or newsletter.

Ship of Fools
http://ship-of-fools.com
A very popular site but not for anyone extra-sensitive about their faith. A sort of religious Private Eye magazine.

Using Cartoons in Web Evangelism
http://www.gospelcom.net/guide/web-cartoon.html
Lots of good advice and links to cartoon websites.

HUMOUR - GENERAL

Darwin Awards
http://www.darwinawards.com
Darwin Awards celebrate the theory of evolution by commemorating the remains of those who have improved our gene pool by removing themselves from it in really stupid ways.

Funny
http://www.funny.co.uk
On-line comedy directory with links to humour all over the web.

Funny-Bone
http://funny-bone.spunge.org
Features free, clean humour for all ages and a free daily mailing.

Humour Database
http://humor.ncy.com
Searchable database of jokes, which are helpfully rated (general, parental guidance etc.) so you can avoid anything that might offend.

Humour Links
http://www.humorlinks.com
A huge resource with search engine and links to over 4,000 comedy sites.

HumourNet
http://www.humournet.com
Join the HumourNet mailing list to exchange jokes or browse through the collections.

Kiss this Guy
http://www.kissthisguy.com
Readers send in their most embarrassing misheard lyrics. Maybe someone should start a similar site for hymns and worship songs.

My humour
http://www.myhumor.org
Jokes and funny stuff for all ages. Proof that humour can be clean and funny at the same time.

Quoteland
http://www.quoteland.com
Hundreds of quotes and humourous sayings to brighten up your sermon (or to read in someone else's sermon).

Scatty.com
http://www.scatty.com
A joke site for kids and all the family.

INTERNET - FREE SERVICES

Cool Freebie Links
http://www.coolfreebielinks.com
Freebies ... freebies ... freebies!

EcuNet

http://www.ecunet.org

Ecunet is a not-for-profit, online network of Christian organizations. You can sign-up to create your own discussion area or join one of the many existing forums.

Every Mail

http://www.everymail.com

Use this free site to compose and send e-mails in a selection of languages.

Free E-Mail Address

http://www.free-email-address.com

Contains reviews of web-based e-mail services (with links).

Free E-mail Providers Page

http://members.tripod.com/~mareka/

Need free e-mail? Pick your free e-mail address from US and outside-US lists. See also http://www.charitynet.org/resources/freemail.html.

Free Fax Service

http://www.tpc.int

Transmit faxes anywhere in the world via the Internet. Coverage is not 100% and the recipient gets an advert attached to your message, but it is free! For commercial services, see http://www.fax.co.uk/, http://www.ukfax.com and http://www.faxaway.com/.

FreeFind Search Engine

http://www.freefind.com

Add a free search engine to find material within your own website. As usual, the snag is advertising on the results page. See also http://www.atomz.com.

Microsoft Network (MSN UK)

http://www.msn.co.uk

Microsoft's network. As well as a good general starting point, MSN offers free e-mail via Hotmail, and free faxing.

Missionboard.com
http://www.missionboard.com/index.cfm
A source for communication among Christian missions, churches and individuals all over the world. You can set up a web page for free.

Pegasus Mail
http://www.pmail.com
An excellent free e-mail program which can be used for simple mailing lists. If you are serious about setting up e-mail lists, look at the Mercury product (from the same author and also free) on this site.

Postmaster
http://www.postmaster.co.uk
Free web-based e-mail from a UK company.

INTERNET - GUIDES, STATISTICS AND SECURITY

COIN
http://www.coin.org.uk
Free UK support for churches on Internet matters.

Computers Don't Bite
http://www.bbc.co.uk/education/cdb/
Handy beginner's guide from the BBC.

Cyber Atlas
http://cyberatlas.internet.com
Statistics on world-wide use of the internet.

Delphi Internet
http://www.delphi.com/navnet/faq/history.html
A brief history of the Internet.

Gallup Organization
http://www.gallup.com
Supplies results of past surveys, so you can keep up to date with trends and ratings or pepper your sermon with statistics.

Get Net Wise
http://www.getnetwise.org
Helpful site that explains how to browse safely and reviews all
the software tools available to filter unwanted content.

Getting onto the Internet
http://www.methodist.org.uk/information/internet.htm
Excellent series of pages from the Methodist church on the
internet, including tips on safety.

International Data Corporatation
http://www.idcresearch.com
The research and consulting arm of International Data Group
(IDG), publisher of Computerworld, PC World and InfoWorld.

Learn the Net
http://www.learnthenet.com/english/
An internet guide and tutorial.

Life on the Internet: Beginner's Guide
http://www.screen.com/start/guide
Index to various sections dedicated to the basics of the
Internet.

Microsoft security
http://www.microsoft.com/security
Details of Microsoft security options with a superb beginners'
section.

Modem Help
http://www.modemhelp.com
Help for your modem, whatever make or model.

NOP
http://www.maires.co.uk
Site includes latest research on UK internet usage, demo-
graphics and likely trends.

Rough Guide to the Internet
http://www.roughguides.com
Home of the Rough Guide books, including an on-line version
of the guide to the Internet complete with a directory of top
sites.

Search Engine Watch
http://searchenginewatch.com/facts/kids.html
Links here to child-safe search options and articles that explain how filtering of Internet sites works.

Urban Legends and Folklore
http://urbanlegends.about.com/science/urbanlegends/
Has many stories and information about internet hoaxes and email scams

Web Novice
http://www.webnovice.com
Get to grips with the Internet – a plain-speaking guide. Your next stop after reading this book!

What is?
http://whatis.com
Internet jargon explained. Sort out your POP3s from your SMTPs.

Zone Alarm
http://www.zonelabs.com
Home of the popular firewall which can prevent attacks on your computer while you are browsing the Internet. The software is free for personal and non-profit use.

Electronic Frontier Foundation http://www.eff.org

Electronic Privacy Information Center http://www.epic.org

World Wide Web Consortium: Security
http://www.w3.org/Security/faq/www-security-faq.html

ISPS - CHRISTIAN

Azariah Internet Ministries
http://www.azariah.org.uk
E-mail and internet access, mail forwarding, list servers, web space and general computing advice to local churches and individuals.

CatholiCity
http://www.catholicity.com
A community of Catholic organizations. The site offers free, limited homepages to selected, authentically Catholic organizations.

Charis Internet Services
http://www.charis.co.uk
Christian ISP based in Birmingham, UK.

ChristianWeb.net
http://www.christianweb.net
Free Internet resources include e-mail accounts, Christian yellow pages, site directory and classified advertising.

Church UK
http://www.churchuk.net
Christian ISP with some useful services such as simple web page creation, sub-domains and site redirection.

In Jesus
http://www.injesus.com
Enables groups to interact and provides facilities for setting up on-line giving for your own ministry.

Jireh Internet Services
http://www.jireh.co.uk
UK Christian ISP. Handles dialup connections, hosting and page design.

True Path
http://www.truepath.com
A US-based Christian ISP which offers free web hosting.

Word Net
http://www.wordnet.co.uk
UK Christian Internet company specializing in website design and hosting.

WWJD.net
http://www.wwjd.net
Dedicated to spreading the word of God on the Internet. It offers free home pages, e-mail, banners and Christian chat.

XALT ISP
http://www.xalt.co.uk
XALT provide connections to the Internet and free web space, with a percentage of the phone bill being passed back to Christian causes.

Netreach http://www.netreach.co.uk

Wyre Compute http://www.wyrecompute.com

ISPS – GENERAL

ADSL Guide
http://www.adslguide.org.uk
Your guide to fast ADSL connections in the UK.

Directory of Internet Service Providers
http://www.thedirectory.org
Directory of over 10,000 ISPs, with breakdowns by country.

E-Mail Today
http://www.emailtoday.com
News of latest advances in e-mail technology plus directory of services and e-mail providers.

Fish.co.uk
http://www.fish.co.uk
An ISP with a difference – all its profits support Christian Aid's work to reduce poverty worldwide.

List, The
http://thelist.internet.com
Your quest to find the right ISP should begin with The List: a searchable database of all the current ISPs either in the US or around the world. Over 6,000 ISPs.

W3C – The World Wide Web Consortium
http://www.w3.org
Official guardians of the web. Look here for HTML specifications and papers.

PC Pro http://www.pcpro.co.uk

LEADERSHIP

Christian Leadership World
http://www.teal.org.uk
Free on-line training resources to help Christian leaders.

Effective Teams
http://www.teams.org.uk
Help teams achieve more, support each other, and enjoy working together. Tools, downloads and training materials – all for free.

Leadership Journal
http://www.leadershipjournal.net
Offers 'practical biblical advice, insights, and humour to encourage the church leader'. Contains sample articles addressing issues such as preaching and pastoral care.

Leadership University
http://www.leaderu.com
Apologetics training resources.

Next Wave
http://www.next-wave.org
Monthly interdenominational online magazine on the nature of ministry, faith and leadership in the 21st century.

Pastors.com
http://www.pastors.com
Sermons, free e-mail, books and weekly e-newsletter.

School of Christian Leadership
http://www.worldchristians.org
Training resources focused on mission.

Administry http://www.administry.co.uk

MAGAZINES AND JOURNALS –
CHRISTIAN

Beyond Magazine
http://www.beyondmag.com
Magazine whose goal is to engage a highly visual generation.

Books and Culture
http://www.christianitytoday.com/books/
Christian magazine that seeks to offer 'a Christian perspective on key issues, and informed analysis of books and ideas that are shaping our society'.

Campus Life
http://www.christianitytoday.com/campuslife/
Magazine from the Christianity Today stable.

Christian History
http://www.christianitytoday.com/history/
Seeks to 'make the heritage of Christianity come to life'. Contains sample articles on such issues as Christian involvement in the abolition of slavery and modern urban decay.

Christianity Today
http://www.christianitytoday.com
Top Christian magazine with community sections (women, men, singles, church leaders ...), interest channels (music, spirituality ...) and a link to their many sister magazines.

Compass
http://gvanv.com/compass/comphome.html
Catholic journal that seeks to be 'a forum for lively debate on contemporary, social and religious questions.'

Dirty Hippy Liberal Christian Home Journal
http://student-www.uchicago.edu/~mbaldwin/dirty.html
Advocates liberal, socially active Christianity. Extensive archive of articles addresses abortion and the pro-life stance, American prison population statistics, gays in the Church, and other controversial topics.

Discipleship Journal
http://www.gospelcom.net/navs/NP/dj/
Magazine from the Navigators that focuses on developing deeper relationships with Christ.

Evangelicals Now
http://www.e-n.org.uk
Monthly evangelical newspaper, published in the UK.

Fides Quaerens Internetum – Journals
http://www.bu.edu/people/bpstone/theology/journals.html
List of Christian theological journals.

Guideposts
http://www.guideposts.org
Guideposts say they are more than a magazine: 'We're your daily inspiration on the web – for both you and your kids. You'll find a prayer companion, magazine articles, extracts from bestselling books, even fellowship.'

Heartlight
http://www.heartlight.org
A weekly electronic publication dedicated to bringing practical help to inspire positive Christian living.

Leadership Journal
http://www.leadershipjournal.net
Offers 'practical biblical advice, insights, and humour to encourage the church leader'. Contains sample articles addressing issues such as preaching and pastoral care.

Life and Work
http://www.lifeandwork.org
Official Church of Scotland magazine.

Maranatha Christian Journal
http://www.mcjonline.com
News and views: an online magazine that won the 1998 'Best of the Christian Web' award.

Next Wave
http://www.next-wave.org
Monthly interdenominational online magazine on the nature of ministry, faith and leadership in the 21st century.

Sojourners Online
http://www.sojourners.com
Non-denominational Christian organization urging grassroots activism, informed by personal faith and directed toward the goal of social justice and discovery of 'the intersection of faith, politics, and culture'.

Spirituality for Today
http://www.spirituality.org
Interactive monthly magazine addressing a variety of matters concerning the Catholic Church. (Not only for a Catholic audience.)

Third Way Magazine
http://www.thirdway.org.uk
A virtual home for rigorous Christian thinking on politics, society and culture. Third Way advertises itself as a magazine for people who haven't lost faith in God or lost touch with the world.

Woman Today Online
http://www.christianwomentoday.com
Christian women's magazine: Bible study, advice, stories, devotions.

Youth Work
http://www.youthwork.co.uk
The website of Youthwork magazine, Britain's most widely read resource for Christian youth ministry. Articles and ideas.

Banner, The http://www.thebanner.org

Campus Journal http://www.gospelcom.net/rbc/cj/

Catholic Teacher's Gazette
http://www.cartrefc.demon.co.uk

Christian Century http://www.christiancentury.org

Christian Computing http://www.gospelcom.net/ccmag/

Christian Herald http://www.christianherald.org.uk

Christian Home and School
http://www.gospelcom.net/csi/chs/

Church Schools http://www.churchschools.co.uk

Closer Look, A http://www.acloserlook.com/9802acl/

Commonweal http://www.commonwealmagazine.org

Evangelical Times http://www.evangelical-times.org

Insights http://insights.uca.org.au

Interpretation: A Journal of Bible and Theology
http://www.interpretation.org

Journal for Christian Theological Research
http://apu.edu/~CTRF/jctr.html

Light Magazine
http://ds.dial.pipex.com/town/square/ac848/light.htm

Other Side, The http://www.theotherside.org

St. Anthony Messenger
http://www.americancatholic.org/navigation/Messenger

Tabletalk http://www.gospelcom.net/ligonier/tt/

Today's Word http://www.crusade.org/cgi/word.cgi

Worldwide Challenge Magazine
http://www.wwcmagazine.org

MAGAZINES AND JOURNALS −

GENERAL

Electronic News Stand
http://enews.com
Directory of links to 2,000+ magazines, plus home to another
200 or more with sample articles and subscription forms.

Fathers Direct
http://www.fathersdirect.com
UK online magazine for all fathers, written by fathers.

Financial Times http://www.news.ft.com

Magazine Rack
http://www.magazine-rack.com
Features links to lots of on-line magazines, presented as a graphical, virtual magazine rack.

News Rack
http://www.newsrack.com
Comprehensive search for magazines and newspapers around the globe. Locate the website for the Church Times or the Chorley Citizen.

Pathfinder
http://www.pathfinder.com
There's too much here to squeeze into a short description. Time Magazine is just a section of this site! An excellent on-line magazine.

MAPS AND TRAVEL

Biblelands
http://www.mustardseed.net
Multimedia tour of the Holy Land. From Egypt and Israel to Rome.

Big Book
http://www.bigbook.com
Lists over 11 million US businesses, plus street maps, reviews and free home pages.

Destination: Earth
http://www.earth.nasa.gov/
Official site of NASA's Earth Science enterprise. With educational materials and images, it has a great section for children.

Embassy Web
http://www.embassyweb.com
This site gives access to a large searchable database containing details of diplomacy personnel worldwide.

Embassy World
http://www.embassyworld.com
Embassy and consulate search engine.

Garden Tomb
http://www.gardentomb.com
Information site on the Garden Tomb in Jerusalem.

International Christian Embassy Jerusalem
http://www.intournet.co.il/icej/
Embassy site for Christians in Jerusalem.

Library Map Collection
http://www.lib.utexas.edu/Libs/PCL/Map_collection/
Map_collection.html
The place to find world maps of every description including
nautical, political and topograhic.

Mapblast
http://www.mapblast.com
US and Canadian street maps.

Maranatha Tours (Euro) Ltd.
http://www.maranatha.co.uk
Travel tours for groups visiting Israel or Christian heritage sites
in the UK and Europe.

National Geographic Society
http://www.nationalgeographic.com
Excellent site full of geographical facts and resources
including downloadable maps.

National Map Centre
http://www.mapsworld.com
Over 800 editable maps from regions around the world.

Nexus
http://www.nexustour.co.uk
Aims to meet the travel requirements of religious and cultural
groups, irrespective of denomination and destination.

UK Street Map
http://www.streetmap.co.uk
Provides address searching and street map facilities for the
UK. Handy for directing visitors to your church.

UpMyStreet
http://www.upmystreet.com
Fascinating site which allows you to find information – and businesses – in your local area. UpMyStreet.com helps you pick and probe at the latest published statistics about your community.

Virtual Jerusalem
http://www.imaginevr.co.il/vrjerusa.htm
Tour of Jerusalem, the 3,000-year-old City of David and cross-roads for three of the world's major religions – Judaism, Islam and Christianity. You will need Viscape software, which can be downloaded from the site.

Christian Guild Holidays http://www.cgholidays.co.uk

MISCELLANEOUS

Animal Immortality Book and Pet Resources
http://www.creatures.com
Tips on pet care and animal stories plus a book about animals receiving eternal life.

Athletes in Action
http://sports.crosswalk.com/aia/
Well-presented site for Christians with an interest in athletics.

Bible Quizzes
http://www.biblequizzes.com
Quizzes on a variety of topics. Includes crosswords and a Bible planner.

Biblical Holidays
http://biblicalholidays.com
Hundreds of pages about 'Biblical Holidays' and innovative ideas for celebrating them.

Christian Jugglers Association
http://www.juggling.org/~cja/
It's marvellous what a search engine will choose as its first result to the question, 'How do I become a Christian?'!

Christmas in the Holy Land
http://www.Jesus2000.com/christmas.htm
An opportunity to view video clips of Christians from all over the world gathering in Bethlehem to celebrate the birth of Jesus Christ.

Ecclesiological Society, The
http://www.eccl-soc.demon.co.uk
The society for those who love church buildings.

Fellowship of Christian Athletes
http://www.fca.org
Well-presented site that is easy to navigate.

Funders Online
http://www.fundersonline.org
Independent information on funding resources.

FundRaising Export
http://www.fundraisingexpert.com
Fundraising ideas and advice.

Garden of Praise
http://gardenofpraise.com/garden.htm
The creators of this site believe that the gardener works with God to grow something beautiful for all to see and to cause his name to be glorified.

Get ordained
http://ulc.org/ulc/ordain.htm
Just click on the button to become an ordained minister with the Universal Life Church. Beats three years of hard study at theological college.

Good Steward, The
http://www.thegoodsteward.com
Biblical principles of stewardship: time, money and the environment.

Meet-O-Matic
http://www.meetomatic.com
Free meeting organizer via a website.

Rosemary Conley Fitness Clubs
http://www.conley.co.uk
Advice on losing weight.

Sistine Chapel, The
http://www.christusrex.org/www1/sistine/0-Tour.html
The Sistine Chapel has its own virtual museum with multiple views of the masterpiece.

UK Fundraising
http://www.fundraising.co.uk
Guidance and resources for UK charity and non-profit fundraisers.

MISSION - APOLOGETICS AND EVANGELISM

2001 principle, The
http://www.2001principle.net
A scientific and philosophical study of the origin and creation of the universe. Lots of food for thought based around the 2001 film.

Adherents.com
http://www.adherents.com
Thousands and thousands of statistics that tell you membership and congregational figures for over 1,300 religions, churches, denominations, faith groups and movements.

Alpha
http://www.alpha.org.uk
Developed at Holy Trinity Church, London, Alpha is a 15-session practical introduction to the Christian faith. The church itself is at www.htb.org.uk.

American Scientific Affiliation (ASA)
http://asa.calvin.edu./ASA/
A fellowship of men and women who have a commitment to integrity in the practice of science.

Apologetics, Evangelism and Creationism
http://mcu.edu/library/apologet.htm
Extensive list of links to articles and sites.

Billy Graham Institute of Evangelism
http://www.wheaton.edu/bgc/ioe/ioehome.html
This is the Institute of Evangelism at Wheaton College. If you want Billy Graham, go to http://www.billygraham.org/. The Institute promotes research, study and training to assist in reaching the world with the gospel.

Business Men's Fellowship UK
http://www.bmf-uk.com
Helps men speak to their work colleagues about their personal relationship with God.

Chick Publications
http://chick.com
Wear a Chick T-shirt for Christ and evangelize in McDonalds!

Christian Answers Network
http://www.christiananswers.net
Provides Christian answers to contemporary questions: Bible archaeology, Bible and theology, family and marriage, social issues and government … Even if the approach is not your style, the answers could start a discussion.

Christian Apologetics
http://ccel.org/contrib/exec_outlines/ca.html
Pages on the historical Jesus by Mark Copeland.

Christian Research Institute
http://www.equip.org
CRI exists to provide Christians worldwide with carefully researched information and reasoned answers that encourage them in their faith.

Christian Students in Science
http://www.csis.org.uk
Promotes discussion in the student community on issues relating to science and faith.

Christian Surfers UK
http://www.csuk.freeserve.co.uk
Shares the gospel of Jesus Christ with the surfing communities in the UK.

Christian Think Tank
http://www.webcom.com/~ctt/
A serious attempt to confront the questions of believers and sceptics with reflections on philosophy, theology, spirituality and apologetics.

Christian Viewpoint for Men
http://www.cvmen.org.uk
Provides training, encouragement and resources to men seeking to bring other men to faith in Christ.

Christians in Science
http://www.cis.org.uk
A professional Christian group for all who are concerned about science/faith issues

Church.co.uk
http://www.church.co.uk
An innovative project from Oasis which introduces people to Christian faith and worship.

Crossroads Project, The
http://www.crossrds.org
Helping the church at large effectively explain and defend the Christian message in today's culture

Damaris Trust, The
http://www.damaris.org
Resources on films, books and music relating the Bible to contemporary culture

DigiTracts – The Digital Gospel
http://www.digitracts.com
Various presentations of the gospel on-line. The site encourages you to share these e-tracts with your friends and family.

Evangelism.uk.net
http://www.evangelism.uk.net
Suggestions and ideas to UK Christians and churches to encourage and enable their evangelistic thinking and action.

Facing the Challenge
http://www.facingthechallenge.org
Training Christians to understand contemporary culture and respond in an effective, Bible-based way

Faith Movement
http://www.faith.org.uk
A Roman Catholic movement seeking to promote a synthesis between orthodox Catholicism and our modern scientific culture.

Genesis Research and Education Foundation
http://www.genesis.dircon.co.uk
A research organization investigating aspects of origins from the perspectives of science, archaeology and theology

In Defense of the Faith
http://www.gty.org/~phil/resourcz.htm
Christian apologetic and theological helps for the thinking Christian.

Institute for Christian Research
http://www.icr.org
Devoted to research, publication and teaching in those fields of science particularly relevant to the study of origins.

Jesus Film Project
http://www.jesusfilm.org
The Jesus Film Project seeks to give everyone in the world a chance to hear the gospel in their own language through a film version of St Luke's Gospel. In the UK use http://www.jesusvideo.co.uk.

Leadership University
http://www.leaderu.com
Apologetics training resources.

Marcus Honeysett
http://www.mhoneysett.freeserve.co.uk/html/FullIndex.htm
Some excellent articles about relating culture and evangelism

newWay.org
http://www.newwway.org
Very useful articles and other resources on how to communicate.

Reaching the Generations for Jesus
http://home.pix.za/gc/gc12/
Research and discussion on the various generations of young people growing up today: Generation X (born 1961–82), Generation Y (1982–2003) and Generation Z (2003–2025).

Reaching the Unchurched Network
http://www.run.org.uk
Led by practitioners for practitioners, RUN's focus is to inspire, equip and encourage church leaders to prioritise reaching the unchurched.

Reasons to Believe
http://www.reasons.org
Resources from the ministry of Hugh Ross, answering skeptics, encouraging believers.

Reasons to Believe
http://www.reasons.org
The mission of Reasons to Believe is to show that science and faith are allies and not enemies.

Rebuild
http://www.rebuild.org.uk
Rebuild exists to help local churches make a lasting difference in their communities.

SASRA
http://www.sasra.org.uk
Personal evangelism amoung the UK's armed forces.

School of Christian Leadership
http://www.worldchristians.org
Training resources focused on mission.

Science and Religion Forum
http://www.srforum.org
An ecumenical organization promoting discussion between scientific understanding and religious thought.

Science and Spirit
http://www.science-spirit.org
The home site of the magazine devoted to cutting-edge science, balanced with the wisdom of a world of faiths.

Telling the Truth Project
http://www.clm.org/ttt/home.html
Pooling the best of Christian scholarship and propelling it to a global audience via the net.

Through the Roof
http://www.throughtheroof.org
Disability outreach of Joni Eareckson Tada in the UK.

Unravelling Wittgenstein's Net – a Christian Thinktank
http://www.christian-thinktank.com
A large number of text resources on reasons for Christian faith

Web Evangelism
http://www.brigada.org/today/articles/web-evangelism.html
Excellent guide to using websites for evangelism. If you are setting up your own church or mission website, read this first!

Web Evangelism Bulletin
http://www.gospelcom.net/guide/webevangelismbulletin.html

Web Evangelism Net
http://www.webevangelism.net
Information and links on using the Internet for evangelism. Companion site to the book 'Using your Church Web Site for Evangelism'.

Whitefield Institute, The
http://www.uccf.org.uk/wi
Exists to discover ways in which Christians can have a positive role in today's world and to provide resources to make this possible.

Women Today International
http://www.womentoday.org
Dedicated to help women reach their homes, communities, states and the world for Christ.

Y2000
http://www.y-2000.com
Using the Millennium to make Jesus better known.

Zacharias Trust (UK), The
http://www.zactrust.org
Training in evangelism.

Agape UK http://www.agape.org.uk

Billy Graham Online http://www.billygraham.org

British and Foreign Bible Society
http://www.biblesociety.org.uk

Christians in Sport http://www.christiansinsport.org.uk

Creation Research Society http://www.creationresearch.org

Creation Resources Trust http://www.c-r-t.co.uk

Global Consultation On World Evangelization
http://www.ad2000.org/gcowe95/

Guide to Web Evangelism, A
http://www.brigada.org/today/articles/web-evangelism.html

International Organization for Migration (IOM)
http://www.iom.int

Luis Palau Evangelistic Association
http://www.gospelcom.net/lpea/

Message to Schools http://www.message.org.uk

Refugee Net http://www.refugeenet.org

United Beach Missions http://www.ubm.org.uk

United Nations Population Information Network (POPIN)
http://www.undp.org/popin/

Victory Tracts and Posters
http://www.victory10.freeserve.co.uk

World Christian Resources Directory
http://www.missionresources.com

MISSION - ORGANIZATIONS

Arab World Ministries
http://www.gospelcom.net/awm
Useful set of links on ministry among Muslims.

Bible Site, The
http://www.thebiblesite.org
Donate Bibles to persecuted Christians worldwide.

Brigada
http://www.brigada.org
Focuses on worldwide mission, with links to other missionary organizations and helpful guidelines for missionaries.

Campus Crusade for Christ International
http://www.ccci.org
Well-presented site on the work of Campus Crusade with links to their international ministries. Some on-line resources and the Four Spiritual Laws in scores of languages.

Christian Enquiry Agency
http://www.christianity.org.uk
Seeks to provide information to people outside the Churches who wish to find out more about the Christian faith.

Christian Research
http://www.christian-research.org.uk
Source of information and statistics on the UK Church.

Christian Vision and Christian Voice
http://www.christian-vision.org
UK charity promoting Christianity around the world by setting up radio stations and by using the Internet.

Christians Aware

http://www.christiansaware.co.uk

Ecumenical Christian organization working to build bridges between various nations and cultures. CA specialises in promoting overseas visits and exchanges between Christians in the UK and churches around the world.

Church Pastoral Aid Society (CPAS)

http://www.cpas.org.uk

UK mission society mainly working with Anglican churches. Best known for its youth and children's work (Explorers, Climbers, Scramblers, Pathfinders and CYFA).

DAWN

http://www.jesus.org.uk/dawn/

Weekly reports on church planting and mission success.

Everypeople.net

http://www.everypeople.net

Comprehensive information about worldwide missions.

Focus Radio

http://www.facingthechallenge.org/focus.htm

A media agency producing resources relating the Bible to contemporary culture, including the Facing the Challenge course.

Fusion

http://www.fusion.uk.com

Fusion is a student-led movement that encourages 'grass roots' evangelism on campuses and a positive view of the world and a Christian's responsibility to reach out to it.

Great Commission Air

http://www.greatcommissionair.org

Provision of safe and efficient air transport for Christian missions and humanitarian relief.

International Coalition for Religious Freedom

http://www.religiousfreedom.com

This site features a country-by-country analysis of the state of religious freedom.

InterVarsity Christian Fellowship

http://www.gospelcom.net/iv/

US, University-based Christian organization. Features mission opportunities, the journal Student Leadership and links to college chapter websites.

Missionboard.com

http://www.missionboard.com/index.cfm

A source for communication among Christian missions, churches and individuals all over the world. You can set up a web page for free.

Missions by Modem International

http://www.mbmintl.org

Provides Christian based, computerized educational and inspirational resources to those ministering among difficult peoples in hard places.

Operation Mobilisation

http://www.om.org

OM's site, with details of their ministry and publications worldwide.

OSCAR

http://www.oscar.org.uk

OSCAR is an acronym of `One Stop Centre for Advice and Resources' and is a gateway to useful UK related information, advice and resources on mission.

Scripture Union

http://www.scriptureunion.org.uk

Christian publications with special ministry to children and young people.

SPCK

http://www.spck.org.uk

A mission society known throughout the world for its grants, support of theological education and distribution of Christian literature.

UCCF
http://www.uccf.org.uk
Universities and Colleges Christian Fellowship supports
Christians in British college education. Has a mission focus
and runs a number of graduate programmes.

Worldwide Evangelization for Christ
http://www.cin.co.uk/wec/

Youth With a Mission UK
http://www.ywam.org.uk
Draws people from a variety of backgrounds to work in a vast
spectrum of evangelistic activities.

Action Partners http://www.actionpartners.org.uk

AD 2000 and Beyond http://www.ad2000.org

Agape Europe http://agapeeurope.org

AIMS http://www.aims.org

American Missionary Fellowship
http://www.americanmissionary.org

American Tract Society http://www.gospelcom.net/ats/

Anglican Board of Missions – Australia
http://www.accnet.net.au/abm/

Arab World Ministries http://www.gospelcom.net/awm/

Baptist Missionary Society http://www.rpc.ox.ac.uk/bms/

Barnabus Outreach Trust http://www.go-4th.com

Bible Mission International http://www.bethany.co.uk/bmi/

Board of Mission: Uniting Church of Christ in Australia
http://www.uca.org.au/nsw/bom/

British and Foreign Bible Society
http://www.biblesociety.org.uk

Caleb Project http://www.calebproject.org

Campus Crusade for Christ, Canada
http://www.crusade.org

Capernwray Missionary Fellowship
http://www.capernwray.co.uk

Centre for Mission Direction http://www.cmd.org.nz

Christian Military Fellowship http://www.cmf.com

Christian Missions (SIM) http://www.sim.org

Church Mission Society http://www.cms-uk.org

Cooperative Baptist Fellowship http://www.cbfonline.org

Council for World Mission http://www.cwmission.org.uk

Crusade for World Revival http://www.cwr.org.uk

East to West http://www.e2w.dircon.co.uk

Emmaus Road, International http://www.eri.org

**Foreign Mission Board of the Southern Baptist
Convention** http://www.imb.org

Frontier Internship in Mission http://tfim.org

Frontiers http://www.frontiers.org

General Board of Global Ministries – Methodist Church
http://gbgm-umc.org/gbgma.stm

Global Missions International
http://www.globalmissions.org

Gospel for Asia http://www.gfa.org/indexgfl.htm

Greater Europe Mission http://www.gospelcom.net/gem/

ICCC – International Christian Chamber of Commerce
http://www.iccc.net

Institute for Ecumenical and Cultural Research
http://www.csbsju.edu/iecr/

International Bible Society http://www.gospelcom.net/ibs/

International Bulletin of Missionary Research
http://www.omsc.org

International Mission Board http://www.imb.org

International Teams http://www.iteams.org

Interserve http://www.interserve.org

J.John, Philo Trust http://www.philo.ndirect.co.uk

Lausanne Committee for World Evangelism
http://www.lausanne.org

Lausanne Movement http://www.lausanne.org

London Insititute for Contemporary Christianity
http://www.licc.org.uk

Military Ministry http://www.militaryministry.com

Mission Aviation Fellowship http://www.maf.org

Mission To Unreached Peoples
http://www.mup.org/mupinfo

Mission: America http://www.missionamerica.com

Navigators http://www.gospelcom.net/navs/

New Tribes Mission http://www.ntm.org

Oasis Trust http://www.u-net.com/oasis/

Officers' Christian Fellowship http://www.ocfusa.org

OMF International http://www.omf.org

Outreach Unlimited Ministries http://www.u-net.com/~oum/out.htm

Pioneers http://www.pioneers.org

Prayer Warriors International
http://www.prayerwarriors.org.uk

Qua Iboe Fellowship http://web.ukonline.co.uk/qua.iboe/

Red Sea Mission Team
http://ourworld.compuserve.com/homepages/rsmt_uk/

Reform Ireland http://www.reform-ireland.org

Slavic Gospel Association http://www.sga.org

Summer Institute of Linguistics http://www.sil.org

United Society for the Propagation of the Gospel
http://www.uspg.org.uk

United States Center for World Mission
http://www.uscwm.org

Unreached Peoples http://www.bethany-wpc.org/profiles/home.html

World Missions Far Corners
http://www.worldmissionsfarcorners.com

World Team http://www.xc.org/wt/

Worldwide Evangelical Gospel Outreach
http://www.iu.net/wego/

Wycliffe Associates (UK)
http://www.globalnet.co.uk/~wa_uk/

Wycliffe Bible Translators http://www.wycliffe.org

Youth With A Mission International http://www.ywam.org

MUSIC - CHRISTIAN

About Christian Music
http://christianmusic.about.com
Portal site for Christian music from those nice About people.

American Gospel Music Directory
http://www.americangospel.com

Anglican Church Music
http://churchmusic.org.uk
This site aims to be a central source of information for Anglican and Episcopal church music, with resources for church musicians, singers and congregation members.

Anglican Church Music
http://www.churchmusic.org.uk
Information, resources and links for Anglican and Episcopal Church musicians and clergy.

Anglican Online Hymnal
http://www.oremus.org/hymnal/
Public domain texts from nine Anglican hymnals from the second half of the twentieth century.

Black Gospel Music
http://afgen.com/gospel.html
Site offers articles, information, books and CDs from Tommy Dorsey to Bobby Jones.

CCLI music links
http://www.ccli.com/WorshipResources/
Music links from Christian Copyright Licensing International.

CCM Online
http://www.ccmcom.com
Publisher of Christian music magazines. Includes previews, tours, directory of band pages and a chat forum.

Choral Directory
http://members.tripod.com/~choral/
Directory of British cathedral and church choirs.

Christian Bands
http://www.cnet.clara.net/links/bands.htm
Brief list of UK Christian bands.

Christian Copyright Licensing International (CCLI)
http://www.ccli.co.uk
Information on CCLI's copyright schemes for churches in various countries. The UK site is at http://www.ccli.co.uk/.

Christian Music Guide
http://christianmusic.about.com/musicperform/
christianmusic/
About's guide to Christian music.

Christian Music Online
http://cmo.com
Dedicated to providing the latest information on the Christian music world.

Christian Music Place
http://christianmusic.org/cmp/
Information on Christian artists, albums, Christian music festivals, Chrisitian concerts, recording and distributing your own Christian music.

Classical Midi Organ Stop
http://users.gmi.net/~wgraeber/
MIDI files and links to other sites.

Creative Church
http://www.creativechurch.org.uk
Extensive and regularly updated listing of Christian contemporary music, drama scripts and video clips. Registration fee required.

Cross Rhythms
http://www.crossrhythms.co.uk
UK-based multimedia Christian music ministry with radio station, magazine and festival.

Cyber Hymnal
http://www.cyberhymnal.org
Nearly 3,000 Christian hymns and songs from many denominations. There are lyrics, sound, background information, photos, links, MIDI files and music scores you can download.

Dove Awards
http://www.doveawards.com
The Dove Awards for Gospel music are awarded each Spring and act as a showcase for performers of Christian music.

Freedom Ministries
http://www.freedomministries.org.uk
As they put it: 'Standing against the flood of rock-idiom music in the Church.'

Friends of Cathedral Music, The
http://www.fcm.org.uk
A society whose aim is to assist cathedrals in maintaining their traditional sung services.

Gospel Train
http://www.gospeltrain.com
This site brings you soul and gospel music.

Gregorian Chants
http://www.music.princeton.edu/chant_html/
Learn about this Christian tradition of liturgical song from the Medieval period.

Hymnsite.com
http://www.hymnsite.com
The hymn and psalm tunes at this site are in the public domain and may be freely downloaded. Hymns are linked with Bible passages.

ICUK
http://www.icuk.com
Aims to showcase Christian contemporary music in the UK.

Jamsline
http://www.jamsline.com
Information site on Christian music.

Lutheran Hymnal
http://www.lutheran-hymnal.com
Lutheran hymnals presented in MIDI, in MP3, in lyrics and in sheet music.

Oremus Hymnal
http://www.oremus.org/hymnal/
This online hymnal contains texts and MIDI files of tunes used in much of the English-speaking world, with particular emphasis on the Anglican tradition.

Phatt
http://www.phatt-music.com/phatt
Promotes those in musical ministry.

Praise TV
http://www.praisetv.com
Glossy US site for Christian music.

Resources for the Church Musician
http://www.pldi.net/~murrows/publish.htm

Ringing World Online
http://www.luna.co.uk/~ringingw/
Gives you a weekly fix of news, gossip and useful information about bell ringing.

SolidGospel.com
http://www.solidgospel.com
Gospel music with song of the day. Find and listen to your favourite artist.

Songs of Praise
http://songsofpraise.org
Song site with MP3s, MIDIs and even translations.

Sonicplace
http://www.sonicplace.com
A place to listen to Christian music on-line.

Spirit Music
http://www.spiritmusic.co.uk
Supplier of contemporary Christian music to the UK and beyond.

Sunhawk.com
http://www.sunhawk.com
Music download site, with free 'Solero' music viewing software for downloading, playing and printing sheet music.

Tastyfresh: Christian Dance Music
http://www.tastyfresh.com
Large Christian dance music site. Keep up with the latest UK and US releases.

UK Gospel Music
http://www.avnet.co.uk/goodsela/gospel/
Information on gospel music events throughout the UK. Offers a small selection of links to other sites.

Worship Together
http://www.worshiptogether.com
Worship resources, including free songs and music software.

Alliance Music http://www.alliancemusic.co.uk

American Hymnody Collection
http://www.bju.edu/resources/library/hymnofrm.htm

Christian Guitar Resources http://www.christianguitar.ws

Christian Karaoke
http://www.christiankaraoke.strayduck.com/page1.htm

Christian-music.co.uk http://www.christian-music.co.uk

Graham Kendrick http://www.grahamkendrick.co.uk

Guild of Church Musicians
http://www.quarks.co.uk/TGOCM/

Integrity Music Inc. http://www.integritymusic.com

Maranatha! Music http://www.maranathamusic.com

Message to Schools http://www.message.org.uk

Psalmody International http://www.psalmody.org

Royal School of Church Music http://www.rscm.com

Sarum College Centre for Liturgical Organ Studies
http://www.sarum.ac.uk/organstudies/

MUSIC - GENERAL

All Music Guide
http://www.allmusic.com
Nearly half a million albums, over 3 million tracks, 160,000 reviews on nearly 1,000 musical styles.

Ask MP3
http://www.askmp3.com
All you wanted to know about MP3, and a bit more besides.

AudioFind
http://www.audiofind.com
Great resource for finding music, lyrics, artists, song titles and albums.

Aus Music Guide
http://www.amws.com.au
Huge music directory for Australia.

Billboard
http://www.billboard.com
Definitive collection of US charts, including internet downloads and searches.

ChoralNet
http://www.choralnet.org
An excellent site for all things choral.

Classical Music on the Net
http://www.musdoc.com/classical/
Your guide to everything classical. Spend an evening here when choir practice is cancelled.

Classical Net
http://www.classical.net
Excellent resource, with lists of composers' works and nearly 4,000 links to other sites.

Classical Search
http://www.classicalsearch.com
The Internet's most comprehensive search engine for classical music. Created by the people who publish the British and International Music Yearbook, it provides links to over 25,000 music-related web sites worldwide.

Dotmusic
http://www.dotmusic.com
UK and worldwide charts from top magazines.

Emusic
http://www.emusic.com
Music download site

Great Guitar Sites on the Web
http://www.guitarsite.com
Links to over 1,000 sites for guitars, chords, tablature, bands and MP3.

Let's Sing It
http://www.letssingit.com
Large lyrics database.

Lycos Music Search
http://music.lycos.com/downloads/
Search for music and audio files on the Internet that use the common MP3 format.

MIDI Explorer
http://www.musicrobot.com
Allows you to search for MIDI files on the Internet.

MP3.com
http://www.mp3.com
With over 20 million items to download, MP3 is a rich source of music and recorded speech.

Music Boulevard
http://www.musicblvd.com
Music Boulevard offers a wide selection of music, all categorized by genre.

Music Yellow Pages On-line
http://www.musicyellowpages.com
Provides a database for the music, audio, lighting and entertainment industries.

PeopleSound
http://www.peoplesound.com
Tracks by thousands of aspiring artists. Sign up your church band here.

Telly Tunes
http://www.tellytunes.net
Need the music for the theme tune from your favourite TV programme?

Ultimate Band List
http://www.ubl.com
Like the name says, they try to offer a comprehensive music directory.

Royal College of Organists http://www.rco.org.uk

NETWORKS, COMMUNITIES AND CENTRES

2000 Teen Chat
http://www.2000-teen-chat.com/main
General chat site for teenagers.

711 Web Cafe Christian Chat Network
http://www.711webcafe.net
US-based Christian chat forums.

Best of the Christian Web-Chat Directory
http://www.botcw.com/search/Chat_Rooms/

List of Christian chat rooms.
Carmelite Friars UK
http://www.carmelite.org
Information on Carmelite spirituality and the movement worldwide.

Chat-o-Rama
http://www.solscape.com/chat
One of the most comprehensive listings of general chat sites on the web.

Christian Cafe
http://thechristiancafe.com
Single Christians looking for love, romance, friends, fellowship, pen-pals, partners and relationships in a virtual cafe. See also a site with a similar name and aims: http://www.christian-cafe.com.

Christian Chat
http://www.christianchat.co.uk
Its name says it all. There's also a US site at http://christian-chat.com.

Christian Chat Network
http://www.cchat.net
Drop by if you need a friend or a safe place to chat.

Christian ChatLine
http://www.christianchatline.com
Another Christian chat site

Christian Connection
http://www.christianconnection.co.uk
A website dedicated to creating opportunities for friendship, dating and matchmaking for likeminded Christian singles of all denominations across the UK and Ireland.

Christian Connection US
http://www.christian.email.net
A Christian singles dating network. They claim it's the largest Christian singles site on the web.

Christian Friendship Fellowship
http://www.digitalchurch.co.uk/cff/
A non-profit making registered charity which provides a specialised ministry and outreach to Christians on their own.

Christian Singles Worldwide
http://www.christiansingles.com
Supports single Christians who want to correspond with other Christians.

Christians Online
http://www.conline.net
A Christian community web site where you can search for Christian penpals, ask others to pray for you or use the chat facilities.

Church Net UK WebChat
http://www.churchnet.org.uk/webchat/
UK Christian chat forum.

Corrymeela Community
http://www.corrymeela.org.uk
A dispersed community from all Christian traditions.

Crosswalk Chats
http://chat.crosswalk.com
Useful to create your own kid's chatroom.

EcuNet
http://www.ecunet.org
Ecunet is a not-for-profit, online network of Christian organizations. You can sign-up to create your own discussion area or join one of the many existing forums.

In the Beginning
http://www.serve.com/larryi/begin.htm
Christian resource site, offering church search facility, Christian music and radio, discussion and chat groups, and devotional material.

Integrity
http://www.integrityusa.org
Offers a voice for the full inclusion of homosexual persons in the Episcopal Church in the USA.

Iona Community
http://www.iona.org.uk
Rebuilding of the common life through work and worship, prayer and politics, the sacred and the secular.

IRC Net
http://www.irc.net
A good starting point if you want to find out about IRC or download the software.

KidChatters
http://www.kidchatters.com
Chatroom suitable for children from six to twelve years.

KidzChatz
http://www.kidzchatz.com
Chatroom for children from all over the planet.

Lesbian and Gay Christian Movement
http://www.lgcm.org.uk
Encourages fellowship, friendship, and support among individual lesbian and gay Christians. The movement also aims to help the whole Church re-examine its understanding of human sexuality.

meta-list
http://www.meta-list.org
An international moderated forum on science and religion sponsored by the John Templeton foundation

New Day Introductions
http://www.wordnet.co.uk/personal.html
A Christian introduction agency.

On-line Communities in the UK
http://www.communities.org.uk
Aims to address issues of sustainability, social inclusion and healthier economies by focusing on the use of new communications technologies.

Orthodox Community of St Aidan, Manchester
http://home.clara.net/orthodox/
Dedicated to making Orthodox Christianity more widely known.

Schoenstatt Fathers
http://www.schoenstatt.org.uk
A community of Catholic priests working in pastoral activity throughout the world.

Society of the Divine Savior: the Salvatorians
http://www.sds.org
An international Roman Catholic religious community.

Taize Community
http://www.taize.fr
Information in 22 languages on this famous community.

Talk about it
http://www.geocities.com/Athens/Academy/9894
A place to chat about your problems and find advice via IRC (Internet Relay Chat).

Tel-a-Teen
http://www.tel-a-teen.org
Help for teenagers with problem relationships. Chat with trained peers and find a listening ear.

Wilderness
http://home.onestop.net/wilderness/
Radical Christian peace community in Britain.

Wilibrord's Christian Chat Sites
http://members.tripod.com/~Erala/chat.html
Links to a range of places on the web where Christians gather
to talk, debate and have fellowship.

Worth Abbey
http://web.ukonline.co.uk/worth.abbey/
An English Benedictine monastery in a changing world.

Ashburnham Christian Trust
http://www.ashburnham.org.uk

Barnabas Trust http://www.barnabas.org.uk/HomePage.htm

Bruderhof Communities http://www.bruderhof.org

Capernwray Hall http://www.capernwray.org.uk

Carberry Conference Centre
http://dspace.dial.pipex.com/carberry/

Christian Chat Rooms dot com
http://www.christianchatrooms.com

Christian Conference Trust http://www.cct.org.uk

Christian Motorcyclists Association
http://www.bike.org.uk/cma/

ChristianLinks chat http://chat.christianlinks.com

Fellowship of Scientists (USA)
http://solon.cma.univie.ac.at/~neum/sciandf/fellow

Holy Joes http://www.holyjoes.com

Hothorpe Hall http://www.hothorpe.co.uk

Order of St Benedict http://www.osb.org/osb/

Scargill House http://www.scargillhouse.co.uk

NEWS - CHRISTIAN

Amity News Service
http://is7.pacific.net.hk/~amityhk/
News and views from the China Christian Council.

Anglican Communion News Service (UK)
http://www.anglicancommunion.org/acns/
Excellent Christian news site with a mailing list so that you
can keep up to date.

Anglicans Online
http://www.anglican.org/online/
Anglican news and resources, with material for youth minis-
ters and young Anglicans, a section on music and religious
orders.

Catholic News Service
http://www.catholicnews.com
The Catholic News Service is the primary source of national
and world news that appears in the US Catholic press.

Christian Broadcasting Network
http://www.cbn.com
US Christian site for news, information and entertainment.
The site also provides articles on issues such as health and
spirituality.

Christian Daily News
http://www.christiandailynews.org
News site produced by Christian Word Ministries. Either read
it on-line or subscribe to an e-mail list.

Christian Reporter
http://crnews.pastornet.net.au/crnews/
International Christian News service based in Australia.

Church Net UK News Service
http://www.churchnet.org.uk/news/
UK Church news.

Church News Service
http://ourworld.compuserve.com/homepages/aphenna/
Resources for harassed church newsletter editors.

Church Times
http://www.churchtimes.co.uk
UK's leading Anglican weekly.

Crosswalk Sports
http://sports.crosswalk.com
Click on the sport of your choice for news, articles and information.

Ecumenical News International
http://www.eni.ch
Daily news about religion and the ecumenical movement. Site has good archives.

Episcopal Life
http://www.dfms.org/episcopal-life/
The national newspaper of the Episcopal Church.

Methodist Recorder
http://www.methodistrecorder.co.uk
A good news site with a reasonable selection of links. 'The world's most influential Methodist newspaper.'

Parish Pump
http://www.parishpump.co.uk
Source of information and articles for busy church magazine editors.

Religion Today
http://www.religiontoday.com
Religion news from the US and around the world – and search the archives of important past religion stories.

Religious News Service
http://www.religionnews.com
This news service specialises in religious news. It covers all religions.

Tablet
http://www.thetablet.co.uk
A Roman Catholic weekly newspaper which has been reporting on events of significance for over 150 years. Offers a very varied selection of articles.

Universe, The
http://www.the-universe.net
Leading UK site for Catholic news and issues. Reports international stories, humanitarian issues and Catholic comment.

Worldwide Faith News
http://www.wfn.org
Searchable database of news reports, announcements, general information, and policy statements from various Christian groups.

Catholic World News http://www.catholic.net

Christian Information Network http://www.cin.co.uk

Church of England Newspaper
http://www.churchnewspaper.com

Episcopal News Service http://www.dfms.org/ens/

Jesus Army Streetpaper
http://www.jesus.org.uk/spaper.html

LifeLine News http://www.lifelinenews.net

Observer, The http://www.observer.co.uk/international

Vatican News http://www.vatican.va/news_services/

World Association for Christian Communication
http://www.wacc.org.uk

NEWS - GENERAL

ABC Australia News
http://www.abc.net.au/news
View the world from the other side with ABC Australia news.

About on News and Events
http://uknews.about.com/aboutuk/uknews
About's roundup of UK news and events.

All Newspapers.com, Inc.
http://www.allnewspapers.com
Find today's headline news, business reports, sports events and more. Also links local, national and international news sources.

Ananova
http://www.ananova.com
Leading UK news site.

Australian Broadcasting Corporation
http://www.abc.net.au/news/

BBC
http://www.bbc.co.uk
One of the UK's top sites with lots of news and comment. Turn the TV off to browse through it!

BBC World Service
http://www.bbc.co.uk/worldservice/index.shtml
Available in 43 languages, this website is in a league of its own.

Business Wire
http://www.businesswire.com
This is a fast and free news-based service. You can retrieve news stories by topic or date so you can find news specific to your industry.

Crayon
http://www.crayon.net
Create your own custom paper from hundreds of local, national, and international on-line sources.

Fish for News
http://www.fish4news.co.uk
Scan through over 800 papers across the UK.

Infobeat
http://www.infobeat.com
Tired of sifting through news pages just to get to the bits you want? Infobeat allows you to receive personalized news reports via e-mail.

Internet News
http://www.internetnews.com
A daily net newspaper that tracks all the internet related stories and events.

Kidon Media-Link
http://www.kidon.com/media-link/index.shtml
This site tries to give a complete directory of newspapers and other news sources on the Internet.

MediaInfo
http://www.mediainfo.com/emedia/
News and comment with an excellent database of newspapers around the world.

News Rack
http://www.newsrack.com
Comprehensive search for magazines and newspapers around the globe. Locate the website for the Church Times or the Chorley Citizen.

News365
http://www.news365.com
News and information at your fingertips – 10,000 news media sites and 300 topics. Search topic or region.

NewsNow
http://www.newsnow.co.uk
The latest headlines from leading news sources, updated every five minutes.

NewsTrawler
http://www.newstrawler.com
A parallel search engine that retrieves the summaries of articles from the archives of hundreds of online information sources around the world such as newspapers, journals and magazines.

PA NewsCentre
http://www.pa.press.net
UK news, parliamentary proceedings, weather and sport.

Paperboy
http://www.thepaperboy.com
Wonderful source of online newspapers around the world. UK papers, national and local, are well represented. It even incudes a 'translator' for foreign papers.

Reuters
http://www.reuters.com
The world's number one news agent, still leading the pack with an excellent news site by virtue of its headlines, financial news and search engine.

USA Today
http://www.usatoday.com/news/world/nw1.htm
World news and views from the popular American newspaper.

Wired News
http://www.wired.com
Internet and computer related news.

Channel 4 News http://www.channel4news.co.uk

Economist, The http://www.economist.com

Guardian Online http://www.guardian.co.uk

Guardian Unlimited http://www.guardian.co.uk

Independent, The http://www.independent.co.uk

ITN News http://www.itn.co.uk

New Statesman http://www.newstatesman.co.uk

New York Times http://www.nytimes.com

Scotsman http://www.thestar.com

Sunday Times http://www.sunday-times.co.uk

Sydney Morning Herald http://www.smh.com.au

Telegraph http://www.telegraph.co.uk

Times Educational Supplement http://www.tes.co.uk

Times, The http://www.thetimes.co.uk

Washington Post http://www.washingtonpost.com

NEWSGROUPS

Deja News
http://www.deja.com
Deja is the only searcher dedicated exclusively to searching
Usenet newsgroups. Users can search the Usenet as far back
as March, 1995 with a simple interface. Now part of the
Google search engine.

Liszt
http://www.liszt.com
Searchable directory of over 90,000 mailing lists. There is a
Christian section at http://www.liszt.com/select/Religion/
Christian/.

meta-list
http://www.meta-list.org
An international moderated forum on science and religion
sponsored by the John Templeton foundation

Miami Christian University Virtual Library
http://mcu.edu/library/
A directory site, but with only a few descriptions of the sites
listed. However, the range (if not the number) is wide and
includes e-mail discussion lists and Usenet groups.

news.newusers.questions
http://www.geocities.com/ResearchTriangle/Lab/6882/
A useful starting point if your are interested in newsgroups.

Newsgroups
http://www.deja.com
The name of the newsgroup reveals its subject matter, so a
simple list of relevant groups is sufficient. Not all newsgroups
are available on every newsgroup server. If you have difficulties, look at the groups via Deja.

Publicly Accessible Mailing Lists
http://paml.net
Thousands of specialist e-mail discussion groups organized by
name and subject.

Soc.Religion.Christian
http://geneva.rutgers.edu/src/
Web home page for one of the main Christian newsgroups.

OTHER BELIEFS

AAHoroscopes
http://www.aahoroscopes.com
Site explains astrology, meaning of signs and provides weekly horoscopes.

Academic Info: Religion
http://www.academicinfo.net/religindex.html
An annotated directory of resources for the academic study of religion.

Academic Jewish Studies
http://h-net2.msu.edu/~judaic/
The site contains articles, a resources library, a newsletter and an on-line discussion group. It is useful for people who want to look at Jewish Studies in depth or who have a general interest in comparative religion.

Answering for Islam
http://www.afi.org.uk
Addresses common issues about Islamic religion and culture.

Answering Islam
http://answering-islam.org.uk
An individual's site with some good cross links to Islamic sites.

Apologetics Index
http://www.apologeticsindex.org
Vast database and glossary of information on cults, sects, new religious movements, doctrines, apologetics and counter-cult organizations.

Arab World Ministries
http://www.gospelcom.net/awm
Useful set of links on ministry among Muslims.

BeliefNet
http://about.beliefnet.com
Portal site for general spiritual belief. As its byline says, 'we all believe in something'. See also http://home.about.com/religion, which is another general religion site from about.com.

Buddhist Society
http://www.thebuddhistsociety.org.uk
Details of the life and teachings of the Buddha, plus information on membership, publications, classes and courses.

Buddhist Studies WWW Virtual Library
http://www.ciolek.com/WWWVL-Buddhism.html
Comprehensive library of Buddhist resources.

Centre for Jewish-Christian Relations
http://www.cjcr.org.uk
Centre for exploration of Jewish-Christian relations from Bible times to today.

Christian Apologetics and Research Ministry
http://www.carm.org
Aims to equip Christians with good information on Christian doctrine and various religious movements such as Mormonism and the Jehovah's Witnesses.

Cult Awareness & Information Centre
http://www.caic.org.au/
Wide range of cults and -isms are listed here. Not every group mentioned on this site is considered a destructive cult. Some are 'benign -isms'.

Current Affairs of Muslims
http://www.cam.org.uk
Comprehensive coverage of all the important news relating to Muslims.

Fate and Fortune
http://www.fateandfortune.com
Vast collection of Tarot, Runes, Dreams, Feng Shui, I-Ching, Horoscopes, Palms and Love Spells.

First and Last Ministries
http://www.firstandlast.org.uk
The site includes topics, news and views, for the evangelization of Jehovah's Witnesses, plus help and support for those studying with, or leaving, the Watch Tower Society.

Fort: Panth Khalsa
http://www.panthkhalsa.org
Information on the Sikh nation, famous Sikhs, code of conduct, human rights and Sikhs world-wide.

God Channel
http://www.godchannel.com
"The purpose of this site is to provide God with a focused virtual presence on Earth." That's what the site says and it's worth a look to see what is going on (and being believed) out there.

Hindu Universe
http://www.hindunet.org/home.shtml
Lots of information on Hinduism.

Hinduism Today
http://www.hinduismtoday.kauai.hi.us
On-line magazine for Hindus.

Infidels
http://www.infidels.org
An on-line community of non-believers who aim to promote metaphysical naturalism.

Interfaith Calendar
http://www.interfaithcalendar.org
An easy to use calendar listing the sacred times for world religions.

Into the Light
http://www.itl.org.uk
A Christian view of the Bible and Christianity in response to questions and misconceptions of those from an Islamic background.

Investigating Islam
http://www.islamic.org.uk
Interpreting Islam and attempts to refute Christianity.

Islam Online
http://www.islam-online.net
Portal site for Islam that aims to give information about Islam, its culture and current affairs.

Islamic Resources
http://www.latif.com
Links to Islamic FAQs, announcements, conferences and social events, Qur'an teachings, Arabic news and the Cyber Muslim guide.

Jewish-Christian Relations
http://www.jcrelations.com
Lots of information, resources, articles and links.

Jewish.co.uk
http://www.Jewish.co.uk
Information on UK Jewish community, synagogues, festivals, culture, food etc.

Jews for Jesus
http://www.jews-for-jesus.org
They exist, they say, 'to make the Messiahship of Jesus an unavoidable issue to Jewish people worldwide.'

Maven: Jewish Portal
http://www.maven.co.il/
Links to all things Jewish.

Mormon Church in the UK
http://www.geocities.com/Athens/Acropolis/8825/
Information about the Church of Jesus of Latter-Day Saints in the UK.

Mormonism Research Ministry
http://www.mrm.org
An evangelical Christian ministry which challenges the claims of The Church of Jesus Christ of Latter-day Saints.

Muslim Directory
http://www.muslimdirectory.co.uk
Plenty of interesting information on this site for followers and
non-followers alike.

Muslim-Christian Debate
http://www.debate.org.uk
Muslim and Christian apologetic articles.

National Hindu Students Forum
http://www.nhsf.org.uk
Promotes Hindu interests and encourages debate.

Ontario Consultants on Religious Tolerance
http://www.religioustolerance.org
Many religious sites on the internet are created by committed
believers. The aim of this site is to describe dozens of faith
groups as accurately as possible from a neutral stance, from
Asatru to Christianity to Zoroastrianism.

Pagan Links: UK
http://www.ukpaganlinks.mcmail.com
Information and resources for pagans living in the UK.

Qur'an Browser
http://www.stg.brown.edu/webs/quran_browser/pqeasy.shtml
On-line Qur'an.

Rastafarian Religion
http://www.rasta-man.co.uk/religion.htm
Explains origins and main features of Rastafarian religion.

RE-XS for Schools
http://re-xs.ucsm.ac.uk
Offers information and links on over 20 religions and belief
systems, major contemporary moral issues and RE teaching.

Reachout Trust
http://www.reachouttrust.org
Building bridges to those caught up in the cults, occult and
New Age.

Religion and Religious Studies
http://www.clas.ufl.edu/users/gthursby/rel/
Information and links for study and interpretation of religions.

Religions and Scriptures
http://www.wam.umd.edu/~stwright/rel/
Scriptures from around the world.

Religious Movements Page, The
http://religiousmovements.lib.virginia.edu/profiles/profiles.htm
Profiles of more than two hundred religious movements.

Religious Studies Page
http://www.clas.ufl.edu/users/gthursby/rel/
Information and links for study and interpretation of religions.

Religious Studies Resources on the Internet
http://fn2.freenet.edmonton.ab.ca/~cstier/religion/toc.htm
Links to general religious studies sites and to specific faith sites.

Sada Punjab
http://www.sadapunjab.com
Sikh religious writings and Punjabi music, including Punjabi jukebox, literature and language.

Spirit Web
http://www.spiritweb.org
Encourages general spiritual consciousness.

Spotlight Ministries
http://www.spotlightministries.co.uk
Focuses on cults, spiritual abuse, the new age, the occult, and false teachings. Has an extensive list of useful links.

Swedenbourg Society
http://www.swedenborg.org.uk
Established in 1810 to print and publish works of Emanuel Swedenborg, a mystic.

Watchman Fellowship
http://www.watchman.org
A ministry of Christian discernment, focusing on cults and new religious movements.

Wilfrid Laurier University
http://www.wlu.ca/~wwwrandc/internet_links.html
Comprehensive list of religious studies links.

Yahoo: Religions
http://www.yahoo.com/society_and_culture/religion/
Yahoo offers a wide selection of links to other faiths and beliefs.

Zipple
http://www.zipple.com
The Jewish Yahoo, connecting Jews globally via technology, content, commerce, news, editorial.

American Academy of Religion http://www.aar-site.org

Answers to Jehovah's Witnesses
http://www.holyscriptures.com

Baha'i Faith http://www.miracles.win-uk.net/Bahai/

Buddhist Society in the UK http://www.buddsoc.org.uk

Church of Jesus Christ of Latter-day Saints
http://www.lds.org

Church of Latter-day Saints (UK) http://www.lds.org.uk

Hare Krishna http://www.ksyberspace.com/liverpool/

His Holiness Sakya Trizin http://www.eclipse.co.uk/~rs1042/

Jewish Bible Association http://www.jewishbible.org

Messianic Testimony http://www.charitynet.org/~messianic/

Muslim Coalition http://www.muslimcoalition.com

Muslim-Christian Debate Website, The
http://www.debate.org.uk

Pagan Way Information Network
http://www.users.globalnet.co.uk/~petand/

Reform Synagogues of Great Britain
http://www.refsyn.org.uk

Scientology http://www.scientology.org

Sikh Net http://www.sikh.net

Spiritualist Association of Great Britain
http://www.users.globalnet.co.uk/~kluski/sagb.htm

Unitarian and Free Churches: UK
http://www.unitarian.org.uk

Unitarian Universalist Association http://uua.org

POLITICS AND GOVERNMENT

AJAX
http://www.sagal.com/ajax
Details of every US government site.

Arab Net
http://www.arab.net
All the Arab nations and their governments are represented on this site.

CARE (Christian Action Research and Education)
http://www.care.org.uk
CARE is a Christian organization providing caring work in the community.

CCTA Government Information
http://www.open.gov.uk
The place to find any UK government authority.

Christian Coalition of America
http://cc.org
Conservative political group which pushes a strong pro-family agenda.

Christian Coalition, The
http://www.cc.org
This American organization was founded to influence policy and promote Christian values in government.

Christian Solidarity Worldwide
http://www.csw.org.uk
Takes up the cases of persecuted Christians through political lobbying and support.

Demos
http://www.demos.co.uk
Political think tank in the UK.

Europa
http://www.europa.eu.int
European governments and information.

Family Research Council
http://www.frc.org
Promotes the traditional family unit and the Judeo-Christian value system upon which it is built.

FedWorld
http://www.fedworld.gov
Locate US federal government information, contacts and documents.

Great American Web Site, The
http://www.uncle-sam.com
This home page gives access to information about most areas of American government. It is compiled by a non-government agency.

International Christian Concern
http://www.persecution.org
Seeks religious liberty for Christian believers persecuted for their faith.

Movement for Christian Democracy
http://www.mcdpolitics.org
Promotes debates, political education, policies, campaigns, and research in order to feed Christian perspectives into national policies to shape British politics.

New Economics Foundation
http://www.neweconomics.org
Independent think tank working to construct a new economy centred on people and the environment

Number 10
http://www.number10.gov.uk
News from Downing Street, briefings and speeches.

Official Government Websites
http://www.psr.keele.ac.uk/official.htm
Lists most ot the world's governmental web sites.

One World
http://www.oneworld.org
A community of over 350 leading global justice organizations. Good for links to organizations such as Oxfam and Save the Children.

Orange Order
http://www.geocities.com/CapitolHill/1684/orange.html
Explanation of the Christian roots and nature of the Orange Order.

Oultwood
http://www.oultwood.com/localgov
Lists local government sites from around the world.

Peace Brigades International
http://www.igc.apc.org/pbi/
Explores and implements non-violent approaches to peace-keeping and support for basic human rights.

United Nations
http://www.un.org
Daily news updates, pictorial history, documents and maps, information on peace missions and descriptions of UN departments and offices.

Voice of the Martyrs
http://www.persecution.com
The Church still faces persecution. Richard Wurmbrand's group strives to bring practical and spiritual assistance to those persecuted and ensures they are never forgotten.

Amnesty International http://www.amnesty.org

Australian Democrat Party http://www.democrats.org.au

Australian Labour Party http://www.alp.org.au

Australian Liberal Party http://www.liberal.org.au

Australian National Party http://www.npa.org.au

British Conservative Party http://www.conservatives.com

British Labour Party http://www.labour.org.uk

British Liberal Democrat Party http://www.libdems.org.uk

Cabinet Office http://www.cabinet-office.gov.uk

Canadian Goverment http://canada.gc.ca

Christian Campaign for Nuclear Disarmament
http://www.gn.apc.org/ccnd/

Commission on Global Governance http://www.cgg.ch

Conservative Christian Fellowship
http://ourworld.compuserve.com/homepages/CCFHUB/

Department of Trade and Industry http://www.dti.gov.uk

Fellowship of Reconciliation http://www.nonviolence.org

G7 and G8 http://www.g7.utoronto.ca

Home Office http://www.homeoffice.gov.uk

Human Rights International http://www.hri.ca

Human Rights Watch http://www.hrw.org

Inter-Church Committee for Refugees
http://www.web.net/~iccr/

International Labour Organization (ILO)
http://www.ilo.org

International Law http://www.un.org/law/

International Organization for Migration (IOM)
http://www.iom.int

Movement for Christian Democracy
http://www.mcdpolitics.org

National Assembly for Wales http://www.wales.gov.uk

New Zealand Goverment http://www.govt.nz

Open Doors http://www.solcon.nl/odi/ODUK/

Organisation for Economic Cooperation and Development (OECD) http://www.oecd.org

Plaid Cymru http://www.plaidcymru.org

Refugee Net http://www.refugeenet.org

Scottish Parliament http://www.scottish.parliament.uk

Statistics from the UK Government
http://www.statistics.gov.uk

UN Social Policy and Development
http://www.un.org/esa/socdev/

United Nations Conference on Trade and Development
http://www.unctad.org/en/

United Nations High Commissioner for Human Rights
http://www.unhchr.ch

United Nations Organization http://www.un.org

United Nations: Humanitarian Affairs
http://www.un.org/ha/

United Nations: Human Rights http://www.un.org/rights/

US Democrat Party http://www.democratic-party.org

US House of Representatives http://www.house.gov/

US Republican Party http://www.rnc.org

US Senate http://www.senate.gov

US Town Hall Party http://www.townhall.com

White House http://www.whitehouse.gov

World Bank http://www.worldbank.org

REFERENCE - GENERAL

All Words
http://www.allwords.com
Guide for word lovers: for academic use and for fun, including crossword solver.

Allexperts
http://www.allexperts.com
When you need a theologian to help you out, try the God section at Allexperts, where you can send your questions via e-mail to a number of experts in various fields.

Art Guide
http://www.artguide.org
An extensive list of art galleries and and exhibitions in the UK with loads of information about individual artists.

Bartlett's Quotations
http://www.bartleby.com/100/
Searchable database of quotations.

Britannica On-Line
http://www.britannica.com
The best web sites, leading magazines, related books and the complete Encyclopaedia Britannica.

Cal State
http://library.csun.edu
On-line tools to search humanities, business and science data-bases. Very useful for accessing full text of general reference books such as encyclopaedias, dictionaries and handbooks.

Cambridge Dictionary
http://dictionary.cambridge.org
Look up words, descriptions and pronunciation in this comprehensive online resource.

Canon Law
http://canonlaw.anglican.org
Canon Law and Ecclesiastical Law in the Anglican Communion and in the Episcopal Church.

Census On-line
http://www.census-online.com
Useful links to US census data.

Chambers Electronic Encyclopedia
http://www.encyclopedia.com
An extraordinary amount of information showing at a screen near you. More than 17,000 articles provide free, quick and useful information on almost any topic.

CIA's World Factbook
http://www.odci.gov/cia/publications/factbook/
Huge database of facts and figures, political, economic and social indicators, geography etc. Not much about spying here, but useful facts for prayer and mission.

Columbia Encyclopedia
http://www.encyclopedia.com
More than 14,000 articles from the Concise Columbia Electronic Encyclopedia.

COPAC: University Research Library Catalogue
http://copac.ac.uk/copac/
Unified access to the catalogues of some of the largest university research libraries in the UK and Ireland.

Dictionary.com
http://www.dictionary.com
Online dictionary and related resources

Economic Net
http://www.economicnet.com
Finance news and resources, including banks.

English Server–Reference Links
http://eserver.org/reference/
Reference links from the English Server at Carnegie Mellon University.

Gallup Organization
http://www.gallup.com
Supplies results of past surveys, so you can keep up to date with trends and ratings or pepper your sermon with statistics.

Grolier
http://gme.grolier.com
The Grolier Multimedia Encyclopedia On-Line.

Info Please
http://www.infoplease.com
Need a fact? Here's the place to look. The religious section only has a few statistics, but may help if you want to check when Donus was Pope.

Library of Congress Studies
http://lcweb2.loc.gov/frd/cs/cshome.html
A library full of information on nations, their history and culture.

Libweb – Library WWW Servers
http://sunsite.berkeley.edu/Libweb/
More than 1,100 libraries in more than 45 countries on six continents are said to be listed here. Libweb covers most UK on-line university libraries.

Museum Network
http://www.museumnetwork.com
Worldwide directory of museums and their teaching materials.

Museums around the World
http://www.icom.org/vlmp/world.html
Directory of museums on the Internet sorted by country.

One Look
http://www.onelook.com
Search more than six hundred online dictionaries at once.

Quotations Archive
http://www.aphids.com/quotes/
The Quotations Archive is a comprehensive, searchable database of general purpose quotations. See also http://www.aphids.com/quotes/links.html for links to other sites.

Research It
http://www.itools.com/research-it/
A collection of on-line research tools. Search dictionaries, translate words, find quotations and more.

US Census Bureau
http://www.census.gov
Masses of US statistics.

VideoZone
http://www.videozone.co.uk
You can search the movies by actor/actress, subject or title, and then order on-line.

Weather Channel, The
http://www.weather.com
Forecasts for over 1,600 cities worldwide as well as numerous radar and satellite maps.

Web of On-line Dictionaries
http://www.facstaff.bucknell.edu/rbeard/diction.html
Over 800 dictionaries in 150 languages.

British Library http://portico.bl.uk

British Library: OPAC 97 http://opac97.bl.uk

Christian Sign Language Reference Site
http://www.jireh.demon.co.uk

Encyclopaedia Britannica http://www.britannica.com

Library of Congress
http://lcweb.loc.gov/homepage/lchp.html

National Art Library, Victoria and Albert Museum, UK
http://www.nal.vam.ac.uk

Smithsonian, The http://www.si.edu/

SEARCH – CHRISTIAN
DIRECTORIES AND GATEWAYS

1–4–All
http://www.jesus.org.uk/search/
Useful page from the Jesus Army which allows you to choose which of the main Christian search directories to search.

711.Net Christian Internet Assistance
http://www.711.net
5000+ sites with 300+ alphabetical and topical categories. Each entry has only a brief description.

About
http://www.about.com
A general directory organized by subject and each area over-seen by a 'guide'. Positive towards Christianity, with special lists for Catholicism, Protestantism and general Christianity. A good place to start (used to be The Mining Co.).

All in One Christian Index
http://www.allinone.org
Compilation and rating of major Christian search and direc-tory sites. Includes topical indexes, regional indexes and a site submission form.

Aussie Christian Search Engine
http://www.crosscape.com.au/search/
Search Australian Christian web pages. This is a search engine not a directory of sites, so do not be surprised if non-Christian sites will also be listed.

Australian Churches
http://www.vision.net.au/~kevin_keep/churches.htm
Australian churches by state, alphabetically.

Best of the Christian Web
http://www.botcw.com
Over 5,000 sites with good descriptions and ratings. Includes an articles archive, chat room and Christian software news.

Christian Community
http://www.ccgroups.com
A searchable directory of Christian lists and newsletters

Christian Link Collection
http://www.makarios.nu/
A slightly different list of links – these are organized by church tradition: Anglican, Catholic, Lutheran and Orthodox.

Christian Links http://www.christianlinks.com

Christian Portal
http://www.711.net
Help with searching the incredible number of products and services by businesses supporting and benefiting the Christian community.

Christian Ring of Rings
http://nav.webring.yahoo.com/hub?ring=chrrings&list
List of Christian web rings – that is, Christian sites which link to each other to encourage moving from one site to the next.

Christian Suppliers
http://www.christiansuppliers.com
Directory of suppliers for UK churches and Christian organizations.

Christian Topics
http://www.christiantopics.com
If you want to conduct a search with a particular topic in mind, try this search engine.

ChristiaNet
http://www.christianet1.com
The Christian Businesses Directory is designed to assist Christians in locating products and services in the US and Canada.

Christianity Today
http://www.christianitytoday.com/search
Large search engine and directory from Christianity Today in the US. Over 20,000 links. An excellent starting point although the site descriptions are only brief.

Christianlinks
http://www.christianlinks.com
US-based search engine for Christian sites. Each entry has a short description.

Church Net UK
http://www.churchnet.org.uk
UK search and directory. There are only brief descriptions, but this is a good place to start for UK material.

Church of England Yellow Pages
http://www.blackburn.anglican.org/yellow_pages
An A–Z directory of Anglican churches and church organizations throughout the UK. Lists addresses, telephone numbers and clergy.

CrossSearch
http://www.crosssearch.com
Straightforward, well-organized directory of several thousand Christian sites and over 100 different categories. Reasonable annotation given for each listing.

Crosswalk
http://omnilist.crosswalk.com
Good search engine (5,000+) with reasonable descriptions.

Down Under Christian Directory
http://www.ozemail.com.au/~phopwood/
Directory of Australian Christian life. Includes links to congregations, theology statements, sample sermons and an archive of related news articles.

Find a Church
http://www.findachurch.co.uk
Helps you to find a local UK church, whether they have a website or not.

Fish Net
http://www.fni.com/xstart/
Small list, but includes educational institutions and legal links.

GCN Search
http://www.gcnhome.com/asp/search.asp
Large database and reasonable descriptions. Includes radio, literature and film.

God on the Net
http://www.godonthenet.com
On-line version of this directory, with a submission form to add your favourite sites. Tell us what you would like to see in the next edition.

GOSHEN
http://www.goshen.net
The largest Christian search engine with over 1 million visitors a month! Has index to denominations, churches, education and community groups.

Gospel Communicators Network
http://www.gospelcom.net
Gospel Communications Network (Gospelcom) is an alliance of Christian ministries founded to proclaim the gospel in cyberspace. This means, they say, more than just web pages of links, but an alliance of organizations with life-enriching resources.

HIS-Net Christian Network
http://www.his-net.com
Mid-size directory with reasonable descriptions.

ICLNet
http://www.iclnet.org/pub/resources/xn-dir.html
Directory of Christian and theological colleges in the US.

In the Beginning
http://www.serve.com/larryi/begin.htm
Christian resource site, offering church search facility, Christian music and radio, discussion and chat groups, and devotional material.

Internet Christian Library
http://www.iclnet.org
The library was formerly known as The Institute for Christian Leadership. It offers links to Christian sites and resources around the web. The look may not be slick, but the content is excellent. ICLnet still contains one of the largest and most complete.

Internet for Christians
http://www.gospelcom.net/ifc/
List of Christian resources and Christian e-mail mailing lists

Internet Padre, The
http://www.internetpadre.com
The primary aim of this site is to provide a trusted resource for links and resources from a thoroughly Catholic perspective.

Kingdom Seek
http://www.kingdomseek.co.uk
UK Christian search directory.

Miami Christian University Virtual Library
http://mcu.edu/library/
A directory site, but with only a few descriptions of the sites listed. However, the range (if not the number) is wide and includes e-mail discussion lists and Usenet groups.

Net Ministries
http://netministries.org
Another US-based directory with 9,000+ entries, but not as good as some of the others. Offers free web space for churches and charities with a simple form to create a home page.

Omnilist
http://members.aol.com/clinksgold/
Not the most exhaustive list, but it helpfully breaks its recommendations down into 'gold' and 'silver' sites. Browse through the 'gold' entries to find some excellent material.

OurChurch.com
http://www.ourchurch.com
Directory with over 9,000 entries with search by category or keyword. Has an easy-to-use site builder and free church and charity website hosting.

Peter's Net
http://www.petersnet.net
A Catholic search and document library.

RE Directory
http://www.theredirectory.org.uk
Directory of RE sites and organizations.

Scottish Christian.com
http://www.scottishchristian.com
Directory of Christian sites in Scotland.

Serve Him
http://servehim.com
Helpful single page with links to many of the top Christian web sites. They would like you to make this your browser's start page.

Theology Library
http://www.mcgill.pvt.k12.al.us/jerryd/cathmob.htm
A collection of over 4,800 links in the spirit of the Second Vatican Council.

UK Christian Handbook Online
http://www.ukchristianhandbook.org.uk
Online version of the definitive directory of Christian organizations and services.

UK Christian Net
http://www.uk-christian.net
Small search directory for UK Christian groups.

UK Christian Web
http://www.christianweb.org.uk
Directory of UK Christian sites.

UK-Church.Net
http://uk-church.net/uk-listings.htm
Search page for UK churches, whether they are on the net or not.

UKCH Online
http://www.ukchristianhandbook.org.uk
On-line version of the very useful UK Christian Handbook. Find contact details for virtually every UK Christian organization.

University of St. Mary of the Lake
http://www.vocations.org/library
Excellent links to other Catholic sites and documents.

Webway at Premier Radio
http://www.premier.org.uk/webway/directory.html
Over 400 UK Christian sites arranged alphabetically, but with little annotation.

World Council of Churches
http://www.wcc-coe.org
Excellent links to national churches and organizations around the world.

XALT
http://www.xalt.co.uk
Portal site with articles, links, directory (sites, jobs and acco-
modation) plus news.

YouthPastor.Com
http://youthpastor.com
Directory specializing in helping harassed youth workers with
links and resources.

Christian Best http://www.christianbest.com

Christian Only http://www.his-net.com

Christian World Daily http://www.themissionary.net/pages/

Church 2000 http://www.church2000.org/Links/

Icthus http://www.icthus.co.uk

Jesus Army: Lists and Searches
http://www.jesus.org.uk/search/

New Zealand Christian Internet Directory
http://www.search.nzcid.org.nz

Surf-in-the-Spirit http://www.surfinthespirit.com

SEARCH – E-MAIL AND PHONE

192.com
http://www.192.com
Comprehensive service for tracking down names and
addresses. You can ask to be notified if people look up your
own details.

AnyWho Directory Services
http://www.anywho.com
Residential, business and government white and yellow pages
listings for US and Canada.

Big Book
http://www.bigbook.com
Lists over 11 million US businesses, plus street maps, reviews
and free home pages.

Big Foot
http://www.bigfoot.com
The web's largest directory of e-mail addresses, with US, UK, German and French versions.

Big Yellow
http://www.bigyellow.com
US business and shopping directory.

Charities Direct
http://www.caritasdata.co.uk
Alphabetical list of UK charities with contact information.

Charity Commission
http://www.charity-commission.gov.uk
Full register of UK charities with addresses and aims.

Christian E-mail Mailing Lists
http://www.gospelcom.net/ifc/mail/view/
Search or browse this directory of over 500 Christian e-mail lists.

Electronic Yellow Pages
http://www.eyp.co.uk
UK business phone directory.

International Directories
http://www.infobel.be/inter/world.asp
All the white and yellow page telephone directories available on the web.

Liszt
http://www.liszt.com
Searchable directory of over 90,000 mailing lists. There is a Christian section at http://www.liszt.com/select/Religion/Christian/.

PhoneNet UK
http://www.bt.com/phonenetuk/
British Telecom's on-line phone directory.

Publicly Accessible Mailing Lists
http://paml.net
Thousands of specialist e-mail discussion groups organized by name and subject.

Reverse Phone Directory
http://www.reversephonedirectory.com
This site will identify a name and address from a US telephone number.

Switchboard
http://www.switchboard.com
Find people and businesses in the US.

Telstra Yellow Pages
http://www.yellowpages.com.au
Australian business phone directory.

WorldPages.com
http://www.worldpages.com
Extensive search facility for US and Canadian white and yellow page listings.

Yell
http://www.yell.co.uk
UK Yellow Pages on-line. This is the biggest UK-specific directory and combines a company A–Z, film finder and business phone directory.

Yellow Pages Superhighway
http://www.bestyellow.com
This site has a database equivalent to 300 printed yellow pages books for US national and international business.

Phonenumbers.net http://www.phonenumbers.net

SEARCH – GENERAL

About

http://www.about.com

A general directory organized by subject and each area over-
seen by a 'guide'. Positive towards Christianity, with special
lists for Catholicism, Protestantism and general Christanity. A
good place to start (used to be The Mining Co.).

AltaVista

http://altavista.com

AltaVista is extremely fast and comprehensive. It searches the
entire text of web pages and Usenet articles so the vast
number of hits returned can be overwhelming.

AOL Search

http://search.aol.com

Searching for AOL users.

Argus Clearinghouse

http://www.clearinghouse.net

A concise archive of 'value-added topical guides which identify, describe, and evaluate Internet-based information
resources'. These guides are evaluated and indexed by category. You can also search for keywords, titles and authors.

Ask Jeeves

http://www.askjeeves.com

Search engine that allows you to ask questions in plain
English. Some of the responses to queries may not be very
useful, but it often offers interesting links to pursue.

Ask Jeeves for Kids

http://www.ajkids.com

Excellent search engine for children which allows them to
type in sentences such as, 'Why is the sky blue?'

Charity Net

http://www.charitynet.org/resources/charitylinks/

If you need to find details on a charity, try CharityNet with its
2,000+ international non-profit links.

Copernic

http://www.copernic.com

Search engine for your PC that searches all of the main internet search engines

Deja News

http://www.deja.com

Deja is the only searcher dedicated exclusively to searching Usenet newsgroups. Users can search the Usenet as far back as March, 1995 with a simple interface. Now part of the Google search engine.

DirectHit

http://www.directhit.com

Direct Hit is a bit different: it runs a popularity contest. Their popularity figures work by tracking the links that Internet users actually select from lists of search results.

DogPile

http://www.dogpile.com

Meta-search engine which uses other search engines to locate items and then collates the results. As they say, "All results, no mess."

Down-Under Yellow Pages

http://www.yellowpages.com.au/

This site offers listings of companies in Australia.

EuroSeek

http://www.euroseek.net

European search and directory. If it's European sites you want, see also http://www.euroferret.com.

Excite

http://www.excite.com

Excite is a feature-rich web site offering the benefits of both a powerful search engine and a well-organized index. Has local varieties in specific countries, for example http://www.excite.co.uk in the UK.

Family Search Internet
http://www.familysearch.org
Use this site to search for family names and events on the renowned and extensive Mormon database.

FeMiNa
http://www.femina.com
Lists sites that are 'women friendly'. A searchable front end provides access to hundreds of sites which are also organized into browsable categories. Has a good list of Christian sites.

Go
http://go.com
Portal site from Disney and InfoSeek.

HotBot
http://www.hotbot.com
With HotBot you can use Boolean operators without having to type in the terms.

Kresch
http://kresch.com/search/search.htm
From Kresh's single page you can search the main engines or use their own search engines at once.

LineOne
http://www.lineone.net
Good general starting point for UK surfers. Lots of content, with some restricted to members only.

LookSmart
http://www.looksmart.com
Directory from the Reader's Digest. Easy to navigate and each site entry has a comment. Probably the nearest rival to Yahoo in terms of being 'hand made'.

LookSmart–UK
http://www.looksmart.co.uk
LookSmart in the UK: an excellent general directory.

Lycos
http://www.lycos.com
Offers various services, such as news, city guides and maps. Differs between countries. Also has a search engine for non-text at http://www.lycos.com/lycosmedia.html.

Northern Light
http://www.northernlight.com
Northern Light organizes its search results by creating folders of documents with similar subjects, sources, or types.

NZ.com
http://www.nz.com
Search engine for New Zealand.

Open Directory Project
http://www.dmoz.org
Directory of sites put together by a diverse range of editors. This directory is often used by other search engines as it returns listings that have been evaluated by experienced editors rather than simply looking up key words.

OzSearch
http://www.ozsearch.com.au
Essential web directory and Internet guide for Australians.

Rough Guide to the Internet
http://www.roughguides.com
Home of the Rough Guide books, including an on-line version of the guide to the Internet complete with a directory of top sites.

Search Engine Watch
http://www.searchenginewatch.com
The best place to go to learn about search engines, how to use them and how to make submissions of your own site's details.

Search.com
http://www.search.com
Popular metasearch site offering access to over 200 search engines guides, auctions, storefronts, Usenet archives, news archives and software libraries.

SearchUK
http://www.searchUK.com
Concentrates on searching UK sites.

SoftCom
http://www.sofcom.com.au/Directories/
Australian directory.

Surf Searcher
http://www.surfsearcher.net
Offers a single page from which you can search the main UK search engines and directories. Also search for UK maps, weather and telephone numbers.

SurfSaver
http://www.surfsaver.com
SurfSaver takes the pages of information you collect from the web and organizes it for you in a searchable archive. Pages are saved with graphics, frames, formatting and links.

TOC H – UK Charities
http://www.phon.ucl.ac.uk/home/dave/TOC_H/Charities/
List of UK charity websites.

UK Children's Directory
http://www.ukchildrensdirectory.com
Umbrella site hosting a comprehensive list of links to children's and parenting sites.

UKMax
http://www.ukmax.com
UK search engine allowing you to search for sites within the UK domain only. Has free e-mail using you@britain.com, you@london.com and you@ukmax.com.

UKOnline
http://www.ukonline.com
A good starting site for everything British. Has lists of national and regional newspapers and is also good for travel and timetables.

Yahoo
http://www.yahoo.com
Yahoo is the best-known Internet directory. Yahoo catalogues sites manually, depending largely on user submissions. The site is now looking dated – and its Christianity section is not strong.

Yahooligans
http://www.yahooligans.com
Child-friendly web guide organized into subject groups like dinosaurs, hobbies and homework answers. Excellent.

SERMONS AND PREACHING

ChildrenSermons.com
http://www.childrensermons.com
Over 60 children's sermons provided as a free resource for all. Each sermon has a Bible reference, complete text, and suggested prop.

Christian Articles Archive
http://www.joyfulheart.com
Articles for personal inspiration, Bible study, speakers' illustrations and church newsletters.

Desperate Preacher's Site
http://www.javacasa.com/dps/
This site is dedicated to all who are burning the midnight oil! Sermons are based around the Revised Common Lectionary.

Explore the Word
http://www.exploretheword.com
An excellent site for serious Bible study. Also has notes on history, spirituality and sermons.

Sermon Central
http://www.sermoncentral.com
Over 16,000 full-text sermons and sermon outlines, all indexed by Bible chapter.

Sermon Help
http://www.sermonhelp.com
Offers sermons for every Sunday of the year. All sermons are archived by topic and by Bible passage. Sermons are based on the New Revised Common Lectionary. Subscription needed.

Sermon Illustrations
http://www.sermonillustrations.com
Illustrations that you can search by topic or Bible reading. And while you are browsing, why not pick up a unique e-mail address from clergy.net?

Sermon Links
http://www.sermonlinks.com
Thousands of links to sermons, sermon outlines and devotional material.

Sermon Notes Online
http://www.sermonnotes.com
Sermon Notes can give you a jump start on sermon preparation, offering seeker-sensitive messages and contemporary illustrations. However, it is a subscription service so there is not much here unless you have a password.

Sermon Resources
http://joywell.org/sermon-resources.html
Listing of other sermon sites.

Sermon Search
http://www.sermonsearch.com
Contains a searchable database of 8,000 sermons from contemporary pastors/speakers.

Sermon Shop
http://www.ecunet.org/sermonshop.html
Every week scriptural texts are listed from a variety of Christian lectionaries, where they are then discussed and developed for sermons and other ministry uses.

Sermon.org
http://www.sermon.org
Index and collection of sermons, outlines, articles, lectures and addresses from contemporary Reformed pastors.

Sermons and More
http://www.txdirect.net/~tgarner/
Great sermons from the past, for example Charles Spurgeon and JC Ryle.

Sermons and Stories
http://www.sermons-stories.co.uk
Free access to lectionary-based sermons and stories.

Spurgeon Archive
http://www.spurgeon.org
Claims to be the largest collection of Spurgeon material on the web.

Text This Week, The
http://www.textweek.com
An excellent site which offers links to a wide variety of on-line resources for study and liturgy, indexed according to the scripture lessons in the Revised Common Lectionary.

Worship That Works/Selected Sermons
http://ecusa.anglican.org/worship-that-works/
A weekly sermon series by a wide selection of lay and clergy preachers.

Order of Preachers – Dominicans http://www.op.org

SHOPPING

Acorndirect
http://www.acorndirect.co.uk
Christian books and music by mail order in the UK. 20,000 titles with full search.

Amazon Books
http://www.amazon.com
Currently the world's most successful online bookstore. For Amazon in the UK, look at http://www.amazon.co.uk.

Bargain Christian Books
http://www.bargain-christian-books.com
Discounted Christian books.

Barnes and Noble
http://www.barnesandnoble.com
Main rival to Amazon.com to be the on-line bookstore king.

BigYellow
http://www.bigyellow.com
On-line shopping directory has over 17 million business listings.

Bridal Planner
http://www.bridalplanner.com
Get advice from other brides-to-be plus the inevitable commercialism.

Buyer's Index
http://www.buyersindex.com
US site that searches over 15,000 sources for the best prices.

Christian Resources Exhibition
http://www.crexhib.co.uk
News on forthcoming exhibitions.

Christian Shopping Mall
http://www.christianet.com
Designed to assist Christians in locating products and services.

Christian Suppliers
http://www.christiansuppliers.com
Directory of suppliers for UK churches and Christian organizations.

Christianbook.com
http://www.christianbook.com
On-line bookshop.

ChristianBookshop.com
http://www.christianbookshop.com
On-line bookshop from some of the UK's leading resource providers.

Church House Bookshop
http://www.chbookshop.co.uk
The official bookshop of the Church of England plus a very wide range of other titles.

Church World Direct
http://.http://www.churchworlddirect.com
A global Christian marketplace with products, services and resources for the Christian community.

From Down Under
http://www.timebooksellers.com.au
The best of Australian titles including specialist and rare books.

Gospelcom Shopping
http://www.gospelcom.net/welcome/categories/shopping.shtml
Shopping online from Gospelcom.

GospelDirect
http://www.gospelcom.net/gf/mc/welcome.html
Christian videos, books and software.

Lund Theological Books
http://lundbooks.co.uk
New and secondhand theological books. Buys up academic and clerical libraries. If the book you need is out of print, look here.

Milestone.net
http://www.milestone.net
A portal for people interested in shopping and business opportunities.

Parable Christian Stores
http://www.parable.com
Christian stores for online shopping.

Price Watch
http://www.pricewatch.com
Select an item and this site will connect you with the cheapest retailer.

St Andrews Bookshop
http://www.standrewsbookshop.co.uk
Wide range of Christian titles from a leading independent bookshop.

Wedding Guide
http://www.weddingguide.co.uk
Information, advice and products for planning a wedding.

Wedding Service
http://www.wedding-service.co.uk
Billed as the UK's largest wedding and bride information directory.

Worshipmusic.com
http://www.worshipmusic.com
On-line shop for Christian praise music.

Blackwells http://blackwells.co.uk

BOL http://www.bol.com

Cantate Recordings
http://ourworld.compuserve.com/homepages/cantate/

CLC http://www.clc.org.uk

Dillons Bookstore http://www.dillons.co.uk

Independent Christian Bookstores
http://www.sonshinebookstore.com

W H Smith http://www.whsmith.co.uk

Waterstones http://www.waterstones.co.uk

Wesley Owen http://www.wesleyowen.com

SOCIAL ISSUES

Action for Gay and Lesbian Ordination
http://www.dircon.co.uk/aglo/
AGLO is a single-issue pressure group which campaigns for equality for lesbians, gay men and bisexuals in the Anglican priesthood.

American Family Association
http://www.afa.net
AFA stands for traditional family values, focusing primarily on the influence of television and other media – including pornography – on our society.

Arthur Rank Centre
http://www.arthurrankcentre.org.uk
Resources for the rural community and its churches, including the 'Living Churchyard and Cemetery Project'.

Black Information Link
http://www.blink.org.uk
Comprehensive site on black issues and racism.

Centre for Applied Ethics
http://www.ethics.ubc.ca/resources/business/
Links to general business ethics resources on the web.

Christian Digest
http://www.christiandigest.com
Published by Christian Family Network, it is perhaps most well known for its involvement in fighting the homosexual agenda, same sex marriages, and violence and nudity on network television.

Commission for Racial Equality
http://www.cre.gov.uk
Commission for Racial Equality tackles racial discrimination.

Countryside Matters
http://www.countrysidematters.org.uk
Looks at issues of concern for the farming and rural community.

Ethics for Scientists
http://onlineethics.org
A useful site for scientists and engineers seeking answers to ethical issues. It has case studies, letters and a help line.

Ethics on the Web
http://commfaculty.fullerton.edu/lester/ethics/ethics_list.html
List of links on ethics created by the School of Communications at California State University, Fullerton.

Lesbian and Gay Christian Movement
http://www.lgcm.org.uk
Encourages fellowship, friendship, and support among individual lesbian and gay Christians. The movement also aims to help the whole Church re-examine its understanding of human sexuality.

Life and Peace Institute
http://www.life-peace.org
International and ecumenical centre for peace research and action. Good information and links.

Linacre Centre for Bio Ethics
http://www.linacre.org
Reviews Catholic teaching on euthanasia, abortion, prenatal screening, contraception and genetic engineering.

Pro-Life Resource List
http://www.prolife.org/ultimate/
A comprehensive listing of right-to-life information on the Internet.

RE-XS
http://www.re-xs.ucsm.ac.uk/ethics/
Ethics section of RE-XS for schools which looks at the major moral issues from abortion to wealth and poverty.

Religion & Ethics NewsWeekly
http://www.pbs.org/religionandethics/
Site of American TV programme of the same name.

Safe Space at Greenbelt
http://www.geocities.com/WestHollywood/9381/
The Safe Space is a group of lesbian, gay, bisexual and heterosexual Christians concerned with the relationship between spirituality and sexuality.

Salt of the Earth
http://salt.claretianpubs.org
An online resource for social issues from a Catholic perspective.

Scruples for Marketplace Christians
http://www.scruples.org
A site designed to equip Christians with helpful information, biblical principles and practical skills to enable them to succeed as Christians in the marketplace.

Society, Religion and Technology Project
http://www.srtp.org.uk
Looking at the ethics of technology for a New Millennium from the Church of Scotland.

Society, Religion and Technology Project
http://www.srtp.org.uk/srtpage3.shtml
Examines the ethics of technology, with resources on genetic engineering, cloning, risk and climate change

Ultimate Pro-Life Resource List
http://www.prolifeinfo.org
An extensive directory of right-to-life resources on the Internet.

Ethical Investors http://www.oneworld.org/ethical-investors/

Ethics http://www.cellgroup.com

Ethics for children http://gonow.to/ethics/

Ethics Links
http://www.gac.edu/Academics/philosopy/ethics.html

Ethics Resources on the Net
http://condor.depaul.edu/ethics/ethb1.html

Index on Censorship http://www.oneworld.org/index_oc/

Institute for Values in Society
http://www.sarum.ac.uk/society/

Mission: America http://www.missionamerica.com

SOFTWARE - CHRISTIAN

Angelfire Communications
http://www.angelfire.com/ca/cvanbeek7/
Helpful list of sources for Christian shareware and commercial software.

Christian Computing
http://www.gospelcom.net/ccmag
Magazine that reviews software, hardware and applications for Christian-related tasks.

Church Computer Users Group
http://www.churchcomputer.org.uk
A non-denominational charity that provides help, advice and resources for all who use computers in all aspects of church life.

Free Christian Software Directory
http://www.seriousd.com/freeware.htm
Index of the best sites on the web for locating Christian and Church related freeware. See also http://www.seriousd.com/clipart.htm for clipart.

GOSHEN – Christian Software
http://www.christianshareware.net
The GOSHEN Christian Shareware library site is a good starting point for Bible and Christian software.

Serious Developments
http://www.seriousd.com/freeware.htm
Claims to index the best sites on the web for locating Christian and church-related freeware.

Visual Liturgy
http://www.vislit.com
Software tool for planning worship. The site provides updates to the program and its hymn lists.

Biblesoft http://www.biblesoft.com

Data Developments http://www.data-developments.co.uk

Parsons Technology http://www.parsonstech.com

SOFTWARE - GENERAL

32 Bit
http://www.32bit.com
Archive for the latest and greatest shareware, demos and free software.

AntiVirus Software
http://antivirus.about.com
A valuable site for all users keen to keep up to date with virus problems.

asu.info.apple.com
http://asu.info.apple.com
One of the biggest and most reliable download centres for the Apple Mac range.

Completely Free Software
http://www.completelyfreesoftware.com
No-nonsense, no-frills site for Windows that delivers what it says. Well worth a visit before you buy commercial software.

Cover CDs
http://covercd.co.uk
Features UK computer magazine cover disks and searchable back issue archives.

Download.com
http://www.download.com
Extensive shareware site.

Family Software Spot
http://www.familysoftwarespot.com
Family-related downloads with descriptions, tutorials and advice.

Freewarehome.com
http://www.freewarehome.com
Lists, with descriptions, of totally free software.

iMac, The
http://www.theimac.com
Great for new iMac owners with guides and tutorials in abundance.

InfoMac HyperArchive
http://hyperarchive.lcs.mit.edu/HyperArchive/
Software library for Apple Macs.

Jumbo Shareware
http://www.jumbo.com
As its name suggest, a huge library of downloadable software for all types of computers.

Mac Download
http://www.macdownload.com
The ZDNET Mac downloads web site has all the top shareware and free titles.

Mac OS Zone
http://www.macoszone.com
The place for the newest and best in Macintosh software and demos with thousands of review pages.

MacAddict
http://www.macaddict.com
News, views, guides and trouble-shooting help for Apple Mac computers.

Net Security
http://netsecurity.about.com
Articles, tutorials and news about all aspects of internet and network security.

PC Help Online
http://www.pchelponline.com
The purpose of this site is to avoid searching all over the Internet trying to locate a specific company or information to cure PC woes.

PC Quote
http://www.pcquote.co.uk
Searches for the best prices for PC hardware and software from UK suppliers.

Pegasus Mail
http://www.pmail.com
An excellent free e-mail program which can be used for simple mailing lists. If you are serious about setting up e-mail lists, look at the Mercury product (from the same author and also free) on this site.

Shareware Junkies
http://www.sharewarejunkies.com
A download site that gives evaluations of the software they have available.

Shareware.com
http://www.shareware.com
Large collection of shareware files.

Software Archives
http://www.softwarearchives.com
A huge online database of freeware and shareware programs for your PC.

Top File
http://www.topfile.com
Reviews the best shareware and freeware for Windows.

TUCOWS
http://www.tucows.com
Specialist site for Internet software. Download the latest browsers from here.

Well Connected Mac
http://www.macfaq.com
Guide to Apple Mac software and resources.

Windows
http://windows.about.com
All aspects of PC maintenance covered in an easy-to-understand manner.

SPIRITUALITY

24-7
http://www.24-7prayer.com
A worldwide, non-stop prayer movement

American Catholic
http://www.americancatholic.org
News and articles from the Franciscan friars of Cincinnati.

Apostate Cafe
http://www.apostate.com/religion/
A discussion of Christianity, Gnosticism, theology, heresy, and prayer.

Biographical Sketches of Christians
http://justus.anglican.org/resources/bio/
Stories of the people who, through the centuries, have made the Christian Church what it is today.

CaseStudies
http://www.case-studies.com
Practical lessons about people, God, and life. A mixed bag which may inspire, anger or bore you.

Celtic Christianity
http://www2.gol.com/users/stuart/celtihs.html
Search engine and links on everything Celtic.

Christian Quotation of the Day
http://www.gospelcom.net/cqod/
To start the day with challenge or cheer, look at this Gospelcom site or subscribe via e-mail. Previous quotations are archived, just in case you miss out while on holiday.

Crosswinds
http://www.btinternet.com/~crosswinds/
Seeks to establish a partnership of praying churches across the UK.

Daily Devotions
http://www.devotions.net
Daily, short devotion.

Daily Wisdom
http://www.gospelcom.net/gci/dw/
A daily story, allegory, or commentary on contemporary life and culture.

Devotionals
http://www.devotionals.net
A small selection of devotional material, from the classic Charles Spurgeon's Morning and Evening devotions to Bible reading plans.

Firewatch
http://140.190.128.190/merton/merton.html
Articles and research on the works of Thomas Merton and Christian mysticism.

He is Risen
http://www.execpc.com/~tmuth/easter/
A journey through scripture, art, music and stories which reflect on the miracle of the resurrection of Jesus.

NUPSA
http://www.nupsa.com
An interdenominational Christian prayer ministry that is committed to building a strong, broad-based prayer network.

Spirit Home
http://www.spirithome.com
Resources and links on spirituality and spiritual disciplines.

Words from the Well
http://www.gospelcom.net/peggiesplace/words.htm
Devotionals from Peggie plus a list of other sites.

Confraternity of the Blessed Sacrament
http://www.netcomuk.co.uk/~lnagel/cbs.html

Institute for Christian Spirituality
http://www.sarum.ac.uk/spirituality

Virtual Guide to Easter http://www.the-word.net/links/easter

SUPPORT AND COUNSELLING

Age Concern
http://www.ace.org.uk
Age Concern – practical help, information, advice and resources for the elderly and their carers.

Alcohol Concern
http://www.alcoholconcern.org.uk
National agency on alcohol misuse with advice, publications, news and information service.

Another Empty Bottle
http://www.alcoholismhelp.com
Alcohol problems laid out for alcoholics and their relatives.

Baby Loss
http://www.babyloss.com
UK site offers support and is useful for people who have experienced the devastating loss of a baby.

British Deaf Association
http://www.britishdeafassociation.org.uk
British Deaf Association offers sign language information.

British Epilepsy Association
http://www.epilepsy.org.uk
Offers a wealth of information for sufferers.

CARE (Christian Action Research and Education)
http://www.care.org.uk
CARE is a Christian organization providing caring work in the community.

Care Aware
http://www.careaware.co.uk
All the facts about long term care for the elderly.

Care for the Family
http://www.care-for-the-family.org.uk
Help for those in the UK hurting because of the breakup of their family.

Care Guide
http://www.careguide.uk.com
Over 8000 retirement, residential and nursing homes listed.

Cascade
http://www.cascade.u-net.com
Drug information site run by young people for young people.

Child Poverty Action Group
http://www.cpag.org.uk
Researches family poverty in UK and provides welfare benefits advice and training courses.

Compassionate Friends, The
http://www.tcf.org.uk
The Compassionate Friends support families after the loss of a child.

Connections Christian Counselling Services
http://www.connections.ndirect.co.uk
A UK Christian counselling centre helping people around the world.

Contact a Family
http://www.cafamily.org.uk
Povides support and advice to parents with children with rare diseases and syndromes.

Contact the Elderly
http://www.contact-the-elderly.org
Contact the Elderly takes lonely elderly people to tea each month.

Credit Action
http://www.creditaction.com
Educational charity working nationally to improve money management skills from a biblical perspective.

Daughters of Charity
http://www.daughtersofcharity.org.uk
An international community of women within the Roman Catholic Church who live and work alongside individuals, families and other groups who need support, affirmation and practical help.

Daylight Trust
http://www.aandp.co.uk/daylight/
Ecumenical Christian group which aims to provide support, counselling and spiritual guidance.

Dementia Care Trust
http://www.dct.org.uk
Offers practical support for carers, information and resources with counselling services available for carers.

Dementia Web
http://www.dementia.ion.ucl.ac.uk
Support, advice, information for dementia carers.

Divorce.co.uk
http://www.divorce.co.uk
Advice on mediation, counselling and legal aspects of divorce.

Drugscope
http://www.drugscope.org.uk
Charity involved with drug education in UK schools.

Ellel Ministries International
http://ellelministries.org
A non-denominational group which offers training and ministry in Christian healing, deliverance and counselling.

Guide for Life
http://www.guideforlife.co.uk
Empathic overview of responses and solutions to serious illness, death and bereavement.

Help the Aged
http://www.helptheaged.org.uk
Practical support for the independent elderly person.

Hospital Chaplaincy Gateway
http://www.hospitalchaplain.co.uk
A site dedicated to helping hospital chaplains use the internet and providing links to relevant sites.

Learning Disabilities On-Line
http://www.ldonline.org
Interactive guide to learning disabilities for parents, teachers and children.

Marie Stopes International
http://www.mariestopes.org.uk
Family planning organisation with clinic information, education, resources and publications.

Mencap
http://www.mencap.org.uk
Support and advice services for people with learning disabilities.

MIND
http://www.mind.org.uk
Helps people face up to mental illness.

Miscarriage Association
http://www.the-ma.org.uk
Offers support, advice and practical information to women experiencing miscarriage.

National Association for Christian Recovery
http://www.christianrecovery.com
Helping the Christian community become a safe and helpful place for people recovering from addictions, abuse or trauma.

National Council for Divorced and Separated
http://www.ncds.org.uk
NCDS has groups throughout the UK offering social clubs and events.

NSPCC
http://www.nspcc.org.uk
The NSPCC charity runs a child protection help line.

On-line Guidance
http://www.gospelcom.net/guidance/
Offers short articles on a range of life's most pressing personal issues.

Philippi House
http://www.philippi.co.uk
Aims to provide the highest level of counselling and counselling training.

Problem Pages
http://www.problempages.co.uk
Free UK online problem page with answers from agony aunts and uncles.

Prospects
http://www.prospects.org.uk
Christian voluntary organization which values and supports people with learning disabilities so that they live their lives to the full.

RADAR
http://www.radar.org.uk
Supports over 500 local and national disability organizations.

Relate
http://www.relate.org.uk
Counselling and sex therapy education to support couples and families.

Release
http://www.release.org.uk
Dedicated to meeting the health, welfare and legal needs of drugs users and those who live and work with them.

Samaritans
http://www.samaritans.org.uk
Supports people who are suicidal or in despair.

Shelter
http://www.shelter.org.uk
Advice and practical help to those sleeping rough.

THOMAS
http://www.users.globalnet.co.uk/~edges
THOMAS was created to build a bridge of dialogue between the church and people who are on the margins of society especially those who are homeless, addicted to drugs or involved in crime.

Through the Roof
http://www.throughtheroof.org
Disability outreach of Joni Eareckson Tada in the UK.

True Freedom Trust
http://www.tftrust.u-net.com
Support and teaching ministry for men and women struggling with homosexuality, lesbianism and similar issues.

Victim Support
http://www.victimsupport.com
Helps people cope with the effects of crime with free and confidential support and information.

Young Minds
http://www.youngminds.org.uk
Children's mental health charity for parents, children and professionals.

Anglican Marriage Encounter
http://www.marriageencounter.freeserve.co.uk

Big Issue http://www.bigissue.com

Christian Therapists Network http://www.ctn.org.uk

Department of Social Security http://www.dss.gov.uk

Foundation for the Study of Infant Deaths
http://www.sids.org.uk/fsid

Marriage Resource and National Marriage Week
http://www.marriageresource.org.uk

Mental Health Foundation http://www.mentalhealth.org.uk

Multiple Sclerosis Society http://www.mssociety.org.uk

National Council for One Parent Families
http://www.oneparentfamilies.org.uk

National Deaf Children's Society http://www.ndcs.org.uk

National Society for the Protection of Children against Cruelty http://www.nspcc.org.uk

Neighbourhood Watch
http://www.neighbourhoodwatch.org

Network Counselling and Training
http://www.network.org.uk

Prepare/Enrich Network UK http://www.cmp.mcmail.com

Royal National Institute for the Blind
http://www.rnib.org.uk

Society for the Protection of Unborn Children
http://www.spuc.org.uk

TV/RADIO/FILM

Christian Radio (UK)
http://www.Christianradio.org.uk
All the news and views from a UK Christian perspective.

Christian Radio (US)
http://www.christianradio.com
Extensive list of Christian radio stations in the US and around the world.

Christian Spotlight on the Movies
http://www.christlananswers.net/spotlight/
Reviews and ratings of films from a Christian perspective.

Christian Vision and Christian Voice
http://www.christian-vision.org
UK charity promoting Christianity around the world by setting up radio stations and by using the Internet.

ChristianRock.Net
http://www.christianrock.net
A 24-hour Internet-based Christian rock radio station.

Cinema Guide from Scoot
http://www.cinema.scoot.co.uk
Guide to what's on and when in England, Scotland, Wales and Ireland.

Discovery On-Line
http://www.discovery.com
Site of the Discovery channel with news, teaching resources and fun area for children.

Dove Foundation
http://www.dove.org
Dove reviewers try to help you sort out the wheat from the chaff when choosing the best videos for your family.

Family Radio
http://www.familyradio.com
Non-denominational, educational organization dedicated to preaching. You can listen live, get station listings and programme guides.

Family Style
http://www.familystyle.com
Each film in the guide has been reviewed and objectional material noted.

Film Reviews
http://film.reviews.co.uk
Reviews of the latest movie releases to hit British cinema screens.

Inspired Christian Technologies
http://www.inspired-tech.com/gallery.html
Christian radio and television broadcasts and feature-length motion pictures by RealVideo. Free Christian animated graphics.

International Christian Media Commission
http://www.icmc.org
Information source for Christian involvement in media.

Internet Movie Database
http://uk.imdb.com
Huge movie info database.

Involved Christian Radio Network
http://www.icm.com
You can listen to over fifty radio-based broadcast ministries.

IScriptdb
http://www.iscriptdb.com
A vast resource for tracking down free film scripts on the internet.

Junctionradio.com
http://www.junctionradio.com
An Oasis site for youth groups running online radio websites and raising money for education in developing countries

Live Radio on the Internet
http://www.live-radio.net
Accurate and maintained source of links to radio stations world-wide.

Praise TV
http://www.praisetv.com
Glossy US site for Christian music.

Premier Radio
http://www.premier.org.uk
Listen to London's Christian radio from anywhere around the world.

Radio Locator
http://www.radio-locator.com
An alphabetical list of links to over 1,000 radio stations around the world.

Radio Online
http://www.radio-online.com
State by state directory of American local radio stations on air and online.

Radio Station Guide
http://windowsmedia.com/radiotuner
A radio guide for Windows Media Player

Trans World Radio
http://www.twr.org
Trans World Radio is an international organization that airs more than 1,200 hours of Christian programmes per week. Site has details of the ministry and a few resources.

United Christian Broadcasters
http://www.ucb.co.uk
Broadcast to the UK and Europe through all styles of contemporary music, news, information and teaching programmes.

Virgin Radio Tuner
http://www.virgin.net/radio/
Tune in to radio stations around the globe.

Association of Christians in Broadcasting
http://www.caclb.org.uk

Christian Channel Europe http://www.god-digital.com

Christian Voice http://www.christianvoice.co.uk

CTVC Video http://www.ctvc.co.uk

FEBA Radio http://www.feba.org.uk

Film.com http://www.film.com

Oneplace.com http://www.oneplace.com

Radio Eden http://www.radio-eden.ndirect.co.uk

Truth for Life http://www.gospelcom.net/tfl/

United Christian Broadcasters http://www.ucb.co.uk

WEB DESIGN - CREATING PAGES

Ambit New Media
http://www.ambitnewmedia.com
The author's own web design and hosting company. Look at http://www.church.uk.net for church-specific information.

Aphids Communications
http://www.aphids.com/megasite/
Good guide to web resources and creating sites for churches. Offers three services: database of over 2,000 Christian sites, help on web page design, and an icon and image archive.

ASPin.com
http://www.aspin.com
Source of Active Server Page scripts and applications. Beef up your web site, but check first that your ISP likes ASP.

Association of Christian Web Authors
http://www.webauthors.org
For Christian web designers, beginners to professionals. See also the Good News Web Designers Association at http://gnwda.org.

Atlas of Great Britain
http://uk.multimap.com
Link to this site to place maps on your web site.

CGI Resource Index
http://www.cgi-resources.com
Nearly 2,000 CGI resources to enhance your site, but check first with your ISP before trying to load them.

Christian Webmasters Association (Europe)
http://www.wordnet.co.uk/chtml2.html
Support group for Christians designing websites. List of members and a few reviews of pages.

CNET Builder.com
http://www.builder.com
Excellent resources and links for web designers.

Crosswalk Chats
http://chat.crosswalk.com
Useful to create your own kid's chatroom.

Designing web pages for the disabled
http://www.gospelcom.net/guide/web-disability.html
Very useful advice on how to design pages which are accessible to those with various disabilities.

Family Media Network
http://www.ourchurchtools.com
Software tools to help build more effective church web sites.

Free Webmaster Tools and Resources
http://kresch.com/resources/
Resources and tools to manage your website. All utilities, programs and sites are carefully selected – or so they say.

Gospelcom Webmaster Tools
http://www.gospelcom.net/free/tools/
How to add a Bible gateway and Christian search form to your site.

HTML Reference Library
http://www.htmlib.com
Excellent reference guide to HTML. Download and use alongside your web editor.

My Postcards
http://www.mypostcards.com
Add postcards and greeting cards to your site. The basic service is free.

Service Monitor
http://www.servicemonitor.com
Free web space and add-on tools such as search and chat.

Top Hosts
http://webmaster.tophosts.com
Links to resources on the Internet for web creators.

UK Street Map
http://www.streetmap.co.uk
Provides address searching and street map facilities for the UK. Handy for directing visitors to your church.

Web Page Design for Designers
http://www.wpdfd.com
For established designers in conventional print media who want to understand layout and graphics on the web.

WhyteHouse, The
http://www.whytehouse.com
A place to go for free Christian web graphics and Javascripts.

Wide Area Communications
http://www.widearea.co.uk/designer/
Guidelines for using graphics on the web.

ZyWeb Publisher
http://www.zy.com
If you want to have your own website, and need a bit more than the 'fill in a form' sites can offer, take a look at the popular ZyWeb site.

WEB DESIGN - HOSTING, DOMAINS AND SERVICES

Add Me
http://www.addme.com
Submit your site to 25 search engines free.

All in One Christian Index
http://www.allinone.org
Compilation and rating of major Christian search and directory sites. Includes topical indexes, regional indexes and a site submission form.

Ambit New Media
http://www.ambitnewmedia.com
The author's own web design and hosting company. Look at http://www.church.uk.net for church-specific information.

Anglican Church Music
http://www.churchmusic.org.uk
If you fancy an address such as http://www.churchmusic.org.uk/stmarys/, visit this site to set up free e-mail and web redirection.

Anglican Domain
http://anglican.org
How to use the domain anglican.org for your own website.

Argus
http://www.argus.myth.co.uk
For a small fee, Argus will monitor your website to check it is always up and running.

Basic Ministries
http://www.basicministries.org
Free 5 MB web space from a Christian provider and there are no pop-up ads to spoil it.

CentralNic
http://www.centralnic.com
CentalNic administers the .uk.com, .gb.net, gb.com domain names for UK.COM Ltd. These names are less well known than the .co.uk and you may still find the name you want.

Christian Ring of Rings
http://nav.webring.yahoo.com/hub?ring=chrrings&list
List of Christian web rings – that is, Christian sites which link to each other to encourage moving from one site to the next.

Church UK Internet Project
http://www.churchuk.net
Christian UK ISP offering domain name registration, web hosting and other services.

Church.uk.net
http://www.church.uk.net
Domains and web hosting from the people that run Christianbookshop.com.

Churches Dot Net
http://churches.net
Offers simple free web page generator for US churches and charities.

Domain Name Guide
http://www.igoldrush.com
Guide to domain names in over 200 countries.

Extreme
http://www.extreme-dm.com/tracking/
If you need a discreet way of obtaining statistics on your website visitors, consider this free on-line tracker.

Free Page Hosting
http://www.thefreesite.com/Free_Web_Space/
If you need free web space, look at some of these general community sites. The amount of free space is not the only criterion by which to judge. Do they allow business sites? Have they got an easy-to-use web page generator?

Goldrush
http://www.igoldrush.com/guide/
All the domain name information you'll ever need, and in plain English too.

Gumball Website Tracker
http://www.gumball-tracker.com
Free visitor tracker, statistics and traffic reporting from UK site.

Homestead
http://www.homestead.com
Free website creation and hosting without adverts. Allows multiple authorship of sites, which may suit some churches and organizations. Their excellent web page editor may be used to create pages for non-Homestead sites too.

Internic
http://www.internic.net
Check here to see if the domain name you want is already taken. In the UK try www.nominet.net and www.centralnic.com.

Kresch redirection
http://kresch.com/resources/Web_Hosting/Redirection_Services/
List of sites offering free redirection services.

Lutherans.Net
http://www.lutherans.net
A website for Lutherans with Bible study tools, discussion, prayer and free web space at http://www.luther95.org.

Methodist Church of Great Britain
http://www.methodist.org.uk
Offers advice for churches who want their own pages or would like to use the methodist.org.uk domain.

Net Ministries
http://netministries.org
Another US-based directory with 9,000+ entries, but not as good as some of the others. Offers free web space for churches and charities with a simple form to create a home page.

OurChurch.com
http://www.ourchurch.com
Directory with over 9,000 entries with search by category or keyword. Has an easy-to-use site builder and free church and charity website hosting.

Register.com
http://www.register.com
Register your domain name. Information on domain names at http://www.register.com/domreg/faq/.

SiteOwner.com
http://siteowner.linkexchange.com
Tools such as submission engine, site inspection and meta-tag builder.

UK-Church.Net
http://uk-church.net/go/free_pointer_service.htm
Free redirection service. You end up with a web address like uk-church.net/go/your-church-name.htm.

Visit Web
http://www.visitweb.com
Handy redirection service for e-mail and web pages. Free with no advertising.

VOIS: Voluntary Organisations Internet Server
http://www.vois.org.uk
Hosts a number of charity and voluntary organizations websites.

ServeYou Network Domain Hosting
http://www.serveyou.com

WOMEN – CHRISTIAN AND GENERAL

Anglican Women's Webpage
http://ecusa.anglican.org/women/
Articles, announcements and resources from the ECUSA/Anglican Women's Network.

Catholic Women's Ordination
http://ourworld.compuserve.com/homepages/justitia/
UK-based group of women and men who believe women should be ordained as priests within the Roman Catholic Church.

Center for Women and Religion
http://aquinas.gtu.edu/Centers/cwr/
Multi-denominational site of Graduate Theological Union, Berkeley, California.

Christian + Feminist
http://www.users.csbsju.edu/~eknuth/xpxx/
Dedicated to the proposition that faith and feminism are not mutually exclusive. Articles and some links.

Christian Advice for Women
http://www.liveit.net
Practical advice on running a household and family plus suggestions for keeping spirituality alive.

Christian Women Today
http://www.christianwomentoday.com
Magazine-style site on women's issues and spirituality.

Christian Working Woman
http://www.christianworkingwoman.org
A ministry to bring a fresh Christian perspective to the workplace.

Christianity Today
http://www.christianitytoday.com/women/
Women section on Christianity Today portal.

Every Woman
http://www.everywoman.co.uk
Impartial legal, medical and business advice for women juggling work and life.

Fawcett Library – The National Library of Women
http://www.lgu.ac.uk/fawcett/main.htm
Library at London Guildhall University which documents the changing role of women in society.

FeMiNa
http://www.femina.com
Lists sites that are 'women friendly'. A searchable front end provides access to hundreds of sites which are also organized into browsable categories. Has a good list of Christian sites.

Hearts at Home
http://www.hearts-at-home.org
This is a non-denominational Christ-centred organization designed to give support to mothers at home.

Home-Based Working Moms
http://www.hbwm.com
This site offers support for mothers working at home.

IVillage.com
http://www.ivillage.com
Magazine and network site for women.

Moms Online
http://www.momsonline.com
Plenty of easy-to-prepare menus, child-rearing advice, stories and chat groups.

Mothers with Children
http://www.gospelcom.net/mops/
MOPS gives encouragement to mothers of young children.

Sister Site
http://www.geocities.com/Wellesley/1114/
A clearing house for information on women's religious congregations, the history of religious life, and the contemporary concerns of women in church and society.

WATCH

http://www.watchwomen.com

Promotes the appointment of women at all levels in the Church and supports women in lay and ordained ministries.

Woman Today Online

http://www.christianwomentoday.com

Christian women's magazine: Bible study, advice, stories, devotions.

Womankind

http://www.womankind.org.uk

UK charity dedicated to women's development and human rights globally.

Women of Faith

http://www.womenoffaith.com

The purpose of Women of Faith is to equip women to reach out to others and become an even more vital part of their communities and churches.

Women on Crosswalk

http://women.crosswalk.com

This Christian community looks at women in the news and in history. It offers daily study guides written for women and inspiring stories of women who made a difference.

Women Today International

http://www.womentoday.org

Dedicated to help women reach their homes, communities, states and the world for Christ.

Women's Ministry

http://www.womensministry.net

An ideas and resource site.

Women.com

http://www.women.com

General on-line magazine.

WWWomen

http://www.wwwomen.com

Magazine and search site for women. 'The home of virtual women,' it says.

European Women's Lobby http://www.womenlobby.org

National Association for Female Executives
http://www.nafe.com

United Nation's Women Watch
http://www.un.org/womenwatch/

Web-World Women http://www.webworldwomen.com

WORSHIP AND LITURGY

Adoremus
http://www.adoremus.org
The Society for the Renewal of the Sacred Liturgy wants to rediscover and restore the 'beauty, the holiness, the power of the Church's rich liturgical tradition'.

Anglican Liturgical Library
http://www.oremus.org/liturgy/
A useful liturgical library with a collection of authorized and other texts used in the Church of England, in the wider Anglican Communion and elsewhere.

Book of Common Prayer
http://justus.anglican.org/resources/bcp/
Chad Wohler's fine coverage of the development of the English and American Prayer Books, starting in 1552.

Daily Office
http://www.missionstclare.com
An online version of the Daily Office available in English and Spanish.

Easter in Cyberspace
http://www.njwebworks.com
A directory of Christ-centred Easter and Lent web sites.

Easter: Christ is Risen
http://entourages.com/barbs/Easter.htm
The biblical story of the resurrection of Christ, links to Easter readings, places to visit, information and more.

Family Worship
http://www.familyworship.org.uk
Resources, songs, and teaching materials from Ichthus Christian Fellowship in London aimed at helping the whole church to worship together.

Lectionary Page, The
http://www.io.com/~kellywp/
A liturgical calendar with links to the lessons from the Episcopal lectionary.

Lift Up Your Hearts
http://www.worship.on.ca/
Excellent list of sites relating to worship. Everything from Altar bread recipes and Byzantine images, right through the alphabet.

Netword
http://www.netword.org.uk
Tries to provide quality liturgical resources for use in Catholic parishes and schools.

Praise Net
http://www.praise.net
Wants to become the leading provider of worship resources on the World Wide Web.

Prayer Book Society
http://www.prayerbookuk.com
Seeks to promote the worship enshrined in the Book of Common Prayer and to defend its doctrine. (The Prayer Book Society of the USA is at http://www.episcopalian.org/pbs1928/.)

Prayer Books
http://justus.anglican.org/resources/
Links to on-line Anglican resources from the Society of Archbishop Justus.

Priestly Society of Saint Pius X
http://www.sspx.org
Founded by Archbishop Lefebvre. The site explains its doctrine and worship.

Songs of Praise
http://songsofpraise.org
Song site with MP3s, MIDIs and even translations.

Text This Week, The
http://www.textweek.com
An excellent site which offers links to a wide variety of on-line resources for study and liturgy, indexed according to the scripture lessons in the Revised Common Lectionary.

Visual Liturgy
http://www.vislit.com
Software tool for planning worship. The site provides updates to the program and its hymn lists.

Wild Goose Publications
http://www.ionabooks.com
Worship resources from the Iona Community

Institute for Liturgy and Mission
http://www.sarum.ac.uk/ILM/

Praxis http://www.sarum.ac.uk/praxis/

Y O U T H - C H R I S T I A N

Aim for Success
http://www.aimforsuccess.org
A site which promotes sexual abstinence until marriage.

Apple Sauce Kids
http://home.dmv.com/~aplsauce/
Resources for anyone who works with children and young people. Everything is copyright free.

Big Bang
http://sr11.xoom.com/verybigbang/
An alternative Christian youth e-zine.

Boys Brigade
http://www.boys-brigade.org.uk
This Christian organization for 6–18 year-olds is the oldest voluntary uniformed youth organization in the world – now embracing the most up-to-date technology.

Cafe Reality
http://www.gospelcom.net/yfc/students/
Youth for Christ discussion and support pages.

Campus Life
http://www.christianitytoday.com/campuslife/
Magazine from the Christianity Today stable.

Careforce
http://www.careforce.co.uk
Serves evangelical churches and organizations by placing Christian volunteers aged 18–25 where their help is most needed in the UK and Ireland.

Catholic Youth Resources
http://www.microserve.net/~fabian/ym.html
A handful of pointers to Catholic youth resources on the web.

Christian Games Forum
http://www0.delphi.com/christiangames/
For Christian games enthusiasts to play on-line, chat etc. Includes adventure and RPG-type games.

Christian Gaming
http://www.christiangaming.com
As the URL hints, this site's about Christian gaming. See also The Purple Yak at http://www.purpleyak.com.

Christian Students in Science
http://www.csis.org.uk
A UK site to promote discussion in the student community on issues relating to science and faith.

Christian Students' Netlinks
http://www.surf.to/netlinks/
Links to some of the best sites of interest to Christian students.

Christian Teen Corner
http://www.wolfeborobible.com/teen.html
On-line Bible studies and advice for teens.

Christian Youth News
http://www.christianteens.net/cyn/
A magazine for teenagers that features articles on the issues that are important to them as well as interviews with Christian artists, album reviews and more.

Christian Youth Resources
http://web.1earth.net/~youth/
Youth resources from Australia.

Church Lads and Church Girls Brigade
http://www.church-brigade.syol.com
A uniformed Anglican youth organization offering fun and fellowship for boys and girls between the ages of 5 and 21.

Church Pastoral Aid Society (CPAS)
http://www.cpas.org.uk
UK mission society mainly working with Anglican churches. Best known for its youth and children's work (Explorers, Climbers, Scramblers, Pathfinders and CYFA).

Crosswalk Games
http://games.crosswalk.com
Traditional and arcade-style games.

Crusaders
http://www.crusaders.org.uk
Crusaders is an interdenominational Christian Youth Organisation working with children and young people across the UK.

Egad Ideas
http://www.egadideas.com
Claims to be the Internet's largest collection of free games, activities and ideas for those who work with today's youth.

FURY
http://www.fury.ws
FURY stands for Fellowship of United Reformed Youth. Site has details of events and affiliated groups.

Fusion
http://www.fusion.uk.com
Fusion is a student-led movement that encourages 'grass roots' evangelism on campuses and a positive view of the world and a Christian's responsibility to reach out to it.

InterVarsity Christian Fellowship
http://www.gospelcom.net/iv/
University-based Christian organization. Features mission opportunities, the journal Student Leadership and links to college chapter websites.

MAYC
http://www.mayc.org.uk
News, events, resources and on-line chat from the Methodist Church youth section.

RE-XS
http://www.re-xs.ucsm.ac.uk/ethics/
Ethics section of RE-XS for schools which looks at the major moral issues from abortion to wealth and poverty.

Reaching the Generations for Jesus
http://home.pix.za/gc/gc12/
Research and discussion on the various generations of young people growing up today: Generation X (1961–82), Generation Y (1982–2003) and Generation Z (2003–2025).

Religious Education Sources
http://members.aol.com/wardfreman/alevelre/
Links to sources for UK secondary school religious education topics.

Rock Solid
http://www.yfc.co.uk/rocksolid.htm
Programme to help local churches reach out to young people.

Silly Olympics
http://www.youth.co.za/olympics/
Did you know the record for downing a can of fizzy drink is 6.45 seconds?

Sloppy Noodle
http://sloppynoodle.com
Magazine site for young people.

Soul Survivor Watford
http://www.soulsurvivor.com
Through festivals and events, Soul Survivor provide a place for young people to get connected with God in lifestyles of worship that make sense to them.

UCCF
http://www.uccf.org.uk
Universities and Colleges Christian Fellowship supports Christians in British college education. Has a mission focus and runs a number of graduate programmes.

WCRP – Youth
http://www.geocities.com/Vienna/2848/
World Conference on Religion and Peace site 'dedicated to promoting co-operation for peace and justice among the members of the world's religions'.

World Bible Quiz Association
http://www.wbqa.org
Resources for using Bible quizzes to motivate young people to learn and live as Christians.

World Student Christian Federation
http://www.wcc-coe.org/wscf/
The WSCF is a meeting place for young Christians from all churches and nations. Founded in 1895, it has over 300,000 members in more than 80 countries.

Youth For Christ

http://www.gospelcom.net/yfc/

YFC want to see every young person have the opportunity to make an informed decision to be a follower of Jesus Christ. Site has information on YFC worldwide.

Youth Linc

http://www.youthlinc.com

A directory for those involved in ministry to high school youth in the US.

Youth Ministry Central

http://www.youthspecialties.com

A list of web sites, including descriptions where necessary, that are useful for youth workers.

Youth Ministry Games Index

http://www.pastor2youth.com/gamesindex.html

Over 700 games for free use.

Youth Ministry Resources

http://www.jonathansresources.com

Collection of ideas and other youth resources.

Youth Specialities

http://www.gospelcom.net/ys/

Organization that supports Christian evangelical youth ministries in the US. Includes information on national meetings and seminars of youth workers, a mailing list and message boards for online discussions.

Youth Work

http://www.youthwork.co.uk

The website of Youthwork magazine, Britain's most widely read resource for Christian youth ministry. Has articles and ideas.

YouthPastor.Com

http://youthpastor.com

Directory specializing in helping harassed youth workers with links and resources.

YouthSearch
http://www.christianteens.net/search/
Links to over 100 youth sites, sorted by category.

Youthworker
http://www.gospelcom.net/ys/ywj/
Contemporary journal for youth ministry. Articles, reviews, subscription details.

Zjam
http://zjam.com
Extensive US web site for Christian teenagers.

Christian Student Equipper http://www.angelic.org

Covenanters
http://dspace.dial.pipex.com/town/avenue/vr30/

Disclosure from Scripture Union http://www.subtle.co.uk

Frontier Youth Trust http://www.fyt.org.uk

Teen Mania Ministries http://www.teenmania.org

YMCA http://www.ymca.org.uk

YMCAs in England http://www.ymca.org.uk

Youth Ministry International
http://www.gospelcom.net/ymi/

Youth With A Mission International http://www.ywam.org

YOUTH - GENERAL

Careers Research and Advisory Centre
http://www.crac.org.uk
Gives young people career advice.

Cascade
http://www.cascade.u-net.com
Drug information run by young people for young people.

Drugscope
http://www.drugscope.org.uk
Charity involved with drug education in UK schools.

Fun-Attic
http://www.funattic.com
Indoor/outdoor games and lots of activities just for the fun of
it.

Internet Public Library: Youth Division
http://www.ipl.org/youth/
General information for young people from US on-line library.
Has a teen section at http://www.ipl.org/teen/.

Medina Valley Centre
http://www.medinavalleycentre.org.uk
An outdoor education centre offering environmental education and field studies for schools, colleges and universities. It
offers RYA sailing courses and sailing and activity holidays.

MindFun.com
http://www.mindfun.com
Trivia questions and trivia games.

Site, The
http://www.thesite.org.uk
One of the UK's biggest web resources for young people with
content on drugs, alcohol, education, entertainment, health,
money, sex, sport and work. Lists of organizations, fact sheets,
features and hotlinks.

Sixthform UK
http://www.sixthform.co.uk
Guidance on careers and help on studying.

Student Unions
http://www.namss.org.uk/student.htm
Directory of Student Unions, student and young people's sites
in the UK.

Useless Knowledge
http://www.uselessknowledge.com
Just what it says: trivia, quotes, imponderables and useless
knowledge. But maybe just the thing for youth games and
quizzes.

Youth Information
http://www.youthinformation.com
National Youth Agency promotes young people's personal
and social development.

Youth Work Resources
http://www.youthworker.org.uk
Aims to provide tools for quality youth work in both Christian
and secular environments.

National Youth Association http://www.nya.org.uk

8

Alphabetical Index of Sites

1–4–All
http://www.jesus.org.uk/search/
192.com
http://www.192.com
2-in-2-1
http://www.2-in-2-1.co.uk
2000 Teen Chat
http://www.2000-teen-chat.com/main
2001 principle, The
http://www.2001principle.net
24-7
http://www.24-7prayer.com
32 Bit
http://www.32bit.com
711 Web Cafe Christian Chat Network
http://www.711webcafe.net
711.Net Christian Internet Assistance
http://www.711.net

A
AAHoroscopes
http://www.aahoroscopes.com
ABC Australia News
http://www.abc.net.au/news
ABC's of Parenting
http://www.abcparenting.com
About
http://www.about.com
About Christian Music
http://christianmusic.about.com
About on Ancient History
http://www.ancienthistory.about.com

About on News and Events
    http://uknews.about.com/aboutuk/uknews
Abundant Life Kids
    http://members.truepath.com/KIDS/
Academic Info: Religion
    http://www.academicinfo.net/religindex.html
Academic Jewish Studies
    http://h-net2.msu.edu/~judaic/
Acorndirect
    http://www.acorndirect.co.uk
Action for Gay and Lesbian Ordination
    http://www.dircon.co.uk/aglo/
Action Partners
    http://www.actionpartners.org.uk
Acts 17.11
    http://www.acts17-11.com/studies.html
AD 2000 and Beyond
    http://www.ad2000.org
Add Me
    http://www.addme.com
Adherents.com
    http://www.adherents.com
Administry
    http://www.administry.co.uk
Adoremus
    http://www.adoremus.org
ADSL Guide
    http://www.adslguide.org.uk
Agape Europe
    http://agapeeurope.org
Agape UK
    http://www.agape.org.uk
Age Concern
    http://www.ace.org.uk
Aim for Success
    http://www.aimforsuccess.org
AIMS
    http://www.aims.org
AJAX
    http://www.sagal.com/ajax
Alcohol Concern
    http://www.alcoholconcern.org.uk
Alex Catalogue of Electronic Texts
    http://sunsite.berkeley.edu/alex/
All in One Christian Index
    http://www.allinone.org

All Music Guide
    http://www.allmusic.com
All Nations Christian College
    http://www.allnations.ac.uk
All Newspapers.com, Inc.
    http://www.allnewspapers.com
All Words
    http://www.allwords.com
Allexperts
    http://www.allexperts.com
Alliance Music
    http://www.alliancemusic.co.uk
Alliance of Lesbian and Gay Anglicans
    http://www.alga.org
Alpha
    http://www.alpha.org.uk
AltaVista
    http://altavista.com
Amazing Discoveries in Bible Archaeology
    http://www.concentric.net/~extraord/archaeology.htm
Amazing Facts
    http://amazing-facts.org
Amazon Books
    http://www.amazon.com
Ambit New Media
    http://www.ambitnewmedia.com
American Academy of Religion
    http://www.aar-site.org
American Baptist Churches in the USA
    http://www.abc-usa.org
American Catholic
    http://www.americancatholic.org
American Family Association
    http://www.afa.net
American Gospel Music Directory
    http://www.americangospel.com
American Hymnody Collection
    http://www.bju.edu/resources/library/hymnofrm.htm
American Medical Association
    http://www.ama-assn.org/consumer/gnrl.htm
American Missionary Fellowship
    http://www.americanmissionary.org
American Scientific Affiliation (ASA)
    http://asa.calvin.edu./ASA/
American Tract Society
    http://www.gospelcom.net/ats/

Amity News Service
    http://is7.pacific.net.hk/~amityhk/
Amnesty International
    http://www.amnesty.org
Amnesty International USA
    http://www.amnestyusa.org
Ananova
    http://www.ananova.com
Angelfire Communications
    http://www.angelfire.com/ca/cvanbeek7/
Anglican Africa
    http://www.anglicanafrica.org/saia/
Anglican Board of Missions – Australia
    http://www.accnet.net.au/abm/
Anglican Catholic Church
    http://www.anglicancatholic.org
Anglican Church Music
    http://www.churchmusic.org.uk
Anglican Church of Canada
    http://www.anglican.ca
Anglican Communion
    http://www.anglicancommunion.org
Anglican Communion News Service (UK)
    http://www.anglicancommunion.org/acns/
Anglican Communion Virtual Tour
    http://www.anglicancommunion.org/virtualtour
Anglican Domain
    http://anglican.org
Anglican Liturgical Library
    http://www.oremus.org/liturgy/
Anglican Marriage Encounter
    http://www.marriageencounter.freeserve.co.uk
Anglican Online Hymnal
    http://www.oremus.org/hymnal/
Anglican Timeline
    http://justus.anglican.org/resources/timeline/
Anglican Women's Webpage
    http://ecusa.anglican.org/women/
Anglicans Online
    http://www.anglican.org/online/
Animal Immorality Book and Pet Resources
    http://www.creatures.com
Another Empty Bottle
    http://www.alcoholismhelp.com
Answering for Islam
    http://www.afi.org.uk

Answering Islam
http://answering-islam.org.uk
Answers to Jehovah's Witnesses
http://www.holyscriptures.com
Antiochian Catholic Church in America
http://www.geocities.com/athens/forum/7951/
Antiochian Orthodox Christian Archdiocese of North America
http://antiochian.org
AntiVirus Software
http://antivirus.about.com
AnyWho Directory Services
http://www.anywho.com
AOL Search
http://search.aol.com
Aphids Communications
http://www.aphids.com/megasite/
Apologetics Index
http://www.apologeticsindex.org
Apologetics, Evangelism and Creationism
http://mcu.edu/library/apologet.htm
Apostate Cafe
http://www.apostate.com/religion/
Apple Sauce Kids
http://home.dmv.com/~aplsauce/
APS Research Guide – Theology
http://www.utoronto.ca/stmikes/theobook.htm
Arab Net
http://www.arab.net
Arab World Ministries
http://www.gospelcom.net/awm
Archbishop of Canterbury
http://www.archbishopofcanterbury.org
Areopagus Publications
http://www.churchnet.org.uk/areopagus
Argosphere.net
http://www.argosphere.net
Argus
http://www.argus.myth.co.uk
Argus Clearinghouse
http://www.clearinghouse.net
ARM Education Centre
http://www.arm.gov/docs/education/warming.html
Art Guide
http://www.artguide.org
Art Today
http://www.arttoday.com

Artcyclopedia
http://www.artcyclopedia.com
Arthur Rank Centre
http://www.arthurrankcentre.org.uk
Ashburnham Christian Trust
http://www.ashburnham.org.uk
Ask Jeeves
http://www.askjeeves.com
Ask Jeeves for Kids
http://www.ajkids.com
Ask MP3
http://www.askmp3.com
ASPin.com
http://www.aspin.com
Assemblies of God
http://www.ag.org
Assemblies Website
http://www.assemblies.org.uk
Associate Reformed Presbyterian Church
http://www.arpsynod.org
Association of Christian Teachers
http://www.christian-teachers.org
Association of Christian Web Authors
http://www.webauthors.org
Association of Christians in Broadcasting
http://www.caclb.org.uk
Association of Vineyard Churches
http://www.vineyard.org.uk
asu.info.apple.com
http://asu.info.apple.com
Athletes in Action
http://sports.crosswalk.com/aia/
Atlantic Fish
http://members.tripod.com/~chr4/
Atlas of Great Britain
http://uk.multimap.com
Audio-Bible
http://www.audiobible.com
AudioFind
http://www.audiofind.com
Aus Music Guide
http://www.amws.com.au
Aussie Christian Search Engine
http://www.crosscape.com.au/search/
Australian Broadcasting Corporation
http://www.abc.net.au/news/

Australian Churches
    http://www.vision.net.au/~kevin_keep/churches.htm
Australian Democrat Party
    http://www.democrats.org.au
Australian Labour Party
    http://www.alp.org.au
Australian Liberal Party
    http://www.liberal.org.au
Australian National Party
    http://www.npa.org.au
Awesome Library
    http://www.awesomelibrary.org
Ayer Company Publishers
    http://www.scry.com/ayer/
Azariah Internet Ministries
    http://www.azariah.org.uk

B
Baby Loss
    http://www.babyloss.com
Baby World
    http://www.babyworld.co.uk
Back to the Bible
    http://www.backtothebible.org/minute/
Baha'i Faith
    http://www.miracles.win-uk.net/Bahai/
Baker Book House
    http://www.bakerbooks.com
Banner of Truth
    http://www.banneroftruth.co.uk
Banner, The
    http://www.thebanner.org
Baptist Men's Movement
    http://easyweb.easynet.co.uk/~aeptypog/bmmhp.html
Baptist Missionary Society
    http://www.rpc.ox.ac.uk/bms/
Baptist Org
    http://www.baptist.org
Baptist Union of Great Britain
    http://www.baptist.org.uk
Baptist World Alliance
    http://www.bwanet.org
Barbour Publishing
    http://www.barbourbooks.com
Bargain Christian Books
    http://www.bargain-christian-books.com

Barnabas Trust
http://www.barnabas.org.uk/HomePage.htm
Barnabus Outreach Trust
http://www.go-4th.com
Barnados
http://www.barnados.org.uk
Barnes and Noble
http://www.barnesandnoble.com
Bartlett's Quotations
http://www.bartleby.com/100/
Basic Ministries
http://www.basicministries.org
BBC
http://www.bbc.co.uk
BBC Education Webguide
http://www.bbc.co.uk/education/webguide/
BBC Education Webguide: Religion
http://www.bbc.co.uk/religion/
BBC Schools
http://www.bbc.co.uk/education/schools
BBC World Service
http://www.bbc.co.uk/worldservice/index.shtml
Belief, Culture and Learning Information Gateway
http://www.becal.net
BeliefNet
http://about.beliefnet.com
Believer.com
http://www.believer.com
Berean Bible Studies Page
http://www.afn.org/~leo/
Berit's Best Sites for Children
http://www.beritsbest.com
Best Environmental Resources Directories
http://www.ulb.ac.be/ceese/meta/cds.html
Best of the Christian Web
http://www.botcw.com
Best of the Christian Web-Chat Directory
http://www.botcw.com/search/Chat_Rooms/
Beyond Magazine
http://www.beyondmag.com
BibArch
http://www.bibarch.com
Bible Answer Machine
http://bibleanswermachine.ww7.com
Bible Browser
http://mama.stg.brown.edu/webs/bible_browser/pbeasy.shtml

Bible Cards
http://www.bibleverseart.com
Bible College of Wales
http://members.netscapeonline.co.uk/philaedwards
Bible Gateway
http://bible.gospelcom.net
Bible Gateway, The
http://www.bible.gospelcom.net
Bible Information Online
http://www.bibleinfo.com
Bible Learning Centre
http://www.biblelearning.org
Bible Mission International
http://www.bethany.co.uk/bmi/
Bible on the Web
http://www.bibleontheweb.com
Bible Quizzes
http://www.biblequizzes.com
Bible Quizzes from TwoPaths
http://www.twopaths.com/biblequizzes.html
Bible Reading Fellowship
http://www.brf.org.uk
Bible Site, The
http://www.thebiblesite.org
Bible Studies Foundation
http://www.bible.org
Bible Studies from Yes Lord Ministries
http://ourworld.compuserve.com/homepages/YesLord/
Bible Study
http://www.biblestudy.org
Bible Verse Art
http://bibleverseart.com
Bible Visuals
http://www.nd.edu/~kcoblent/theo.html
Bible-Links Page
http://www1.uni-bremen.de/~wie/bibel.html
Biblelands
http://www.mustardseed.net
BiblePower
http://www.biblepower.com
Bibles: Public Domain Reference
http://www.bible.org/docs/public/readme.htm
Biblesoft
http://www.biblesoft.com
BibleVerse Art.com
http://bibleverseart.com

Biblical Archaeology Society
http://www.bib-arch.org
Biblical Hebrew Made Easy
http://www.biblicalhebrew.com
Biblical Holidays
http://biblicalholidays.com
Biblical Studies Foundation
http://www.bible.org
BiblicalParenting.com
http://www.biblicalparenting.com
Big Bang
http://sr11.xoom.com/verybigbang/
Big Book
http://www.bigbook.com
Big Foot
http://www.bigfoot.com
Big Issue
http://www.bigissue.com
Big Yellow
http://www.bigyellow.com
Billboard
http://www.billboard.com
Billy Graham Institute of Evangelism
http://www.wheaton.edu/bgc/ioe/ioehome.html
Billy Graham Online
http://www.billygraham.org
Biographical Sketches of Christians
http://justus.anglican.org/resources/bio/
Birdies RE Resource Centre
http://www.ajbird.demon.co.uk
Birmingham Bible Institute
http://www.charis.co.uk/bbi/
Black Gospel Music
http://afgen.com/gospel.html
Black Information Link
http://www.blink.org.uk
Blackwells
http://blackwells.co.uk
Blue Letter Bible
http://www.blueletterbible.org
Blue Mountain
http://www.bluemountain.com
Board of Mission: Uniting Church of Christ in Australia
http://www.uca.org.au/nsw/bom/
BOL
http://www.bol.com

Book Aid
http://www.bookaid.org
Book of Common Prayer
http://justus.anglican.org/resources/bcp/
BookFinder.com
http://www.bookfinder.com
Books and Culture
http://www.christianitytoday.com/books/
Books and Literature
http://digital.library.upenn.edu/books/
Books On Line
http://www.books-on-line.com
Boys Brigade
http://www.boys-brigade.org.uk
Bridal Planner
http://www.bridalplanner.com
Brigada
http://www.brigada.org
Britannica On-Line
http://www.britannica.com
British and Foreign Bible Society
http://www.biblesociety.org.uk
British Conservative Party
http://www.conservatives.com
British Deaf Association
http://www.britishdeafassociation.org.uk
British Epilepsy Association
http://www.epilepsy.org.uk
British Labour Party
http://www.labour.org.uk
British Liberal Democrat Party
http://www.libdems.org.uk
British Library
http://portico.bl.uk
British Library: OPAC 97
http://opac97.bl.uk
British Red Cross, The
http://www.redcross.org.uk
Bruderhof Communities
http://www.bruderhof.org
Buddhist Society
http://www.thebuddhistsociety.org.uk
Buddhist Society in the UK
http://www.buddsoc.org.uk
Buddhist Studies WWW Virtual Library
http://www.ciolek.com/WWWVL-Buddhism.html

Business Men's Fellowship UK
    http://www.bmf-uk.com
Business Wire
    http://www.businesswire.com
Buyer's Index
    http://www.buyersindex.com
Byzantine Images
    http://www.bway.net/~halsall/images.html
Byzantine Orthodox Christian Icon Studio
    http://www.sacredicons.com

C

Cabinet Office
    http://www.cabinet-office.gov.uk
Cafe Reality
    http://www.gospelcom.net/yfc/students/
CAFOD
    http://www.cafod.org.uk
Cal State
    http://library.csun.edu
Caleb Project
    http://www.calebproject.org
CALM Online
    http://www.calmonline.org.uk
Calvin College
    http://www.calvin.edu/
Cambridge Dictionary
    http://dictionary.cambridge.org
Cambridge Theological Federation
    http://www.theofed.cam.ac.uk
Cambridge University Press
    http://www.cup.cam.ac.uk
Campus Crusade for Christ International
    http://www.ccci.org
Campus Crusade for Christ, Canada
    http://www.crusade.org
Campus Journal
    http://www.gospelcom.net/rbc/cj/
Campus Life
    http://www.christianitytoday.com/campuslife/
Campus Tours
    http://www.campustours.com
Canadian Conference of Catholic Bishops
    http://www.cccb.ca
Canadian Conference of Mennonite Brethren Churches
    http://www.mbconf.ca/

Canadian Council of Churches
  http://www.web.net/~ccchurch/
Canadian Goverment
  http://canada.gc.ca
Canon Law
  http://canonlaw.anglican.org
Cantate Recordings
  http://ourworld.compuserve.com/homepages/cantate/
Capernwray Hall
  http://www.capernwray.org.uk
Capernwray Missionary Fellowship
  http://www.capernwray.co.uk
Carberry Conference Centre
  http://dspace.dial.pipex.com/carberry/
CARE (Christian Action Research and Education)
  http://www.care.org.uk
Care Aware
  http://www.careaware.co.uk
Care for the Family
  http://www.care-for-the-family.org.uk
Care Guide
  http://www.careguide.uk.com
Careers Research and Advisory Centre
  http://www.crac.org.uk
Careforce
  http://www.careforce.co.uk
Carmelite Friars UK
  http://www.carmelite.org
Cartoon Works
  http://www.gospelcom.net/cartoonworks/
Cartoons and Illustrations
  http://www.borg.com/~rjgtoons/cpub.html
Cascade
  http://www.cascade.u-net.com
CaseStudies
  http://www.case-studies.com
Catechism of the Catholic Church
  http://www.christusrex.org/www1/CDHN/ccc.html
Catholic Doctrinal Concordance
  http://www.infpage.com/concordance/
Catholic Encyclopedia, The
  http://newadvent.org/cathen
Catholic Info Net (CIN)
  http://www.cin.org
Catholic Information Center
  http://www.catholic.net

Catholic News Service
http://www.catholicnews.com
Catholic Online
http://www.catholic.org
Catholic Pages
http://www.catholic-pages.com
Catholic Relief Services
http://www.catholicrelief.org
Catholic Resources on the Net
http://www.cs.cmu.edu/People/spok/catholic.html
Catholic Teacher's Gazette
http://www.cartrefc.demon.co.uk
Catholic Women's Ordination
http://ourworld.compuserve.com/homepages/justitia/
Catholic World News
http://www.catholic.net
Catholic Youth Resources
http://www.microserve.net/~fabian/ym.html
CatholiCity
http://www.catholicity.com
CBN
http://www.cbn.com
CCLI music links
http://www.ccli.com/WorshipResources/
CCM Online
http://www.ccmcom.com
CCTA Government Information
http://www.open.gov.uk
Cell Church
http://www.cellchurch.co.uk
Cell Life Resources
http://nlc.hypermart.net/cell/
Cell-Church Website
http://www.cell-church.org
Celtic Christianity
http://www2.gol.com/users/stuart/celtihs.html
Census On-line
http://www.census-online.com
Center for Reformed Theology and Apologetics
http://www.reformed.org
Center for Women and Religion
http://aquinas.gtu.edu/Centers/cwr/
CentralNic
http://www.centralnic.com
Centre for Applied Ethics
http://www.ethics.ubc.ca/resources/business/

Centre for Jewish-Christian Relations
http://www.cjcr.org.uk
Centre for Mission Direction
http://www.cmd.org.nz
CGI Resource Index
http://www.cgi-resources.com
Chambers Electronic Encyclopedia
http://www.encyclopedia.com
Channel 4 News
http://www.channel4news.co.uk
Charis Internet Services
http://www.charis.co.uk
Charities Direct
http://www.caritasdata.co.uk
Charity Christmas Cards
http://www.charitychristmascards.org
Charity Commission
http://www.charity-commission.gov.uk
Charity Net
http://www.charitynet.org
Chat-o-Rama
http://www.solscape.com/chat
Chick Publications
http://chick.com
Child Alert
http://www.childalert.co.uk
Child Fun
http://www.childfun.com
Child Poverty Action Group
http://www.cpag.org.uk
Children's Bible Study
http://www.childrensbiblestudy.com
Children's Ministry from Kingsway
http://www.childrensministry.co.uk
Children's Society, The
http://www.the-childrens-society.org.uk
ChildrenSermons.com
http://www.childrensermons.com
ChildrensMinistry.net
http://www.childrensministry.net
Chinese Church in London
http://www.ccil.org.uk
Choral Directory
http://members.tripod.com/~choral/
ChoralNet
http://www.choralnet.org

Christ Art
    http://www.christart.com
Christ for the Nations
    http://www.christforthenationsuk.org
Christadelphians
    http://www.christadelphian.org.uk
Christian + Feminist
    http://www.users.csbsju.edu/~eknuth/xpxx/
Christian Advice for Women
    http://www.liveit.net
Christian Aid
    http://www.christian-aid.org.uk
Christian Answers Network
    http://www.christiananswers.net
Christian Apologetics
    http://ccel.org/contrib/exec_outlines/ca.html
Christian Apologetics and Research Ministry
    http://www.carm.org
Christian Articles Archive
    http://www.joyfulheart.com
Christian Bands
    http://www.cnet.clara.net/links/bands.htm
Christian Bed and Breakfast
    http://www.icbbn.com/icbbn.html
Christian Best
    http://www.christianbest.com
Christian Book Promotions Trust
    http://www.christianbookpromotions.org.uk
Christian Broadcasting Network
    http://www.cbn.com
Christian Cafe
    http://thechristiancafe.com
Christian Campaign for Nuclear Disarmament
    http://www.gn.apc.org/ccnd/
Christian Cartoons Showcase, The
    http://www.ChristianCartoons.com
Christian Century
    http://www.christiancentury.org
Christian Channel Europe
    http://www.god-digital.com
Christian Chat
    http://www.christianchat.co.uk
Christian Chat Network
    http://www.cchat.net
Christian Chat Rooms dot com
    http://www.christianchatrooms.com

Christian ChatLine
http://www.christianchatline.com
Christian Church (Disciples of Christ) in the US
http://www.disciples.org
Christian Classics Ethereal Library
http://ccel.org
Christian Coalition of America
http://cc.org
Christian Coalition, The
http://www.cc.org
Christian College Guide
http://www.whatsthebest-college.com
Christian Comics
http://members.aol.com/ChriCom
Christian Comics International
http://members.aol.com/ChriCom/
Christian Community
http://www.ccgroups.com
Christian Computer Art
http://www.cc-art.com
Christian Computing
http://www.gospelcom.net/ccmag/
Christian Conference Trust
http://www.cct.org.uk
Christian Connection
http://www.christianconnection.co.uk
Christian Connection US
http://www.christian.email.net
Christian Copyright Licensing International (CCLI)
http://www.ccli.co.uk
Christian Daily News
http://www.christiandailynews.org
Christian Digest
http://www.christiandigest.com
Christian E-mail Mailing Lists
http://www.gospelcom.net/ifc/mail/view/
Christian Ecology Link
http://www.christian-ecology.org.uk
Christian Education Links and Resources
http://www.tcmnet.com/~cc/edu/edulinks.html
Christian Education Movement
http://www.cem.org.uk
Christian Enquiry Agency
http://www.christianity.org.uk
Christian Focus Publications
http://www.christianfocus.com

Christian Friendship Fellowship
http://www.digitalchurch.co.uk/cff/
Christian Games Forum
http://www0.delphi.com/christiangames/
Christian Gaming
http://www.christiangaming.com
Christian Guild Holidays
http://www.cgholidays.co.uk
Christian Guitar Resources
http://www.christianguitar.ws
Christian Herald
http://www.christianherald.org.uk
Christian History
http://www.christianitytoday.com/history/
Christian History Institute
http://www.gospelcom.net/chi/
Christian Home and School
http://www.gospelcom.net/csi/chs/
Christian Homeschool Forum
http://www.gocin.com/homeschool/
Christian Information Network
http://www.cin.co.uk
Christian Jokes
http://www.christianjokes.co.uk
Christian Jugglers Association
http://www.juggling.org/~cja/
Christian Karaoke
http://www.christiankaraoke.strayduck.com/page1.htm
Christian Leadership World
http://www.teal.org.uk
Christian Link Collection
http://www.makarios.nu/
Christian Links
http://www.christianlinks.com
Christian Links for Kids
http://www.kids-teens.org
Christian Medical and Dental Associations
http://www.cmds.org
Christian Medical Fellowship
http://www.cmf.org.uk
Christian Military Fellowship
http://www.cmf.com
Christian Missions (SIM)
http://www.sim.org
Christian Motorcyclists Association
http://www.bike.org.uk/cma/

Christian Movies Theater On-Line
    http://www.angelfire.com/mt/BibleTruths/MovieCenter.html
Christian Music Guide
    http://christianmusic.about.com/musicperform/christianmusic/
Christian Music Online
    http://cmo.com
Christian Music Place
    http://christianmusic.org/cmp/
Christian Only
    http://www.his-net.com
Christian Origins
    http://www.christianorigins.org
Christian Portal
    http://www.711.net
Christian Postcards
    http://www.christianpostcards.com
Christian Publishing Organisation
    http://www.cpo-online.org
Christian Quotation of the Day
    http://www.gospelcom.net/cqod/
Christian Radio (UK)
    http://www.Christianradio.org.uk
Christian Radio (US)
    http://www.christianradio.com
Christian Reformed Church in North America
    http://www.crcna.org
Christian Reporter
    http://crnews.pastornet.net.au/crnews/
Christian Research
    http://www.christian-research.org.uk
Christian Research Institute
    http://www.equip.org
Christian Resources Exhibition
    http://www.crexhib.co.uk
Christian Ring of Rings
    http://nav.webring.yahoo.com/hub?ring=chrrings&list
Christian Shopping Mall
    http://www.christianet.com
Christian Sign Language Reference Site
    http://www.jireh.demon.co.uk
Christian Singles Worldwide
    http://www.christiansingles.com
Christian Solidarity Worldwide
    http://www.csw.org.uk
Christian Spotlight on the Movies
    http://www.christiananswers.net/spotlight/

Christian Student Equipper
http://www.angelic.org
Christian student groups
http://www.churchnet.org.uk/ukgroups/campus/
Christian Students in Science
http://www.csis.org.uk
Christian Students' Netlinks
http://www.surf.to/netlinks/
Christian Suppliers
http://www.christiansuppliers.com
Christian Surfers UK
http://www.csuk.freeserve.co.uk
Christian Teen Corner
http://www.wolfeborobible.com/teen.html
Christian Therapists Network
http://www.ctn.org.uk
Christian Think Tank
http://www.webcom.com/~ctt/
Christian Topics
http://www.christiantopics.com
Christian Viewpoint for Men
http://www.cvmen.org.uk
Christian Vision and Christian Voice
http://www.christian-vision.org
Christian Vocations
http://www.christianvocations.org
Christian Voice
http://www.christianvoice.co.uk
Christian Wallpapers
http://www.christianwallpapers.freeservers.com
Christian Webmasters Association (Europe)
http://www.wordnet.co.uk/chtml2.html
Christian Women Today
http://www.christianwomentoday.com
Christian Working Woman
http://www.christianworkingwoman.org
Christian World Daily
http://www.themissionary.net/pages/
Christian Youth News
http://www.christianteens.net/cyn/
Christian Youth Resources
http://web.1earth.net/~youth/
Christian-music.co.uk
http://www.christian-music.co.uk
Christianbook.com
http://www.christianbook.com

ChristianBookshop.com
    http://www.christianbookshop.com
ChristiaNet
    http://www.christianet1.com
Christianity On-line – Bible and Reference
    http://www.christianityonline.com/bible/
Christianity On-line Games
    http://www.christianityonline.com/fun/
Christianity Online – Kids
    http://www.christianityonline.com/community/kids/
Christianity Today
    http://www.christianitytoday.com
Christianlinks
    http://www.christianlinks.com
ChristianLinks chat
    http://chat.christianlinks.com
ChristianRock.Net
    http://www.christianrock.net
Christians Abroad
    http://www.cabroad.org.uk
Christians Aware
    http://www.christiansaware.co.uk
Christians in Health Care
    http://www.christian-healthcare.org.uk
Christians in Science
    http://www.cis.org.uk
Christians in Science Education
    http://www.cis.org.uk/cise
Christians in Sport
    http://www.christiansinsport.org.uk
Christians Online
    http://www.conline.net
ChristianWeb.net
    http://www.christianweb.net
Christmas Eternal
    http://members.carol.net/~asmsmsks/xristmas.htm
Christmas in Cyber space
    http://www.njwebworks.net/christmas/
Christmas in the Holy Land
    http://www.Jesus2000.com/christmas.htm
Church 2000
    http://www.church2000.org/Links/
Church Army
    http://www.churcharmy.org.uk
Church Computer Users Group
    http://www.churchcomputer.org.uk

Church House Bookshop
http://www.chbookshop.co.uk
Church House Publishing
http://www.chpublishing.co.uk
Church in Wales
http://www.churchinwales.org.uk
Church Lads and Church Girls Brigade
http://www.church-brigade.syol.com
Church Mission Society
http://www.cms-uk.org
Church Net UK
http://www.churchnet.org.uk
Church Net UK News Service
http://www.churchnet.org.uk/news/
Church Net UK WebChat
http://www.churchnet.org.uk/webchat/
Church News Service
http://ourworld.compuserve.com/homepages/aphenna/
Church of England
http://www.church-of-england.org
Church of England Newspaper
http://www.churchnewspaper.com
Church of England Yellow Pages
http://www.blackburn.anglican.org/yellow_pages
Church of God, International
http://www.cgi.org/cgi/
Church of Jesus Christ of Latter-day Saints
http://www.lds.org
Church of Latter-day Saints (UK)
http://www.lds.org.uk
Church of Scotland
http://www.cofs.org.uk
Church of the Brethren
http://www.brethren.org
Church of the Brethren Network
http://www.cob-net.org
Church of the Nazarene
http://www.nazarene.org
Church of the Province of Southern Africa
http://www.cpsa.org.za
Church Pastoral Aid Society (CPAS)
http://www.cpas.org.uk
Church Schools
http://www.churchschools.co.uk
Church Times
http://www.churchtimes.co.uk

Church UK
    http://www.churchuk.net
Church UK Internet Project
    http://www.churchuk.net
Church Union
    http://www.netcomuk.co.uk/~lnagel/churchunion.htm
Church Union, The
    http://www.churchunion.care4free.net
Church Urban Fund
    http://www.cuf.org.uk
Church World Direct
    http://www.churchworlddirect.com
Church.co.uk
    http://www.church.co.uk
Church.uk.net
    http://www.church.uk.net
Churches Dot Net
    http://churches.net
CIA's World Factbook
    http://www.odci.gov/cia/publications/factbook/
Cinema Guide from Scoot
    http://www.cinema.scoot.co.uk
Classical Midi Organ Stop
    http://users.gmi.net/~wgraeber/
Classical Music on the Net
    http://www.musdoc.com/classical/
Classical Net
    http://www.classical.net
Classical Search
    http://www.classicalsearch.com
CLC
    http://www.clc.org.uk
Closer Look, A
    http://www.acloserlook.com/9802acl/
CNET Builder.com
    http://www.builder.com
COIN
    http://www.coin.org.uk
College is Possible
    http://www.collegeispossible.org
College Quest
    http://www.collegequest.com
CollegeNET
    http://www.collegenet.com
Columbia Encyclopedia
    http://www.encyclopedia.com

Comic Break
http://www.webcom.com/~ctt/comic.html
Comic Relief
http://www.comicrelief.co.uk
Commission for Racial Equality
http://www.cre.gov.uk
Commission on Global Governance
http://www.cgg.ch
Commonweal
http://www.commonwealmagazine.org
Compass
http://gvanv.com/compass/comphome.html
Compassion International
http://www.compassion.com
Compassion UK
http://www.compassionuk.org
Compassionate Friends, The
http://www.tcf.org.uk
Completely Free Software
http://www.completelyfreesoftware.com
Computer-Assisted Theology
http://info.ox.ac.uk/ctitext/theology/
Computers Don't Bite
http://www.bbc.co.uk/education/cdb/
Concerned Women for America
http://www.cwfa.org
Concordia Publishing House (LCMS)
http://www.cph.org
Confraternity of the Blessed Sacrament
http://www.netcomuk.co.uk/~lnagel/cbs.html
Congregational Federation
http://www.congregational.org.uk
Connect Bible Studies
http://www.connectbiblestudies.com
Connections Christian Counselling Services
http://www.connections.ndirect.co.uk
Conservative Christian Fellowship
http://ourworld.compuserve.com/homepages/CCFHUB/
Contact a Family
http://www.cafamily.org.uk
Contact the Elderly
http://www.contact-the-elderly.org
Cool Freebie Links
http://www.coolfreebielinks.com
Cool Planet
http://www.oxfam.org.uk/coolplanet/

Cooperative Baptist Fellowship
    http://www.cbfonline.org
COPAC: University Research Library Catalogue
    http://copac.ac.uk/copac/
Copernic
    http://www.copernic.com
Corrymeela Community
    http://www.corrymeela.org.uk
Council for World Mission
    http://www.cwmission.org.uk
Council of European Bishops Conferences (CCEE)
    http://communio.hcbc.hu
Countryside Matters
    http://www.countrysidematters.org.uk
Covenanters
    http://dspace.dial.pipex.com/town/avenue/vr30/
Cover CDs
    http://covercd.co.uk
Cover to Cover
    http://www.cover2cover.org
Crayon
    http://www.crayon.net
Creation Research Society
    http://www.creationresearch.org
Creation Resources Trust
    http://www.c-r-t.co.uk
Creative Church
    http://www.creativechurch.org.uk
Credit Action
    http://www.creditaction.com
Creeds of Christendom
    http://www.creeds.net
Cross Daily images
    http://graphics.crossdaily.com
Cross Rhythms
    http://www.crossrhythms.co.uk
Cross Search
    http://www.crosssearch.com/Art/Clip_Art/
Crossroads Project, The
    http://www.crossrds.org
CrossSearch
    http://www.crosssearch.com
Crosswalk
    http://omnilist.crosswalk.com
Crosswalk Chats
    http://chat.crosswalk.com

Crosswalk Games
   http://games.crosswalk.com
Crosswalk Sports
   http://sports.crosswalk.com
Crosswinds
   http://www.btinternet.com/~crosswinds/
Crusade for World Revival
   http://www.cwr.org.uk
Crusaders
   http://www.crusaders.org.uk
CTVC Video
   http://www.ctvc.co.uk
Cult Awareness & Information Centre
   http://www.caic.org.au/
Current Affairs of Muslims
   http://www.cam.org.uk
Cyber Atlas
   http://cyberatlas.internet.com
Cyber Hymnal
   http://www.cyberhymnal.org

D
Daily Bible Reading Plan
   http://users.aol.com/bible2007/dailypln.htm
Daily Bible readings
   http://www.americanbible.org/DailyReading/today.cfm
Daily Devotions
   http://www.devotions.net
Daily Office
   http://www.missionstclare.com
Daily Wisdom
   http://www.gospelcom.net/gci/dw/
DaKidz
   http://www.dakidz.com
Damaris Trust, The
   http://www.damaris.org
Darkness to Light
   http://www.dtl.org
Darwin Awards
   http://www.darwinawards.com
Data Developments
   http://www.data-developments.co.uk
Daughters of Charity
   http://www.daughtersofcharity.org.uk
DAWN
   http://www.jesus.org.uk/dawn/

Daylight Trust
    http://www.aandp.co.uk/daylight/
Deja News
    http://www.deja.com
Delphi Internet
    http://www.delphi.com/navnet/faq/history.html
Dementia Care Trust
    http://www.dct.org.uk
Dementia Web
    http://www.dementia.ion.ucl.ac.uk
Demos
    http://www.demos.co.uk
Department of Education and Employment
    http://www.dfee.gov.uk
Department of Health
    http://www.doh.gov.uk
Department of Social Security
    http://www.dss.gov.uk
Department of Trade and Industry
    http://www.dti.gov.uk
Designing web pages for the disabled
    http://www.gospelcom.net/guide/web-disability.html
Desktop Themes
    http://www.infonet.ee/arthemes/
Desperate Preacher's Site
    http://www.javacasa.com/dps/
Destination: Earth
    http://www.earth.nasa.gov/
Devotional Bible Study, A
    http://mydevotion.com
Devotionals
    http://www.devotionals.net
Diaconal Association of the Church of England
    http://www.societies.anglican.org/dace/
Dictionary.com
    http://www.dictionary.com
Dig the Bible
    http://www.digbible.org
DigiTracts – The Digital Gospel
    http://www.digitracts.com
Dillons Bookstore
    http://www.dillons.co.uk
DirectHit
    http://www.directhit.com
Directory of Internet Service Providers
    http://www.thedirectory.org

Dirty Hippy Liberal Christian Home Journal
http://student-www.uchicago.edu/~mbaldwin/dirty.html
Discipleship Journal
http://www.gospelcom.net/navs/NP/dj/
Disclosure from Scripture Union
http://www.subtle.co.uk
Discovery On-Line
http://www.discovery.com
Disney Cards
http://www.postcards.org
Divorce.co.uk
http://www.divorce.co.uk
DogPile
http://www.dogpile.com
Domain Name Guide
http://www.igoldrush.com
Dotmusic
http://www.dotmusic.com
Dove Awards
http://www.doveawards.com
Dove Foundation
http://www.dove.org
Down Under Christian Directory
http://www.ozemail.com.au/~phopwood/
Down-Under Yellow Pages
http://www.yellowpages.com.au/
Download.com
http://www.download.com
Drama for the Church
http://www.drama4church.com
DramaShare
http://www.dramashare.org
Dramatix
http://www.carey.ac.nz/drama/
Drugscope
http://www.drugscope.org.uk

E
E-grace.net
http://www.e-grace.net
E-Mail Today
http://www.emailtoday.com
Early Church Documents
http://web.mit.edu/afs/athena.mit.edu/activity/c/csa/www/
documents/README

Earth Island Institute
    http://www.earthisland.org
Earth Observatory
    http://earthobservatory.nasa.gov
EarthAction
    http://www.oneworld.org/earthaction/
East to West
    http://www.e2w.dircon.co.uk
Easter in Cyberspace
    http://www.njwebworks.com
Easter People
    http://www.robfrost.org/ep.html
Easter: Christ is Risen
    http://entourages.com/barbs/Easter.htm
Ecclesiological Society, The
    http://www.eccl-soc.demon.co.uk
Eco-Congregation
    http://www.tidybritain.org.uk/gfg/
Ecole Initiative
    http://cedar.evansville.edu/~ecoleweb/
Ecology
    http://www.eco-pros.com
Economic Net
    http://www.economicnet.com
Economist, The
    http://www.economist.com
Ecotheology
    http://www.ecotheology.org
EcuLaugh
    http://www.ecunet.org
Ecumenical Links
    http://www.geocities.com/Heartland/Ranch/9925/ecumenical.html
Ecumenical News International
    http://www.eni.ch
Ecumenical Patriarchate of Constantinople
    http://www.goarch.org/patriarchate
EcuNet
    http://www.ecunet.org
Educate the Children
    http://www.educate.org.uk
Education Index
    http://www.educationindex.com
EduNet
    http://www.edunet.com
EduWeb
    http://www.eduweb.co.uk

Effective Teams
    http://www.teams.org.uk
Egad Ideas
    http://www.egadideas.com
Elder Web and AgeInfo
    http://www.elderweb.com
Electric Library
    http://www.elibrary.com
Electronic Frontier Foundation
    http://www.eff.org
Electronic News Stand
    http://enews.com
Electronic Privacy Information Center
    http://www.epic.org
Electronic Yellow Pages
    http://www.eyp.co.uk
Elim Pentecostal Church
    http://www.elim.org.uk
Ellel Ministries International
    http://ellelministries.org
Embassy Web
    http://www.embassyweb.com
Embassy World
    http://www.embassyworld.com
Emmaus Road, International
    http://www.eri.org
Emusic
    http://www.emusic.com
Encyclopaedia Britannica
    http://www.britannica.com
English Server
    http://eserver.org
English Server-Reference Links
    http://eserver.org/reference/
EnviroLink
    http://www.envirolink.org
Environment and Nature
    http://www.nrpe.org
EnviroWeb
    http://envirolink.org
Episcopal Church
    http://www.dfms.org
Episcopal Church in the United States of America
    http://www.ecusa.org
Episcopal Life
    http://www.dfms.org/episcopal-life/

Episcopal Medical Missions Foundation
   http://www.emmf.com
Episcopal News Service
   http://www.dfms.org/ens/
Episcopalian.org
   http://www.episcopalian.org
Ethical Investors
   http://www.oneworld.org/ethical-investors/
Ethics
   http://www.cellgroup.com
Ethics for children
   http://gonow.to/ethics/
Ethics for Scientists
   http://onlineethics.org
Ethics Links
   http://www.gac.edu/Academics/philosopy/ethics.html
Ethics on the Web
   http://commfaculty.fullerton.edu/lester/ethics/ethics_list.html
Ethics Resources on the Net
   http://condor.depaul.edu/ethics/ethb1.html
Europa
   http://www.europa.eu.int
European Christian Environmental Network
   http://www.ecen.org
European Environment Agency, The
   http://www.eea.eu.int
European History
   http://history.hanover.edu/europe.htm
European Institute of Protestant Studies
   http://www.ianpaisley.org
European Women's Lobby
   http://www.womenlobby.org
EuroSeek
   http://www.euroseek.net
Evangelical Alliance
   http://www.eauk.org
Evangelical Covenant Church
   http://www.covchurch.org
Evangelical Environmental Network
   http://homepages.tcp.co.uk/~carling/een/
Evangelical Environmental Network (USA)
   http://www.creationcare.org
Evangelical Free Church of America
   http://www.efca.org
Evangelical Philosophical Society
   http://www.epsociety.org

Evangelical Times
http://www.evangelical-times.org
Evangelicals Now
http://www.e-n.org.uk
Evangelism.uk.net
http://www.evangelism.uk.net
Every Mail
http://www.everymail.com
Every Woman
http://www.everywoman.co.uk
Everypeople.net
http://www.everypeople.net
EWTN
http://www.ewtn.com
Excite
http://www.excite.com
Explore the Word
http://www.exploretheword.com
Extreme
http://www.extreme-dm.com/tracking/

F

Facing the Challenge
http://www.facingthechallenge.org
Fair Trade
http://www.fairtrade.net
Faith Cards
http://faithcards.digitracts.com/faithcard/
Faith Movement
http://www.faith.org.uk
Families.co.uk
http://www.families.co.uk
Family at Go.com
http://family.go.com
Family Click
http://www.familyclick.com
Family Education Network
http://www.familyeducation.com
Family Media Network
http://www.ourchurchtools.com
Family Play
http://www.familyplay.com/activities/
Family Point
http://www.familypoint.com
Family Radio
http://www.familyradio.com

Family Research Council
    http://www.frc.org
Family Search Internet
    http://www.familysearch.org
Family Software Spot
    http://www.familysoftwarespot.com
Family Style
    http://www.familystyle.com
Family Values Network
    http://www.fvn.com
Family Worship
    http://www.familyworship.org.uk
Family.com
    http://www.family.com
FamilyLife
    http://www.familylife.com
Farmington Institute
    http://www.farmington.ac.uk
Fate and Fortune
    http://www.fateandfortune.com
Fathers Direct
    http://www.fathersdirect.com
Fawcett Library – The National Library of Women
    http://www.lgu.ac.uk/fawcett/main.htm
FEBA Radio
    http://www.feba.org.uk
FedWorld
    http://www.fedworld.gov
Fellowship of Christian Athletes
    http://www.fca.org
Fellowship of Reconciliation
    http://www.nonviolence.org
Fellowship of Scientists (USA)
    http://solon.cma.univie.ac.at/~neum/sciandf/fellow
FeMiNa
    http://www.femina.com
Fides Quaerens Internetum – Christian Theology
    http://www.bu.edu/people/bpstone/theology/theology.html
Fides Quaerens Internetum – Journals
    http://www.bu.edu/people/bpstone/theology/journals.html
Film Reviews
    http://film.reviews.co.uk
Film.com
    http://www.film.com
Financial Times
    http://www.news.ft.com

Find a Church
   http://www.findachurch.co.uk
Finding Publishers
   http://www.lights.com/publisher/
Firewatch
   http://140.190.128.190/merton/merton.html
First and Last Ministries
   http://www.firstandlast.org.uk
First Church of Cyberspace
   http://www.godweb.org/index1.html
Fish for News
   http://www.fish4news.co.uk
Fish Net
   http://www.fni.com/xstart/
Fish.co.uk
   http://www.fish.co.uk
Focus on the Family
   http://www.fotf.org
Focus Radio
   http://www.facingthechallenge.org/focus.htm
Food and Agriculture Organization
   http://www.fao.org
Food for the Hungry International
   http://www.fh.org
Foreign and Commonwealth Office
   http://www.fco.gov.uk
Foreign Mission Board of the Southern Baptist Convention
   http://www.imb.org
Fort: Panth Khalsa
   http://www.panthkhalsa.org
Forward Movement Publications
   http://www.forwardmovement.org
Foundation for the Study of Infant Deaths
   http://www.sids.org.uk/fsid
Free Christian drama scripts
   http://www.nlc.net.au/~jw/
Free Christian Images
   http://www.fci.crossnet.se/
Free Christian Software Directory
   http://www.seriousd.com/freeware.htm
Free Church of Scotland
   http://www.freechurch.org
Free E-Mail Address
   http://www.free-email-address.com
Free E-mail Providers Page
   http://members.tripod.com/~mareka/

Free Fax Service
    http://www.tpc.int
Free Page Hosting
    http://www.thefreesite.com/Free_Web_Space/
Free Site: graphics, The
    http://www.thefreesite.com/freegraphics.htm
Free Webmaster Tools and Resources
    http://kresch.com/resources/
Freedom Ministries
    http://www.freedomministries.org.uk
FreeFind Search Engine
    http://www.freefind.com
Freewarehome.com
    http://www.freewarehome.com
Friends of Cathedral Music, The
    http://www.fcm.org.uk
Friends of the Earth
    http://www.foe.org.uk
Friends of the Earth and GM
    http://www.foe.co.uk/campaigns/food_and_biotechnology
From Down Under
    http://www.timebooksellers.com.au
Frontier Internship in Mission
    http://tfim.org
Frontier Youth Trust
    http://www.fyt.org.uk
Frontiers
    http://www.frontiers.org
Fun Brain
    http://www.funbrain.com
Fun-Attic
    http://www.funattic.com
Funders Online
    http://www.fundersonline.org
FundRaising Export
    http://www.fundraisingexpert.com
Funny
    http://www.funny.co.uk
Funny-Bone
    http://funny-bone.spunge.org
FURY
    http://www.fury.ws
Fusion
    http://www.fusion.uk.com

G

G7 and G8
  http://www.g7.utoronto.ca
Gallup Organization
  http://www.gallup.com
Garden of Praise
  http://gardenofpraise.com/garden.htm
Garden Tomb
  http://www.gardentomb.com
GCN Search
  http://www.gcnhome.com/asp/search.asp
General Board of Global Ministries – Methodist Church
  http://gbgm-umc.org/gbgma.stm
Genesis Research and Education Foundation
  http://www.genesis.dircon.co.uk
Genetic Modification Issues
  http://www.gm-info.gov.uk
Get Net Wise
  http://www.getnetwise.org
Get ordained
  http://ulc.org/ulc/ordain.htm
Getting onto the Internet
  http://www.methodist.org.uk/information/internet.htm
Gideons International
  http://www.gideons.org
Global Change master Directory
  http://gcmd.gsfc.nasa.gov
Global Consultation On World Evangelization
  http://www.ad2000.org/gcowe95/
Global March for Jesus
  http://www.gmfj.org
Global Missions International
  http://www.globalmissions.org
Glossary of Religious Terms
  http://www.religioustolerance.org/glossary.htm
Go
  http://go.com
God Channel
  http://www.godchannel.com
God on the Net
  http://www.godonthenet.com
God's Word for Each Day
  http://www.godsworld.org
Goldrush
  http://www.igoldrush.com/guide/

Good Book Company, The
http://www.thegoodbook.co.uk
Good Steward, The
http://www.thegoodsteward.com
Gordon College
http://www.gordon.edu/
GOSHEN
http://www.goshen.net
GOSHEN – Christian Software
http://www.christianshareware.net
Gospel Communicators Network
http://www.gospelcom.net
Gospel for Asia
http://www.gfa.org/indexgfl.htm
Gospel Light
http://www.gospellight.com
Gospel Train
http://www.gospeltrain.com
Gospelcom Shopping
http://www.gospelcom.net/welcome/categories/shopping.shtml
Gospelcom Webmaster Tools
http://www.gospelcom.net/free/tools/
GospelDirect
http://www.gospelcom.net/gf/mc/welcome.html
Govern Your School
http://www.governyourschool.co.uk
Grace Notes
http://www.villageministries.org/grace-notes/
Graham Kendrick
http://www.grahamkendrick.co.uk
Graphic Designers Paradise
http://desktoppublishing.com/design.html
Great American Web Site, The
http://www.uncle-sam.com
Great Commission Air
http://www.greatcommissionair.org
Great Guitar Sites on the Web
http://www.guitarsite.com
Greater Europe Mission
http://www.gospelcom.net/gem/
Greek Orthodox Archdiocese of America
http://www.goarch.org
Greenbelt Festival
http://www.greenbelt.org.uk
Greenpeace International
http://greenpeace.org

GreenSpirit
http://www.greenspirit.org.uk
Gregorian Chants
http://www.music.princeton.edu/chant_html/
Grolier
http://gme.grolier.com
Grow with the Bible
http://www.grow-with-the-bible.org.uk
Gsus On
http://www.gsuson.com
Guardian NetClass
http://education.guardian.co.uk/netclass/
Guardian Online
http://www.guardian.co.uk
Guardian Unlimited
http://www.guardian.co.uk
Guide for Life
http://www.guideforlife.co.uk
Guide to Christian Literature on the Internet
http://www.iclnet.org/pub/resources/christian-books3.html
Guide to Early Church Documents
http://www.iclnet.org/pub/resources/christian-history.html
Guide to Web Evangelism, A
http://www.brigada.org/today/articles/web-evangelism.html
Guideposts
http://www.guideposts.org
Guideposts for Kids
http://www.gp4k.com
Guild of Church Musicians
http://www.quarks.co.uk/TGOCM/
Gumball Website Tracker
http://www.gumball-tracker.com

H

Hall of Church History
http://www.gty.org/~phil/hall.htm
Hare Krishna
http://www.ksyberspace.com/liverpool/
HarperCollins US
http://www.harpercollins.com
HarperCollins UK
http://www.fireandwater.com
He is Risen
http://www.execpc.com/~tmuth/easter/
Health and Safety
http://www.healthandsafety.co.uk

Health Web
http://healthweb.org
Healthfinder
http://www.healthfinder.gov
Healthy Kids
http://www.healthykids.org.uk
Heart Gallery
http://www.heartlight.org/gallery/
Heartlight
http://www.heartlight.org
Hearts at Home
http://www.hearts-at-home.org
Heaven
http://www.catholicdigest.org
Help the Aged
http://www.helptheaged.org.uk
Hindu Universe
http://www.hindunet.org/home.shtml
Hinduism Today
http://www.hinduismtoday.kauai.hi.us
His Holiness Sakya Trizin
http://www.eclipse.co.uk/~rs1042/
HIS-Net Christian Network
http://www.his-net.com
History Channel
http://www.historychannel.com
History Index
http://www.ukans.edu/history/VL/
HistoryNet, The
http://www.thehistorynet.com
Holy Joes
http://www.holyjoes.com
Home Office
http://www.homeoffice.gov.uk
Home-Based Working Moms
http://www.hbwm.com
Homestead
http://www.homestead.com
Hong Kong Christian Council
http://www.hk.super.net/~hkcc
Hospital Chaplaincy Gateway
http://www.hospitalchaplain.co.uk
HotBot
http://www.hotbot.com
Hothorpe Hall
http://www.hothorpe.co.uk

HTML Reference Library
    http://www.htmlib.com
Human Rights International
    http://www.hri.ca
Human Rights Watch
    http://www.hrw.org
Humour Database
    http://humor.ncy.com
Humour from About
    http://christianity.about.com/religion/christianity/cs/christianhumor/
Humour Links
    http://www.humorlinks.com
HumourNet
    http://www.humournet.com
Hymnsite.com
    http://www.hymnsite.com

I

ICCC – International Christian Chamber of Commerce
    http://www.iccc.net
Ichthus Christian Fellowship
    http://www.ichthus.org.uk
ICLNet
    http://www.iclnet.org/pub/resources/xn-dir.html
Icthus
    http://www.icthus.co.uk
ICUK
    http://www.icuk.com
IDS – Institute of Development Studies
    http://www.ids.ac.uk/ids/
Ignatius Press
    http://www.ignatius.com
Illustrated Lectionary Texts
    http://divinity.library.vanderbilt.edu/lectionary/
iMac, The
    http://www.theimac.com
iMVS
    http://www.imvs.com
In Defense of the Faith
    http://www.gty.org/~phil/resourcz.htm
In Jesus
    http://www.injesus.com
In the Beginning
    http://www.serve.com/larryi/begin.htm
Independent Christian Bookstores
    http://www.sonshinebookstore.com

Independent, The
    http://www.independent.co.uk
Index on Censorship
    http://www.oneworld.org/index_oc/
Infidels
    http://www.infidels.org
Info Please
    http://www.infoplease.com
Infobeat
    http://www.infobeat.com
InfoMac HyperArchive
    http://hyperarchive.lcs.mit.edu/HyperArchive/
Insights
    http://Insights.uca.org.au
Inspired Christian Technologies
    http://www.inspired-tech.com/gallery.html
Institute for Christian Research
    http://www.icr.org
Institute for Christian Spirituality
    http://www.sarum.ac.uk/spirituality
Institute for Ecumenical and Cultural Research
    http://www.csbsju.edu/iecr/
Institute for Liturgy and Mission
    http://www.sarum.ac.uk/ILM/
Institute for Values in Society
    http://www.sarum.ac.uk/society/
Integrity
    http://www.integrityusa.org
Integrity Music Inc.
    http://www.integritymusic.com
Inter-Church Committee for Refugees
    http://www.web.net/~iccr/
Interfaith Calendar
    http://www.interfaithcalendar.org
International Bible Society
    http://www.gospelcom.net/ibs/
International Bulletin of Missionary Research
    http://www.omsc.org
International Christian Concern
    http://www.persecution.org
International Christian Embassy Jerusalem
    http://www.intournet.co.il/icej/
International Christian Media Commission
    http://www.icmc.org
International Church of the Foursquare Gospel
    http://www.foursquare.org

International Coalition for Religious Freedom
http://www.religiousfreedom.com
International Committee of the Red Cross (ICRC)
http://www.icrc.org
International Community of the Charismatic Episcopal Church
http://www.iccec.org
International Council of Community Churches
http://www.akcache.com/community/iccc-nat.html
International Data Corporatation
http://www.idcresearch.com
International Directories
http://www.infobel.be/inter/world.asp
International Federation of Red Cross and Red Crescent Societies
http://www.ifrc.org
International Labour Organization (ILO)
http://www.ilo.org
International Law
http://www.un.org/law/
International Mission Board
http://www.imb.org
International Organization for Migration (IOM)
http://www.iom.int
International Orthodox Christian Charities (IOCC)
http://www.ioc.org
International Teams
http://www.iteams.org
International Union of Gospel Missions
http://www.iugm.org
Internet Christian Library
http://www.iclnet.org
Internet Encyclopaedia of Philosophy, The
http://www.utm.edu/research/iep/
Internet for Christians
http://www.gospelcom.net/ifc/
Internet History Sourcebooks
http://www.fordham.edu/halsall/
Internet Movie Database
http://uk.imdb.com
Internet News
http://www.internetnews.com
Internet Padre, The
http://www.internetpadre.com
Internet Public Library
http://ipl.sils.umich.edu
Internet Public Library: Youth Division
http://www.ipl.org/youth/

Internic
    http://www.internic.net
Interpretation: A Journal of Bible and Theology
    http://www.interpretation.org
Interserve
    http://www.interserve.org
InterVarsity Christian Fellowship
    http://www.gospelcom.net/iv/
InterVarsity Press
    http://www.gospelcom.net/ivpress/
Into the Light
    http://www.itl.org.uk
Into the Wardrobe
    http://cslewis.drzeus.net
Investigating Islam
    http://www.islamic.org.uk
Involved Christian Radio Network
    http://www.icm.com
Iona Community
    http://www.iona.org.uk
IPL Online Texts on Religion
    http://readroom.ipl.org/bin/ipl/ipl.books-
    idx.pl?type=deweystem&q1=200
IRC Net
    http://www.irc.net
IScriptdb
    http://www.iscriptdb.com
Islam Online
    http://www.islam-online.net
Islamic Resources
    http://www.latif.com
ITN News
    http://www.itn.co.uk
IVillage.com
    http://www.ivillage.com
IVP Publishers
    http://www.ivpbooks.com

J
J.John, Philo Trust
    http://www.philo.ndirect.co.uk
James Dobson
    http://www.family.org
Jamsline
    http://www.jamsline.com

Jesuit Resources
http://www.jesuit.org
Jesus Army (Jesus Fellowship Church)
http://www.jesus.org.uk
Jesus Army Streetpaper
http://www.jesus.org.uk/spaper.html
Jesus Army: Lists and Searches
http://www.jesus.org.uk/search/
Jesus Christ – Images, Art and Photographs
http://www.clark.net/pub/webbge/jesus.htm
Jesus Film Project
http://www.jesusfilm.org
Jewish Bible Association
http://www.jewishbible.org
Jewish-Christian Relations
http://www.jcrelations.com
Jewish.co.uk
http://www.Jewish.co.uk
Jews for Jesus
http://www.jews-for-jesus.org
Jireh Internet Services
http://www.jireh.co.uk
John Bell's Christian Art Gallery
http://jrbell.crossdaily.com
John Ray Initiative
http://www.jri.org.uk
Jonathan Edwards
http://www.jonathanedwards.com
Journal for Christian Theological Research
http://apu.edu/~CTRF/jctr.html
Journey of Faith
http://www.crusade.org/journey/
Jubilee 2000
http://www.jubilee2000uk.org
Jubilee Kids
http://www.jubilee-kids.org
Jumbo Shareware
http://www.jumbo.com
Junctionradio.com
http://www.junctionradio.com

K
K-House Interactive
http://www.khouse.org
Keys For Kids
http://www.gospelcom.net/cbh/kfk/

Kid Info
    http://www.kidinfo.com
Kid's Sunday School Place
    http://www.kidssundayschool.com
KidChatters
    http://www.kidchatters.com
Kidon Media-Link
    http://www.kidon.com/media-link/index.shtml
Kids and Stuff
    http://www.angelfire.com/ca/kidsandstuff/
Kids Channel
    http://www.kids-channel.co.uk
Kids Domain
    http://www.kidsdomain.co.uk
Kids Earth
    http://kids.earth.nasa.gov
Kids Jokes
    http://www.kidsjokes.co.uk
Kids Web
    http://www.kidsvista.com
Kids' Almanac
    http://kids.infoplease.com
KidsDoctor
    http://www.kidsdoctor.com
KidsHealth
    http://www.kidshealth.org
KidsLink
    http://www.kidslink.co.uk
KidzChatz
    http://www.kidzchatz.com
Kidzweb
    http://www.kidzweb.org
Kingdom Dance Resources
    http://www.bensley.clara.co.uk
Kingdom Seek
    http://www.kingdomseek.co.uk
Kingsway Communications
    http://www.kingsway.co.uk
Kiss this Guy
    http://www.kissthisguy.com
Kresch
    http://kresch.com/search/search.htm
Kresch redirection
    http://kresch.com/resources/Web_Hosting/Redirection_Services/

L

Lausanne Committee for World Evangelism
http://www.lausanne.org
Lausanne Movement
http://www.lausanne.org
Leadership Journal
http://www.leadershipjournal.net
Leadership University
http://www.leaderu.com
Learn the Net
http://www.learnthenet.com/english/
Learning Curve Gallery
http://learningcurve.pro.gov.uk/virtualmuseum
Learning Disabilities On-Line
http://www.ldonline.org
Lectionary Page, The
http://www.io.com/~kellywp/
Leprosy Mission International
http://www.leprosymission.org
Lesbian and Gay Christian Movement
http://www.lgcm.org.uk
LESEA Global: Feed the Hungry
http://www.feedthehungry.org
Let's Sing It
http://www.letssingit.com
Library Map Collection
http://www.lib.utexas.edu/Libs/PCL/Map_collection/Map_
collection.html
Library of Congress
http://lcweb.loc.gov/homepage/lchp.html
Library of Congress Studies
http://lcweb2.loc.gov/frd/cs/cshome.html
Libweb – Library WWW Servers
http://sunsite.berkeley.edu/Libweb/
Life and Peace Institute
http://www.life-peace.org
Life and Work
http://www.lifeandwork.org
Life on the Internet: Beginner's Guide
http://www.screen.com/start/guide
LifeLine News
http://www.lifelinenews.net
Lifelines Drama Group
http://www.lifelines.org.uk
Lift Up Your Hearts
http://www.worship.on.ca/

Light Magazine
http://ds.dial.pipex.com/town/square/ac848/light.htm
Linacre Centre for Bio Ethics
http://www.linacre.org
LineOne
http://www.lineone.net
Lion Publishing
http://www.lion-publishing.co.uk
List, The
http://thelist.internet.com
Liszt
http://www.liszt.com
Live Radio on the Internet
http://www.live-radio.net
London Bible College
http://www.londonbiblecollege.ac.uk
London Insititute for Contemporary Christianity
http://www.licc.org.uk
London Jewish Cultural Centre
http://www.ljcc.org.uk
London Mennonite Centre
http://www.btinternet.com/~lmc/
LookSmart
http://www.looksmart.com
LookSmart – UK
http://www.looksmart.co.uk
Luis Palau Evangelistic Association
http://www.gospelcom.net/lpea/
Lund Theological Books
http://lundbooks.co.uk
Lutheran Church of Australia
http://www.lca.org.au
Lutheran Hymnal
http://www.lutheran-hymnal.com
Lutheran World Federation
http://lutheranworld.org
Lutherans.Net
http://www.lutherans.net
Lutterworth Press
http://www.lutterworth.com
Lycos
http://www.lycos.com
Lycos Music Search
http://music.lycos.com/downloads/
Lycos Picture Search
http://multimedia.lycos.com

M

Mac Download
http://www.macdownload.com
Mac OS Zone
http://www.macoszone.com
MacAddict
http://www.macaddict.com
Magazine Rack
http://www.magazine-rack.com
Mapblast
http://www.mapblast.com
Maranatha Christian Journal
http://www.mcjonline.com
Maranatha Tours (Euro) Ltd.
http://www.maranatha.co.uk
Maranatha! Music
http://www.maranathamusic.com
Marcus Honeysett
http://www.mhoneysett.freeserve.co.uk/html/FullIndex.htm
Marie Stopes International
http://www.mariestopes.org.uk
Mark Goodacre's Web Resources
http://www.ntgateway.com
Marriage Resource and National Marriage Week
http://www.marriageresource.org.uk
Marriage Resources
http://www.marriageresource.org.uk
Maven: Jewish Portal
http://www.maven.co.il/
MAYC
http://www.mayc.org.uk
MediaInfo
http://www.mediainfo.com/emedia/
Medina Valley Centre
http://www.medinavalleycentre.org.uk
Meet-O-Matic
http://www.meetomatic.com
Mencap
http://www.mencap.org.uk
Mennonite Publishing House
http://www.mph.org
Mental Health Foundation
http://www.mentalhealth.org.uk
Message to Schools
http://www.message.org.uk

Messianic Testimony
http://www.charitynet.org/~messianic/
meta-list
http://www.meta-list.org
Methodist Archives and Research Centre
http://rylibweb.man.ac.uk/data1/dg/text/method.html
Methodist Church of Great Britain
http://www.methodist.org.uk
Methodist Recorder
http://www.methodistrecorder.co.uk
Miami Christian University Virtual Library
http://mcu.edu/library/
Microsoft Design Gallery
http://dgl.microsoft.com
Microsoft Network (MSN UK)
http://www.msn.co.uk
Microsoft security
http://www.microsoft.com/security
MIDI Explorer
http://www.musicrobot.com
Milestone.net
http://www.milestone.net
Military Ministry
http://www.militaryministry.com
MIND
http://www.mind.org.uk
MindFun.com
http://www.mindfun.com
Miscarriage Association
http://www.the-ma.org.uk
Miss Maggie
http://www.missmaggie.org
Mission Aviation Fellowship
http://www.maf.org
Mission To Unreached Peoples
http://www.mup.org/mupinfo
Mission: America
http://www.missionamerica.com
Missionboard.com
http://www.missionboard.com/index.cfm
Missions by Modem International
http://www.mbmintl.org
Modem Help
http://www.modemhelp.com
Moms Online
http://www.momsonline.com

Moody College
http://www.moody.edu/
Moorlands Bible College
http://www.moorlands.ac.uk
Moravian Church
http://www.moravian.org
Mormon Church in the UK
http://www.geocities.com/Athens/Acropolis/8825/
Mormonism Research Ministry
http://www.mrm.org
Mothers with Children
http://www.gospelcom.net/mops/
Movement for Christian Democracy
http://www.mcdpolitics.org
MP3.com
http://www.mp3.com
Multiple Sclerosis Society
http://www.mssociety.org.uk
Museum Network
http://www.museumnetwork.com
Museums around the World
http://www.icom.org/vlmp/world.html
Music Boulevard
http://www.musicblvd.com
Music Yellow Pages On-line
http://www.musicyellowpages.com
Muslim Coalition
http://www.muslimcoalition.com
Muslim Directory
http://www.muslimdirectory.co.uk
Muslim-Christian Debate
http://www.debate.org.uk
Muslim-Christian Debate Website, The
http://www.debate.org.uk
My humour
http://www.myhumor.org
My Postcards
http://www.mypostcards.com

N

National Art Library, Victoria and Albert Museum, UK
http://www.nal.vam.ac.uk
National Assembly for Wales
http://www.wales.gov.uk
National Association for Christian Recovery
http://www.christianrecovery.com

National Association for Female Executives
http://www.nafe.com
National Christian Education Council
http://www.ncec.org.uk
National Conference of Catholic Bishops
http://www.nccbuscc.org
National Council for Divorced and Separated
http://www.ncds.org.uk
National Council for One Parent Families
http://www.oneparentfamilies.org.uk
National Council of Churches in the USA
http://ncccusa.org
National Deaf Children's Society
http://www.ndcs.org.uk
National Geographic Society
http://www.nationalgeographic.com
National Grid for Learning
http://www.ngfl.gov.uk
National Hindu Students Forum
http://www.nhsf.org.uk
National Map Centre
http://www.mapsworld.com
National Society for the Protection of Children against Cruelty
http://www.nspcc.org.uk
National Youth Association
http://www.nya.org.uk
Native Web
http://www.nativeweb.org
Natural History Museum
http://www.nhm.ac.uk
Nature Cards
http://www.e-cards.com
Navigators
http://www.gospelcom.net/navs/
Neighbourhood Watch
http://www.neighbourhoodwatch.org
Net Ministries
http://netministries.org
Net Security
http://netsecurity.about.com
Netreach
http://www.netreach.co.uk
Netword
http://www.netword.org.uk
Network Counselling and Training
http://www.network.org.uk

New Advent
http://www.newadvent.org
New College, University of Edinburgh
http://www.div.ed.ac.uk
New Day Introductions
http://www.wordnet.co.uk/personal.html
New Economics Foundation
http://www.neweconomics.org
New Frontier
http://ourworld.compuserve.com/homepages/nfi/
New Frontiers International
http://www.n-f-i.org
New Media Bible
http://www.newmediabible.org
New Statesman
http://www.newstatesman.co.uk
New Testament Gateway, The
http://www.ntgateway.com
New Tribes Mission
http://www.ntm.org
New Wine
http://www.new-wine.org
New York Times
http://www.nytimes.com
New Zealand Christian Internet Directory
http://www.search.nzcid.org.nz
New Zealand Goverment
http://www.govt.nz
News Rack
http://www.newsrack.com
news.newusers.questions
http://www.geocities.com/ResearchTriangle/Lab/6882/
News365
http://www.news365.com
Newsgroups
http://www.deja.com
NewsNow
http://www.newsnow.co.uk
NewsTrawler
http://www.newstrawler.com
newWay.org
http://www.newwway.org
Next Wave
http://www.next-wave.org
Nexus
http://www.nexustour.co.uk

NOP
    http://www.maires.co.uk
Northern Light
    http://www.northernlight.com
NSPCC
    http://www.nspcc.org.uk
Number 10
    http://www.number10.gov.uk
NUPSA
    http://www.nupsa.com
NZ.com
    http://www.nz.com

◊
Oak Hill Theological College
    http://www.oakhill.ac.uk
Oasis Trust
    http://www.u-net.com/oasis/
Observer, The
    http://www.observer.co.uk/international
Officers' Christian Fellowship
    http://www.ocfusa.org
Official Goverment Websites
    http://www.psr.keele.ac.uk/official.htm
Okeanos
    http://faculty.washington.edu/snoegel/okeanos.html
OMF International
    http://www.omf.org
Omnilist
    http://members.aol.com/clinksgold/
Omnilist Education
    http://members.aol.com/clinksgold/omnschol.htm
On-line Bibles
    http://www.geocities.com/Heartland/Acres/3964/bibles/
On-line Books Page, The
    http://digital.library.upenn.edu/books/
On-line Communities in the UK
    http://www.communities.org.uk
On-line Guidance
    http://www.gospelcom.net/guidance/
On-line Icons
    http://www.mit.edu:8001/activities/ocf/icons.html
One Look
    http://www.onelook.com
One World
    http://www.oneworld.org

OneKey
http://www.onekey.com
Oneplace.com
http://www.oneplace.com
Ontario Consultants on Religious Tolerance
http://www.religioustolerance.org
Open Directory Project
http://www.dmoz.org
Open Doors
http://www.solcon.nl/odi/ODUK/
Operation Mobilisation
http://www.om.org
Orange Order
http://www.geocities.com/CapitolHill/1684/orange.html
Order of Preachers – Dominicans
http://www.op.org
Order of St Benedict
http://www.osb.org/osb/
Oremus Hymnal
http://www.oremus.org/hymnal/
Organisation for Economic Cooperation and Development (OECD)
http://www.oecd.org
Orthodox Christian Foundation
http://www.ocf.org
Orthodox Christian Page in America
http://www.ocf.org/OrthodoxPage/
Orthodox Church in America
http://www.oca.org
Orthodox Community of St Aidan, Manchester
http://home.clara.net/orthodox/
Orthodox Presbyterian Church
http://opc.org
OSCAR
http://www.oscar.org.uk
Other Side, The
http://www.theotherside.org
Oultwood
http://www.oultwood.com/localgov
Our Daily Bread
http://www.gospelcom.net/rbc/odb/
OurChurch.com
http://www.ourchurch.com
Outreach Unlimited Ministries
http://www.u-net.com/~oum/out.htm
Oxfam
http://www.oxfam.org.uk

OzSearch
http://www.ozsearch.com.au

P

PA NewsCentre
http://www.pa.press.net

Pagan Links: UK
http://www.ukpaganlinks.mcmail.com

Pagan Way Information Network
http://www.users.globalnet.co.uk/~petand/

Paperboy
http://www.thepaperboy.com

Parable Christian Stores
http://www.parable.com

Parent Soup
http://www.parentsoup.com

Parentalk
http://www.parentalk.co.uk

Parents News Online
http://www.parents-news.co.uk

Parents Online
http://www.parents.org.uk

ParentsPlace.com
http://www.parentsplace.com

Parish Pump
http://www.parishpump.co.uk

Parsons Technology
http://www.parsonstech.com

Pastor Tim's Clean Laughs
http://www.cybersalt.org/cleanlaugh/

Pastoral Press Trinity Music
http://www.pastoralpress.com

Pastors.com
http://www.pastors.com

Pathfinder
http://www.pathfinder.com

PC Help Online
http://www.pchelponline.com

PC Pro
http://www.pcpro.co.uk

PC Quote
http://www.pcquote.co.uk

Peace Brigades International
http://www.igc.apc.org/pbi/

Pegasus Mail
http://www.pmail.com

Peniel Pentecostal Church
    http://www.peniel.org
Pentecostal and Charismatic Churches in the UK
    http://www.upcc.com
Pentecostal World Conference
    http://www.pentecostalworldconf.org
PeopleSound
    http://www.peoplesound.com
Perivale Christian Distributors
    http://www.christnetbooks.co.uk/Peribooks/
Peter Rabbit
    http://www.peterrabbit.co.uk
Peter's Net
    http://www.petersnet.net
Pharm Web
    http://www.pharmweb.net
Phatt
    http://www.phatt-music.com/phatt
Philippi House
    http://www.philippi.co.uk
Philosophy in Cyberspace
    http://www-personal.monash.edu.au/~dey/phil/
PhoneNet UK
    http://www.bt.com/phonenetuk/
Phonenumbers.net
    http://www.phonenumbers.net
Pictures of Earth
    http://seds.lpl.arizona.edu/billa/tnp/pxearth.html
Pioneer
    http://www.pioneer.org.uk
Pioneers
    http://www.pioneers.org
Plaid Cymru
    http://www.plaidcymru.org
Postmaster
    http://www.postmaster.co.uk
Practical Parent
    http://www.practicalparent.org.uk
Praise Net
    http://www.praise.net
Praise TV
    http://www.praisetv.com
Praxis
    http://www.sarum.ac.uk/praxis/
Prayer Book Society
    http://www.prayerbookuk.com

Prayer Books
    http://justus.anglican.org/resources/
Prayer Warriors International
    http://www.prayerwarriors.org.uk
Premier Radio
    http://www.premier.org.uk
Prepare/Enrich Network UK
    http://www.cmp.mcmail.com
Presbyterian Church: USA
    http://www.pcusa.org
President for a Day
    http://www.presidentforaday.org
Price Watch
    http://www.pricewatch.com
Priestly Society of Saint Pius X
    http://www.sspx.org
Pro-Life Resource List
    http://www.prolife.org/ultimate/
Problem Pages
    http://www.problempages.co.uk
Project Earth
    http://www.projectearth.com
Project Gutenburg
    http://promo.net/pg/
Project Wittenberg
    http://www.iclnet.org/pub/resources/text/wittenberg/wittenberg-home.html
Promise Keepers
    http://www.promisekeepers.org
Prophecy Central
    http://www.bible-prophecy.com
Prospects
    http://www.prospects.org.uk
Psalmody International
    http://www.psalmody.org
Publicly Accessible Mailing Lists
    http://paml.net
Pusey House, Oxford
    http://parishes.oxford.anglican.org/puseyhouse/

Q

Qua Iboe Fellowship
    http://web.ukonline.co.uk/qua.iboe/
Quaker Network of Green Concern
    http://www.quakergreenconcern.org.uk/about.html

Quakers
    http://www.quaker.org
Quotations Archive
    http://www.aphids.com/quotes/
Quoteland
    http://www.quoteland.com
Qur'an Browser
    http://www.stg.brown.edu/webs/quran_browser/pqeasy.shtml

R
RADAR
    http://www.radar.org.uk
Radio Eden
    http://www.radio-eden.ndirect.co.uk
Radio Locator
    http://www.radio-locator.com
Radio Online
    http://www.radio-online.com
Radio Station Guide
    http://windowsmedia.com/radiotuner
Rastafarian Religion
    http://www.rasta-man.co.uk/religion.htm
RE Directory
    http://www.theredirectory.org.uk
RE Site, The
    http://www.resite.org.uk
RE-XS
    http://www.re-xs.ucsm.ac.uk/ethics/
RE-XS for Schools
    http://re-xs.ucsm.ac.uk
Reaching the Generations for Jesus
    http://home.pix.za/gc/gc12/
Reaching the Unchurched Network
    http://www.run.org.uk
Reachout Trust
    http://www.reachouttrust.org
Read the Bible in a Year
    http://www.bibleinayear.org
Reasons to Believe
    http://www.reasons.org
Rebuild
    http://www.rebuild.org.uk
Red Cross, The
    http://www.redcross.org
Red Sea Mission Team
    http://ourworld.compuserve.com/homepages/rsmt_uk/

Reform Ireland
    http://www.reform-ireland.org
Reform Synagogues of Great Britain
    http://www.refsyn.org.uk
Reformed Church in America
    http://www.rca.org
Reformed Churches of Australia
    http://www.rca.org.au/
Reformed Ecumenical Council
    http://www.gospelcom.net/rec/
Reformed Episcopal Church
    http://www.recus.org
Refugee Net
    http://www.refugeenet.org
Regents Theological College
    http://www.regents-tc.ac.uk
Register.com
    http://www.register.com
Relate
    http://www.relate.org.uk
Release
    http://www.release.org.uk
ReliefWeb
    http://www.reliefweb.int/w/rwb.nsf
Religion & Ethics NewsWeekly
    http://www.pbs.org/religionandethics/
Religion and Religious Studies
    http://www.clas.ufl.edu/users/gthursby/rel/
Religion Today
    http://www.religiontoday.com
Religion-online.org
    http://www.religion-online.org
Religions and Scriptures
    http://www.wam.umd.edu/~stwright/rel/
Religious Borders
    http://windyweb.com/design/gallery.htm
Religious Christmas in Art
    http://www.execpc.com/~tmuth/st_john/xmas/art.htm
Religious Education Council of England and Wales
    http://re-xs.ucsm.ac.uk/re-council/
Religious Education Sources
    http://members.aol.com/wardfreman/alevelre/
Religious Eduication and Environment Programme
    http://www.reep.org
Religious Icon and Image Archive
    http://www.aphids.com/susan/relimage/

Religious Movements Page, The
http://religiousmovements.lib.virginia.edu/profiles/profiles.htm
Religious News Service
http://www.religionnews.com
Religious Society of Friends (Quakers)
http://www.quaker.org
Religious Studies Page
http://www.clas.ufl.edu/users/gthursby/rel/
Religious Studies Resources on the Internet
http://fn2.freenet.edmonton.ab.ca/~cstier/religion/toc.htm
Reluctant Journey
http://www.gseh65.freeserve.co.uk/contents.htm
Reorganized Church of Jesus Christ of Latter-Day Saints
http://cofchrist.org
Research It
http://www.itools.com/research-it/
Resource Pages for Biblical Studies
http://www.hivolda.no/asf/kkf/rel-stud.html
Resources for Greek Grammar and Exegesis
http://faculty.bbc.edu/RDecker/rd_rsrc.htm
Resources for the Church Musician
http://www.pldi.net/~murrows/publish.htm
Resurrected
http://www.resurrected.co.uk
Reuters
http://www.reuters.com
Reverend Fun
http://www.gospelcom.net/rev-fun/
Reverse Phone Directory
http://www.reversephonedirectory.com
Ringing World Online
http://www.luna.co.uk/~ringingw/
Rocha, A
http://www.arocha.org
Rock Solid
http://www.yfc.co.uk/rocksolid.htm
Roman Catholic Church, Holy See, Vatican City
http://www.vatican.va
Roman Empire
http://www.roman-empire.net
Rosemary Conley Fitness Clubs
http://www.conley.co.uk
Rotary Foundation
http://www.rotary.org
Rough Guide to the Internet
http://www.roughguides.com

Royal College of Organists
  http://www.rco.org.uk
Royal National Institute for the Blind
  http://www.rnib.org.uk
Royal School of Church Music
  http://www.rscm.com

S

Sade Punjab
  http://www.sadapunjab.com
Safe Space at Greenbelt
  http://www.geocities.com/WestHollywood/9381/
Salt of the Earth
  http://salt.claretianpubs.org
Salvation Army (UK)
  http://www.salvationarmy.org.uk
Samaritans
  http://www.samaritans.org.uk
Sarum College Centre for Liturgical Organ Studies
  http://www.sarum.ac.uk/organstudies/
SASRA
  http://www.sasra.org.uk
Sassy's Place for Kids
  http://www.geocities.com/Heartland/Plains/7316/
Save the Children
  http://www.oneworld.org/scf/
Scargill House
  http://www.scargillhouse.co.uk
Scatty.com
  http://www.scatty.com
Schoenstatt Fathers
  http://www.schoenstatt.org.uk
School of Christian Leadership
  http://www.worldchristians.org
Science and Religion Forum
  http://www.srforum.org
Science and Spirit
  http://www.science-spirit.org
Scientology
  http://www.scientology.org
Scotsman
  http://www.thestar.com
Scottish Christian.com
  http://www.scottishchristian.com
Scottish Parliament
  http://www.scottish.parliament.uk

Scripture Union
    http://www.scriptureunion.org.uk
Scruples for Marketplace Christians
    http://www.scruples.org
Search Engine Watch
    http://searchenginewatch.com/facts/kids.html
Search for the Meaning of Christmas
    http://techdirect.com/christmas
Search.com
    http://www.search.com
SearchUK
    http://www.searchUK.com
Seerve Him
    http://servehim.com
Serious Developments
    http://www.seriousd.com/freeware.htm
Sermon Central
    http://www.sermoncentral.com
Sermon Help
    http://www.sermonhelp.com
Sermon Illustrations
    http://www.sermonillustrations.com
Sermon Links
    http://www.sermonlinks.com
Sermon Notes Online
    http://www.sermonnotes.com
Sermon Resources
    http://joywell.org/sermon-resources.html
Sermon Search
    http://www.sermonsearch.com
Sermon Shop
    http://www.ecunet.org/sermonshop.html
Sermon.org
    http://www.sermon.org
Sermons and More
    http://www.txdirect.net/~tgarner/
Sermons and Stories
    http://www.sermons-stories.co.uk
ServeYou Network Domain Hosting
    http://www.serveyou.com
Service Monitor
    http://www.servicemonitor.com
Seventh-Day Adventists
    http://www.adventist.org
Shareware Junkies
    http://www.sharewarejunkies.com

Shareware.com
http://www.shareware.com
SharpWriter.Com
http://www.sharpwriter.com
Shelter
http://www.shelter.org.uk
Shepherd Recordings
http://members.netscapeonline.co.uk/jimwlp/
Ship of Fools
http://ship-of-fools.com
Sikh Net
http://www.sikh.net
Silly Olympics
http://www.youth.co.za/olympics/
Sister Site
http://www.geocities.com/Wellesley/1114/
Sistine Chapel, The
http://www.christusrex.org/www1/sistine/0-Tour.html
Site, The
http://www.thesite.org.uk
SiteOwner.com
http://siteowner.linkexchange.com
Sixthform UK
http://www.sixthform.co.uk
Slavic Gospel Association
http://www.sga.org
Sloppy Noodle
http://sloppynoodle.com
Smart Marriages
http://www.smartmarriages.com
Smithsonian, The
http://www.si.edu/
Soc.Religion.Christian
http://geneva.rutgers.edu/src/
Society for the Protection of Unborn Children
http://www.spuc.org.uk
Society of the Divine Savior: the Salvatorians
http://www.sds.org
Society, Religion and Technology Project
http://www.srtp.org.uk/srtpage3.shtml
SoftCom
http://www.sofcom.com.au/Directories/
Software Archives
http://www.softwarearchives.com
Sojourners Online
http://www.sojourners.com

SolidGospel.com
http://www.solidgospel.com
Songs of Praise
http://songsofpraise.org
Sonicplace
http://www.sonicplace.com
Soul Survivor Watford
http://www.soulsurvivor.com
South African Council of Churches
http://www.sacc.org.za
Southern Baptist Convention
http://www.sbc.net
SPCK
http://www.spck.org.uk
Spirit Home
http://www.spirithome.com
Spirit Music
http://www.spiritmusic.co.uk
Spirit Web
http://www.spiritweb.org
Spiritualist Association of Great Britain
http://www.users.globalnet.co.uk/~kluski/sagb.htm
Spirituality for Today
http://www.spirituality.org
Spotlight Ministries
http://www.spotlightministries.co.uk
Spring Harvest
http://www.springh.org
Spurgeon Archive
http://www.spurgeon.org
Spurgeon's College
http://www.spurgeons.ac.uk
St Andrews Bookshop
http://www.standrewsbookshop.co.uk
St Pachomius Library
http://www.ocf.org/orthodoxpage/reading/St.Pachomius/
St. Anthony Messenger
http://www.americancatholic.org/navigation/Messenger
Stanford Encyclopedia of Philosophy
http://plato.stanford.edu
Statistics from the UK Government
http://www.statistics.gov.uk
STL
http://www.stl.org
Stoneleigh Bible Week
http://www.n-f-i.org/sbw.htm

Student Unions
  http://www.namss.org.uk/student.htm
Student World
  http://www.student-world.co.uk
Study Bible Forum
  http://www.studybibleforum.com
Study, The
  http://www.lexalt.com/spirituallife/thestudy.shtml
StudyWeb
  http://www.studyweb.com
Summer Institute of Linguistics
  http://www.sil.org
Sunday School Lessons
  http://www.sundayschoollessons.com
Sunday Times
  http://www.sunday-times.co.uk
Sunhawk.com
  http://www.sunhawk.com
Surf Searcher
  http://www.surfsearcher.net
Surf-in-the-Spirit
  http://www.surfinthespirit.com
SurfSaver
  http://www.surfsaver.com
Sustainable Development (United Nations)
  http://www.un.org/esa/sustdev/
Swedenbourg Society
  http://www.swedenborg.org.uk
Switchboard
  http://www.switchboard.com
Sydney Morning Herald
  http://www.smh.com.au
Synoptic Problem
  http://www.mindspring.com/~scarlson/synopt/

T
Tablet
  http://www.thetablet.co.uk
Tabletalk
  http://www.gospelcom.net/ligonier/tt/
Taize Community
  http://www.taize.fr
Talk about it
  http://www.geocities.com/Athens/Academy/9894
Talks to Children
  http://www.talks2children.itsforministry.org

Tastyfresh: Christian Dance Music
http://www.tastyfresh.com
Tear Fund
http://www.tearfund.org
Teen Mania Ministries
http://www.teenmania.org
Teknon Trust
http://www.teknon.org
Tel-a-Teen
http://www.tel-a-teen.org
Telegraph
http://www.telegraph.co.uk
Telling the Truth Project
http://www.clm.org/ttt/home.html
Telly Tunes
http://www.tellytunes.net
Telstra Yellow Pages
http://www.yellowpages.com.au
Texas Christian University
http://library.tcu.edu
Text This Week, The
http://www.textweek.com
Theological Research Exchange Network
http://www.tren.com
Theology Library
http://www.mcgill.pvt.k12.al.us/jerryd/cathmob.htm
Third Way Magazine
http://www.thirdway.org.uk
THOMAS
http://www.users.globalnet.co.uk/~edges
Thomas Nelson Publishers
http://www.thomasnelson.com
Through the Roof
http://www.throughtheroof.org
Times Educational Supplement
http://www.tes.co.uk
Times, The
http://www.thetimes.co.uk
Timo's Christian Clipart Site
http://members.theglobe.com/timoclipart/
TOC H – UK Charities
http://www.phon.ucl.ac.uk/home/dave/TOC_H/Charities/
Today in History
http://www.9online.com/today/today.htm
Today's Word
http://www.crusade.org/cgi/word.cgi

Top File
    http://www.topfile.com
Top Hosts
    http://webmaster.tophosts.com
Traidcraft
    http://www.traidcraft.co.uk
Trans World Radio
    http://www.twr.org
True Freedom Trust
    http://www.tftrust.u-net.com
True Path
    http://www.truepath.com
Truth for Life
    http://www.gospelcom.net/tfl/
Truth on Fire
    http://truth-on-fire.com
TUCOWS
    http://www.tucows.com
Tudor History
    http://www.tudorhistory.org
Twentieth Century, The
    http://www.thecentury.com
Two Edged Sword, The
    http://hooray2u.com
Tyndale House
    http://www.tyndale.cam.ac.uk

U
UCCF
    http://www.uccf.org.uk
UK Children's Directory
    http://www.ukchildrensdirectory.com
UK Christian Handbook Online
    http://www.ukchristianhandbook.org.uk
UK Christian Net
    http://www.uk-christian.net
UK Christian Web
    http://www.christianweb.org.uk
UK Fundraising
    http://www.fundraising.co.uk
UK Gospel Music
    http://www.avnet.co.uk/goodsela/gospel/
UK Kids
    http://www.ukkids.co.uk
UK Mums
    http://www.ukmums.co.uk

UK Parents
   http://www.ukparents.co.uk
UK Street Map
   http://www.streetmap.co.uk
UK-Church.Net
   http://uk-church.net/uk-listings.htm
UKCH Online
   http://www.ukchristianhandbook.org.uk
UKMax
   http://www.ukmax.com
UKOnline
   http://www.ukonline.com
Ultimate Band List
   http://www.ubl.com
Ultimate Pro-Life Resource List
   http://www.prolifeinfo.org
Ultimate Veggie Tales Web Site
   http://www.veggietales.net
UN Social Policy and Development
   http://www.un.org/esa/socdev/
Unbound Bible, The
   http://www.unboundbible.org
Under Fives
   http://www.underfives.co.uk
Unitarian and Free Churches: UK
   http://www.unitarian.org.uk
Unitarian Universalist Association
   http://uua.org
United Beach Missions
   http://www.ubm.org.uk
United Christian Broadcasters
   http://www.ucb.co.uk
United Church of Christ
   http://www.ucc.org
United Free Church of Scotland
   http://www.ufcos.org.uk
United Media
   http://www.unitedmedia.com/comics/
United Methodist Church
   http://www.umc.org
United Methodist Church (Unofficial)
   http://www.netins.net/showcase/umsource
United Nation's Women Watch
   http://www.un.org/womenwatch/
United Nations
   http://www.un.org

United Nations Childrens Fund (UNICEF)
    http://www.unicef.org
United Nations Conference on Trade and Development
    http://www.unctad.org/en/
United Nations Development Programme (UNDP)
    http://www.undp.org
United Nations Educational, Scientific and Cultural Organization (UNESCO)
    http://www.unesco.org
United Nations High Commissioner for Human Rights
    http://www.unhchr.ch
United Nations Organization
    http://www.un.org
United Nations Population Information Network (POPIN)
    http://www.undp.org/popin/
United Nations: Human Rights
    http://www.un.org/rights/
United Nations: Humanitarian Affairs
    http://www.un.org/ha/
United Reformed Church: UK
    http://www.urc.org.uk
United Society for the Propagation of the Gospel
    http://www.uspg.org.uk
United States Center for World Mission
    http://www.uscwm.org
Universe, The
    http://www.the-universe.net
University of St. Mary of the Lake
    http://www.vocations.org/library
Unravelling Wittgenstein's Net – a Christian Thinktank
    http://www.christian-thinktank.com
Unreached Peoples
    http://www.bethany-wpc.org/profiles/home.html
UpMyStreet
    http://www.upmystreet.com
Urban Legends and Folklore
    http://urbanlegends.about.com/science/urbanlegends/
US Census Bureau
    http://www.census.gov
US Democrat Party
    http://www.democratic-party.org
US House of Representatives
    http://www.house.gov/
US Republican Party
    http://www.rnc.org
US Senate
    http://www.senate.gov

US Town Hall Party
    http://www.townhall.com
USA Today
    http://www.usatoday.com/news/world/nw1.htm
Useless Knowledge
    http://www.uselessknowledge.com
Using Cartoons in Web Evangelism
    http://www.gospelcom.net/guide/web-cartoon.html

V

Various studies
    http://www.joshhunt.com/goodindex.html
Vatican News
    http://www.vatican.va/news_services/
Victim Support
    http://www.victimsupport.com
Victory Tracts and Posters
    http://www.victory10.freeserve.co.uk
VideoZone
    http://www.videozone.co.uk
Virgin Radio Tuner
    http://www.virgin.net/radio/
Virtual Children's Hospital Home Page
    http://vch.vh.org
Virtual Guide to Easter
    http://www.the-word.net/links/easter
Virtual Jerusalem
    http://www.imaginevr.co.il/vrjerusa.htm
Virtual Religion Index
    http://religion.rutgers.edu/links/vrindex.html
Visit Web
    http://www.visitweb.com
Visual Liturgy
    http://www.vislit.com
Voice of the Martyrs
    http://www.persecution.com
VOIS: Voluntary Organisations Internet Server
    http://www.vois.org.uk
Voluntary Service Overseas
    http://www.vso.org.uk

W

W H Smith
    http://www.whsmith.co.uk
W3C – The World Wide Web Consortium
    http://www.w3.org

Wabash Centre
http://www.wabashcenter.wabash.edu/Internet/front.htm
Washington Post
http://www.washingtonpost.com
WATCH
http://www.watchwomen.com
Watchman Fellowship
http://www.watchman.org
Waterstones
http://www.waterstones.co.uk
WCRP – Youth
http://www.geocities.com/Vienna/2848/
Weather Channel, The
http://www.weather.com
Web Evangelism
http://www.brigada.org/today/articles/web-evangelism.html
Web Evangelism Bulletin
http://www.gospelcom.net/guide/webevangelismbulletin.html
Web Evangelism Net
http://www.webevangelism.net
Web Novice
http://www.webnovice.com
Web of On-line Dictionaries
http://www.facstaff.bucknell.edu/rbeard/diction.html
Web Page Design for Designers
http://www.wpdfd.com
Web-World Women
http://www.webworldwomen.com
Webway at Premier Radio
http://www.premier.org.uk/webway/directory.html
Wedding Guide
http://www.weddingguide.co.uk
Wedding Service
http://www.wedding-service.co.uk
Well Connected Mac
http://www.macfaq.com
Wesley Owen
http://www.wesleyowen.com
Westcott House
http://www.ely.anglican.org/westcott/
What is?
http://whatis.com
Wheaton College
http://www.wheaton.edu/learnres/
Whisper of Thunder, A
http://www.godsbook.com

White House
http://www.whitehouse.gov
Whitefield Institute, The
http://www.uccf.org.uk/wi
WholeFamily Centre
http://www.wholefamily.com
WhyteHouse, The
http://www.whytehouse.com
Wide Area Communications
http://www.widearea.co.uk/designer/
Wild Goose Publications
http://www.ionabooks.com
Wilderness
http://home.onestop.net/wilderness/
Wilfrid Laurier University
http://www.wlu.ca/~wwwrandc/internet_links.html
Wilibrord's Christian Chat Sites
http://members.tripod.com/~Erala/chat.html
Windows
http://windows.about.com
Wired News
http://www.wired.com
Woman Today Online
http://www.christianwomentoday.com
Womankind
http://www.womankind.org.uk
Women of Faith
http://www.womenoffaith.com
Women on Crosswalk
http://women.crosswalk.com
Women Today International
http://www.womentoday.org
Women's Health
http://womenshealth.about.com
Women's Ministry
http://www.womensministry.net
Women.com
http://www.women.com
Word is Alive, The
http://www.geocities.com/Athens/Forum/1853
Word Net
http://www.wordnet.co.uk
Word of Life
http://www.word.org.uk
Words from the Well
http://www.gospelcom.net/peggiesplace/words.htm

World Alliance of Reformed Churches
 http://warc.ch
World Association for Christian Communication
 http://www.wacc.org.uk
World Bank
 http://www.worldbank.org
World Bible Quiz Association
 http://www.wbqa.org
World Christian Resources Directory
 http://www.missionresources.com
World Conservation Union (IUCN)
 http://www.iucn.org
World Council of Churches
 http://www.wcc-coe.org
World Evangelical Fellowship
 http://www.worldevangelical.org
World Health Organization (WHO)
 http://www.who.int/
World Missions Far Corners
 http://www.worldmissionsfarcorners.com
World Relief
 http://www.worldrelief.org
World Service Enquiry
 http://www.wse.org.uk
World Student Christian Federation
 http://www.wcc-coe.org/wscf/
World Team
 http://www.xc.org/wt/
World Trade Organisation (WTO)
 http://www.wto.org
World Vision International
 http://www.wvi.org
World Wide Art Resources
 http://www.world-arts-resources.com
World Wide Fund for Nature
 http://www.panda.org
World Wide Web Consortium: Security
 http://www.w3.org/Security/faq/www-security-faq.html
World Wildlife Fund
 http://www.worldwildlife.org
WorldPages.com
 http://www.worldpages.com
Worldwide Challenge Magazine
 http://www.wwcmagazine.org
Worldwide Evangelical Gospel Outreach
 http://www.iu.net/wego/

Worldwide Evangelization for Christ
    http://www.cin.co.uk/wec/
Worldwide Faith News
    http://www.wfn.org
Worship That Works/Selected Sermons
    http://ecusa.anglican.org/worship-that-works/
Worship Together
    http://www.worshiptogether.com
Worshipmusic.com
    http://www.worshipmusic.com
Worth Abbey
    http://web.ukonline.co.uk/worth.abbey/
WWJD.net
    http://www.wwjd.net
WWW Virtual Library
    http://vlib.org/Overview.html
WWWomen
    http://www.wwwomen.com
Wycliffe Associates (UK)
    http://www.globalnet.co.uk/~wa_uk/
Wycliffe Bible Translators
    http://www.wycliffe.org
Wycliffe Hall, Oxford
    http://www.wycliffe.ox.ac.uk
Wyre Compute
    http://www.wyrecompute.com

X
XALT ISP
    http://www.xalt.co.uk

Y
Y2000
    http://www.y-2000.com
Yahoo
    http://www.yahoo.com
Yahoo: Religions
    http://www.yahoo.com/society_and_culture/religion/
Yahooligans
    http://www.yahooligans.com
Yell
    http://www.yell.co.uk
Yellow Pages Superhighway
    http://www.bestyellow.com
YMCA
    http://www.ymca.org.uk

YMCAs in England
http://www.ymca.org.uk
Young Minds
http://www.youngminds.org.uk
Youth For Christ
http://www.gospelcom.net/yfc/
Youth Information
http://www.youthinformation.com
Youth Linc
http://www.youthlinc.com
Youth Ministry Central
http://www.youthspecialties.com
Youth Ministry Games Index
http://www.pastor2youth.com/gamesindex.html
Youth Ministry International
http://www.gospelcom.net/ymi/
Youth Ministry Resources
http://www.jonathansresources.com
Youth Specialities
http://www.gospelcom.net/ys/
Youth With A Mission International
http://www.ywam.org
Youth With a Mission UK
http://www.ywam.org.uk
Youth Work
http://www.youthwork.co.uk
Youth Work Resources
http://www.youthworker.org.uk
YouthPastor.Com
http://youthpastor.com
YouthSearch
http://www.christianteens.net/search/
Youthworker
http://www.gospelcom.net/ys/ywj/

Z
Zach's Place
http://www.htvwales.com/zacsplace/
Zacharias Trust (UK), The
http://www.zactrust.org
Zipple
http://www.zipple.com
Zjam
http://zjam.com
Zondervan Publishing House
http://www.zondervan.com

Zone Alarm
    http://www.zonelabs.com
ZyWeb Publisher
    http://www.zy.com